PROFESSIONAL EN

"There are many books on recovery but every now and again a book is published that best captures what it takes to recover from addiction. Dr. McGee has done just that. I have been in the field for over four decades and I must say I learned a lot from reading his book and you will too. Get this book and add it to your recovery library. I am certain it will become one of your favorites."

—Allen Berger, PhD, Clinical Director, The Institute of Optimal Recovery and Emotional Sobriety, and author of *12 Stupid Things that Mess Up Recovery* and *12 Smart Things to Do When the Booze and Drugs Are Gone*

"This is a comprehensive, but very readable book, written by an expert clinician, and it certainly tells general readers what one needs to know to move toward recovery from addiction. Both people in need of such help and their family members will find it to be a valuable resource. I highly recommend it!"

—Marc Galanter, MD, Professor of Psychiatry, NYU School of Medicine, and author of *What Is Alcoholics Anonymous?*, *Spirituality and the Healthy Mind*, and *The American Psychiatric Publishing Textbook of Substance Abuse Treatment*

"In this book Dr. McGee briefly sets out the facts of addiction—the self-deceit, harm, and self-absorption, and the unrelenting toll it takes on those who succumb. Even as he describes the devastating consequences of addiction, he just as much, early and powerfully, conveys the immense prospect of hope with treatment and recovery. The problem with addiction is that it hurtles a person into an abyss of despair and self-destruction; the gift of recovery re-confers hope, self-respect, and repair. And better still, it stirs a process of transformation and growth, often beyond our wildest dreams. Dr. McGee, in this compelling book, shows us the way, step by step, how and why this is so."

—Edward J. Khantzian, MD, Professor of Psychiatry, Part-Time, Harvard Medical School, and Past President, the American Academy of Addiction Psychiatry

"The joy of recovery is an important and often missing piece in addiction treatment. Recovery is about building a life that is just too good to give up. The healing power of Love runs through this book like a golden thread."

—William R. Miller, PhD, Emeritus Distinguished Professor of Psychology and Psychiatry, The University of New Mexico, and author of *Motivational Interviewing: How People Change* (with Stephen Rollnick), and *Loving Kindness: Realizing and Practicing Your True Self*

"Whether you are immersed in 12-step mutual help groups or not, you'll appreciate the wisdom and practical guidance of Dr. McGee's 12 Touchstones of Recovery. Addiction is no easy illness and nor is recovery smooth sailing. But Mike makes recovery accessible to all who want to know the what, why, how, where, and when of recovery—joyful recovery. Whether addiction has impacted you or your loved ones, or whether your work is to attract them into treatment and recovery, *The Joy of Recovery* is a hopeful companion to the recovery journey."

—David Mee-Lee, MD, Senior Vice President of The Change Companies and Train for Change, co-founder of the Institute for Wellness Education, and author of *The ASAM Criteria: Treatment Criteria for Addictive, Substance-Related, and Co-Occurring Conditions*

"This book gives a wonderful and much needed approach to the treatment of addiction. It emphasizes the concept that addiction is a bio-psycho-social-spiritual disorder of the brain that requires a bio-psycho-social-spiritual solution. The unique approach of using the Touchstones of Recovery enables patients to incorporate various portions of each Touchstone into their personal recovery program. I highly recommend this book to patients, their families, and professionals. *The Joy of Recovery* gives a new perspective in treating an old disease. This book can turn today's failures into tomorrow's miracles."

—John Harsany, Jr. MD (DFSAM), Medical Director, Riverside County Substance Abuse Program, Dept. of Mental Health Medical Director, Sage Retreat (Hemet Valley Recovery), California Medical Board of Registered Nursing Addiction Medicine Consultant Diversion Division Profession of Addiction Medicine, School of Medicine, University of California—Riverside, California

"Dr. McGee demonstrates a comprehensive understanding of addiction and the necessary steps for recovery in his easy-to-read book, *The Joy of Recovery*. Dr. McGee teaches methods for skillful living through his Touchstone approach. This approach breaks down the individual life skills that one needs to develop to achieve real and lasting recovery. Dr. McGee expertly blends science and spirituality to explain the complexities of addiction and offers the homework necessary to achieve the inner peace required for a life without addiction. This book is a must read for patients in recovery, their families, and their providers."

—Ken Starr, MD ABAM, Addiction Medicine Physician and Founder of the Wellness Group

"*The Joy of Recovery* emphasizes the bio-psycho-social-spiritual aspects of addiction and offers a unique approach using the Touchstones of Recovery to help those who want to recover and prevent relapse. Dr. McGee provides a positive philosophy that is both accessible and useful."

—Stephen M. Melemis, MD, PhD, FRSM, author of *I Want to Change My Life: How to Overcome Anxiety, Depression, and Addiction*

"At last a self-help book that really works. Anyone who reads and applies these teachings can get clean and stay sober."

—Edward Kaufman, MD, founding president of the American Academy of Addiction Psychiatry and current medical director of Northbound Treatment Services

"The *Joy of Recovery* is a wonderful addition to the available lexicon of materials that are designed to help people follow a recovery path, that not only leads to abstinence, but leads to a life filled with joy and meaning. Dr. McGee provides a very practical approach that translates his extensive experience into 'tools and tips' for the reader, at every step along the path. I would not hesitate to recommend this book to those individuals suffering with addiction who are seeking an informed and helpful companion on their journey of hope."

—Kenneth Minkoff, MD, Senior System Consultant, ZiaPartners, Inc., part-time Assistant Professor of Psychiatry, Harvard Medical School

PATIENT ENDORSEMENTS

"I had relapsed before I was introduced to Dr. McGee and the Touchstones of Recovery. I needed more than the fellowship that 12-step programs provide. *The Joy of Recovery* is the next evolutionary step in addiction recovery. This book expands on tried and true methods using 21st-century thinking and practices to make living in recovery a joyful experience." —DN

"*The Joy of Recovery* is a must read for anyone dealing with the hardships of addiction, whether it's for yourself or someone you love. The Touchstones of Recovery, along with Dr. McGee's mental and spiritual fortitude, have given me the strength and encouragement to overcome many obstacles in my life. The Touchstones can be a guide to help change your life forever. They have showed me how to get the most out of my recovery and have changed me into the person I have always wanted to be." —ST

"There actually is joy in recovery. Addiction is such an insidious disease. This book is awesome on so many levels. The ideas of the 12 Touchstones are brilliant. It is easy to read and informative. It teaches how to heal without addicting, how to stay sober with all of life's difficulties. *The Joy of Recovery* is such a perfect title. Dr. McGee's book is special to me because it is another tool for my recovery. I've been given a new life that I love. I entered recovery with Dr. McGee in February 2016. I've been clean and sober for over a year. Working hard on my recovery with Dr. McGee has left me feeling awesome every day. I was beaten all the way down, with pain and fear . . . OMG fear. Dr. McGee was so comforting and compassionate. He really cares. Thank you, Dr. McGee." —DR

"I have suffered from addiction and an overwhelming ungrounded and unfounded fear which caused me to addict throughout my life. Years into my recovery journey with years of continuous sobriety, I was still full of fear and struggled with the Healing Touchstone of recovery. I began suffering from panic attacks that were debilitating, but Dr. McGee and his process, his treatment, and his 12 Touchstones of Recovery (in conjunction with working a program of recovery through a 12-step program) enabled me to overcome my irrational fears and not only to survive in recovery but to thrive. As I continue to persevere, I know that I will utilize the various aspects of the 12 Touchstones of Recovery to continue to grow and work toward achieving my goals of self-fulfillment, making peace with my fear, deepening my spiritual connection with my Higher Power, being a good mother, employee, and a woman of dignity and honor. Recovery, for me, was impossible alone; I needed help from others in recovery, professionals, and tools of recovery. My life has completely transformed and it will continue to transform with God's grace, the support of others in recovery, and the use of the tools I have gathered including the 12 Touchstones of Recovery. I recommend this book to all of those who addict and anyone looking for a guide to help you walk through your journey of recovery." —BD

"Dr. McGee's *The Joy of Recovery* readily articulates the nuts and bolts of why we addict, how we can rectify negative behaviors/habits, and balance a fruitful life of recovery. The 12 Touchstones of Recovery are a great reference tool for the curious, newly sober, and grizzled veterans alike to find and keep on a spiritual path of health, love, and dedication to doing the next right thing. I find myself regularly flipping through *The Joy of Recovery* not only for situational guidance but for reinforcement as to why I choose to live righteously on a daily basis. Simply put, this book is another tool for anyone who is sick and tired of being sick and tired. Love truly is the answer and that begins with *you!*" —MI

"Fundamental parts of changing our life's habits are the Touchstones of Recovery. These Touchstones help those of us who suffer from addiction understand and correct what has brought us to such a destructive lifestyle. Growth, Perseverance, Spirituality, and Love are just some of the Touchstones which are explored in an understanding way. Dr. McGee's book *The Joy of Recovery* is not just for the victim of addiction but also for anyone wishing to understand oneself and become happier." —KY

"This book truly is a display of Dr. McGee's positive philosophy. I have been a patient of Dr. McGee for over a decade; I see him as someone in charge of a lighthouse—a 'beacon' for those of us caught in the destructive storm of addiction. His inspiring guidance has motivated me to achieve a life of balance and integrity. Throughout the book (and his practice), he offers us wisdom without judgment or ridicule. I am truly lucky to have found Dr. McGee and have him by my side, holding my hand, going through the recovery process together. Today, I am alive, I am happy, and I can honestly say it's the way in which he approaches treatment." —HC

"Dr. McGee saved my life and made me have purpose again. I abused substances to deal with my life problems and slipped into a life I was not proud of. Dr. McGee gave me back my life. I will be forever grateful for his wisdom and caring." —FM

Published by
Union Square Publishing
301 E. 57th Street, 4th floor
New York, NY 10022
www.unionsquarepublishing.com

Manufactured in the United States of America, or in the United Kingdom when distributed elsewhere.

McGee, Michael
The Joy of Recovery: A Comprehensive Guide to Healing from Addiction
LCCN: 2018931160
ISBN: 978-1-946928-16-0
eBook: 978-1-946928-17-7

Cover design: Keoki Williams
Interior design: Claudia Volkman
Photo credits: Tom Meinhold / Meinhold Photography
Illustration credits: Daniel Van Bogelen

www.drmichaelmcgee.com

The Joy of Recovery

A Guide to Healing from Addiction

Michael McGee, MD

FREE EBOOK!

Can't wait to release the suffering and start creating more joy in your life?

Go to drmichaelmcgee.com and download your **free copy** of *20 Ways to Realize Joy in Your Life* now!

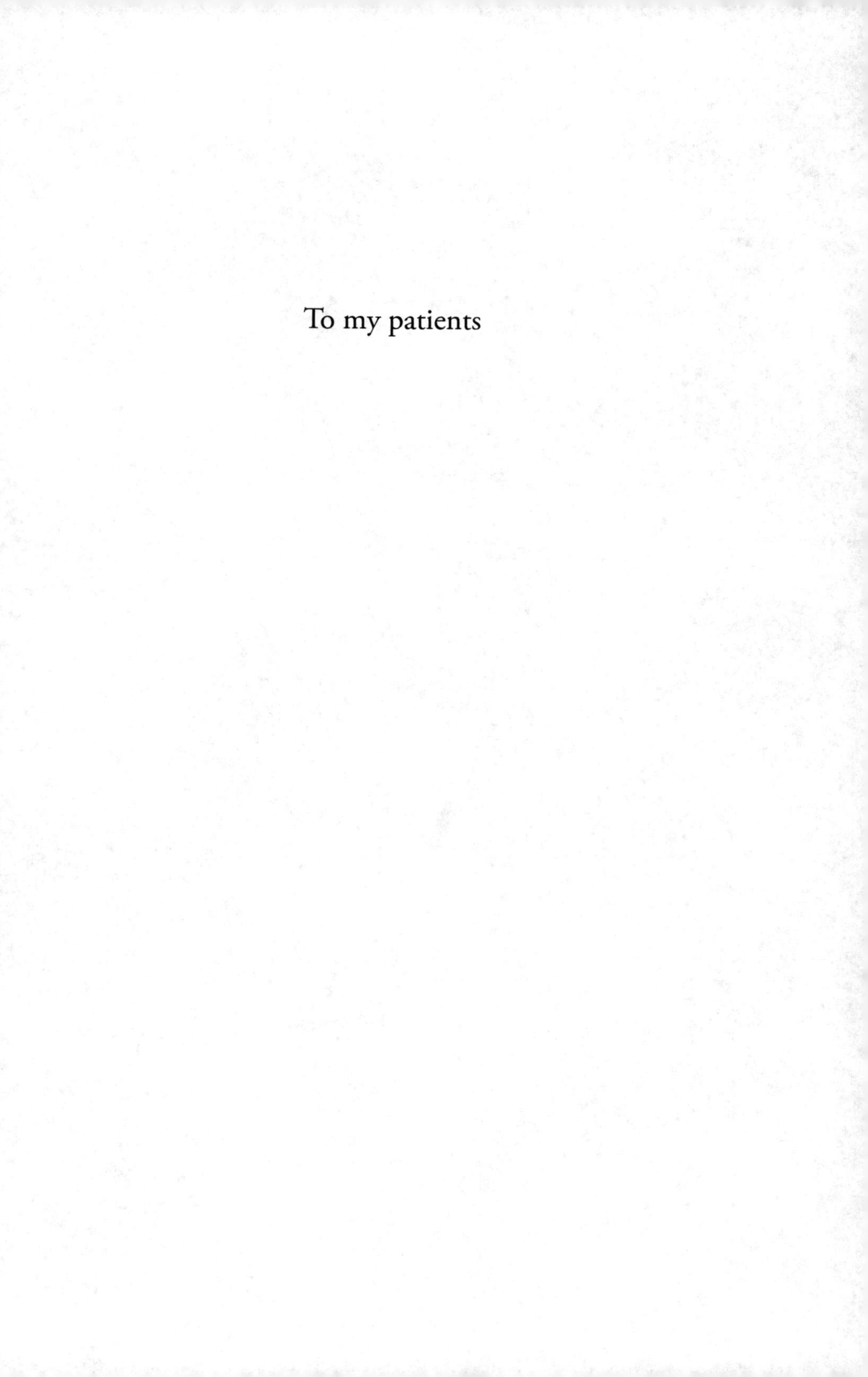

To my patients

ACKNOWLEDGMENTS

A heartfelt thank you to Union Square Publishing for helping to make this book a Reality.

Special thanks to Justin Spizman for his editorial assistance.

Thank you to Keoki Williams of Keoki Design for assistance with the book cover.

Thank you to Daniel Van Bogelen of Strategic Digital Marketing for assistance with the illustrations.

Many thanks to those who provided feedback and helped with the writing of this book. They include Marc Navon, MSW, David Mee-Lee, MD, John Harsany, MD, Reverend Rod Richards, Jon Sapper, and William Miller, PhD.

Many thanks to all my loved ones who have provided so much guidance and support. A special thank you to Linda for your wisdom, inspiration, and encouragement.

Finally, thank you to my patients for the gift of engaging together in profoundly meaningful work. It is that work which inspired this book.

TABLE OF CONTENTS

PREFACE

THE PATH TO TRUE RECOVERY

This is a book about transformation. Within this book, you'll learn how to transform your suffering from addiction into your joy of life. This is a book about hope. Unlike with most other illnesses, recovery from addiction gives you more than you had before your addiction began. Recovery helps to heal the wounds that drove you to addiction in the first place, and you resurface as a better version of yourself. If you address your addiction, your addiction yields a spiritual gift in return. You'll eventually discover a happiness and peace through recovery that you might have never known before.

Addiction varies in severity. Addiction can come in the form of reliance upon substances like alcohol or drugs, or even addictive behaviors. Potentially addictive behaviors might include sexing (harmful and compulsive sexual behavior), gambling, "teching" (compulsive use of the Internet, smartphones, and other technology), overeating, overworking, or overspending (addictive materialism and consumerism).

Addiction is a "solution that almost works," yet makes things far worse in the long run. For many, addiction starts with relieving pain with a pleasurable substance or activity. While natural in practice, sometimes feeling better conflicts with what is true, right, and good. Addiction is a mental illness that compels people to act to feel better now without regard for what is best in their futures. True recovery entails renouncing addictive substances and behaviors and learning to do what is best regardless of cravings and compulsions to do otherwise. True recovery involves learning to savor and nurture Life on Life's terms. People do this by skillfully living life to minimize distress, learning to accept and let go, and implementing more skillful solutions to manage pain.

Recovery entails developing a new way of living. Recovery is a way of Being, Seeing, and Doing. In recovery, you experience wholeness, goodness, and connectedness both internally and externally. This leads to a positive philosophy of life based on experience. You can then begin to live with love and integrity rather than out of fear. Recovery is a spiritual matter at its foundation. It is waking up to Reality in a way that changes everything so that at last you know pure joy, peace, and fulfillment.

This book is a practical "how to" guide to the Being, Seeing, and Doing of recovery. It uses 12 "Touchstones of Recovery" to guide you through the process of healing from addiction. These Touchstones create a "worldview" of recovery. This worldview addresses how you experience and understand your life and the world at large to protect you from the disease of addiction. The goal is to wake up and lovingly engage life. To help you do that, we will spend time focusing on the 12 Touchstones of Recovery outlined below:

1. Work on recovery
2. Create a positive recovery environment
3. Renounce addicting
4. Act with integrity
5. Heal
6. Love
7. Respect Reality
8. Grow
9. Persevere
10. Develop healthy relationships
11. Take accountability
12. Cultivate your spirituality

These Touchstones are an outgrowth of my 30 years of experience as an addiction psychiatrist, my clinical training, and my life experience. Over the years, I have noted common themes of what works for those who discover the joy of recovery, and what doesn't work for those who continue to struggle with addiction. While it is not a one-size-fits-all approach, there are commonalities and patterns to those who turn addiction into recovery. This book represents my professional approach to treating the biological, psychological, social, and spiritual dimensions of addiction and recovery.

Through tapping into the timeless wisdom of the ages, the extensive recovery experience of the many pioneers of recovery, and my patients' successes, you will find a thoughtful and proven approach to overcome a variety of addictions. The Touchstones represent the universal components of a life well lived. They make up a coherent worldview that guides people in their cultivation of their Being, Seeing, and Doing. The value of this book lies both in its universality and in the integration, organization, and presentation of recovery wisdom into practical Touchstones that, if followed, lead to a joyful life. If you work to live your life according to these Touchstones, you will see your life flourish. You will experience the joy of recovery.

Start by reading this book from beginning to end. To get the most out of each Touchstone, take the time to complete the suggested tasks included with each Touchstone. When you are finished reading the book, use it as a reference in your daily recovery work. When you meet with difficulty, identify the relevant Touchstones that bear upon your problem. Then, read through the text for these Touchstones again to refresh your understanding and perspective. You will then be able to more skillfully attend to your difficulty.

Complete the Touchstone self-assessment in the appendix. This will help you identify which Touchstones need the most attention. When you review your life using this assessment, be sure to note the Touchstones that are your strengths. Give yourself credit for your positive attributes, while acknowledging those areas in which you can improve.

After reading this book, use it as a reference to guide your recovery as follows:

1. Use a recovery journal to write about any challenges you are encountering.
2. Then, write any actions you took and actions you did not take that might have contributed to your difficulty.
3. Identify the relevant Touchstones that need attention. Write what you need to do.
4. Share your analysis with a recovery mentor or other trusted person to get their input. Update your recovery plan based on the feedback you receive.

This book is as much a guided and interactive approach to recovery as it is a map and compass along your journey. As you implement these tips and tools, you will heal as your recovery habits and life circumstances improve.

You will find the happiness, serenity, and fulfillment you seek. I will help you along the way.

While working your recovery plan, try the various recovery practices in this book until you figure out what works best for you. Experiment and explore. You will notice that as time progresses and you grow in your recovery, your recovery needs will change.

At first, your work may be crisis stabilization, repairing damage, working to stay sober, developing a healthy support network, and establishing a positive recovery environment. Later on, it will likely transition to developing more meaning, purpose, and fulfillment in your life. As your recovery focus changes, so will your recovery practices. This is as it should be.

You are about to embark on a beautiful and inspiring journey to wellness and health. It might seem challenging at times, but I am hopeful this book will help you to navigate some of the choppy waters ahead. I will do my best to offer you hope, perspective, and resources to reach your goal of overcoming whatever addiction you might face. We are in this together, and I am thankful to share in your recovery.

With gratitude,

Dr. Michael McGee

CHAPTER I

THE RELENTLESS POWER OF ADDICTION

Addiction destroys lives. Roughly a million people die every year from the consequences of alcohol, illicit drug, nicotine, and food addiction.[1][2][3][4][5] Victims of addiction suffer greatly, and often cause substantial suffering in those around them. They are not alone in their fight, and are certainly not alone in the impact of their addiction.

Addiction is a form of cancer that permeates our society. Over 100 million people suffer from substance abuse, food, and behavioral addictions. This amounts to some form of addiction directly affecting nearly a third of our society, and indirectly affecting everyone else through the heartache and economic costs of addiction. Almost every single person in this world knows or loves someone who is or has battled some form of addiction.

Sadly, most people who actually need treatment never receive it. While some might go into remission, far too many suffer unnecessarily and endlessly. It is a repeating trend with no end in sight. For those who do receive treatment, their outcomes are often disappointing, and don't lead to lasting and meaningful change. To that end, we need better treatments made available to more people. Addiction is vast, extensive, and extremely powerful. No one wants to be addicted, but too many just cannot break free.

But hope reigns eternal. Over the past 30 years, I have had the privilege of treating thousands of people who suffered from addiction. I have seen an executive that was once reduced to living under a bridge go on to rebuild his career and start a family. One patient went from being unemployed and homeless to becoming a successful attorney, a homeowner, a landlord, and a loving husband. Another patient was penniless and on the verge of divorce. He went on to become the vice president of a corporation and raise two beautiful children. I have witnessed hundreds of others successfully learn to stop addicting (engaging in the use of addictive substances or engaging in addictive behaviors), heal, repair their lives, and realize their full potential through a steadfast dedication to recovery. I've had the privilege of helping people transform the curse of addiction into a blessing that allowed them, through recovery, to become beautiful people living even more beautiful lives. Recovery is possible for those who want it and are willing to work for it.

The Conflict of Addiction

Our journey through addiction really begins with defining it in the first place. We all likely have some idea of how to define addiction, but the truth is that it comes in many unfortunate shapes and sizes. Addiction is an illness in which you experience strong compulsions or cravings to addict (use an addictive substance or engage in an addictive behavior), combined with a loss of control over your compulsions and cravings. You engage in the addiction to either feel better or not feel worse. Consider that for a second. In no way does addiction make you happy. It just momentarily reduces your pain. But in the end, you'll find yourself worse off because of the destructive consequences of addicting. While you might stop other harmful behaviors, in addiction you continue to addict despite the harm it causes you and others.

Addictions can be to substances such as alcohol or drugs, or to addictive behaviors. People disagree about what are addictive behaviors. If a behavior meets the definition of addiction, then the behavior is a behavioral addiction.

Some people engage in one or more addictive behaviors. Various addictive behaviors include:

- Excessive shopping/spending
- Overeating (including compulsive sugar consumption)
- Gambling
- Compulsive and harmful sexual behaviors
- Excessive Internet use, smart phone use, video game use (compulsive "teching")
- Excessive exercise
- Excessive work
- Compulsive engagement in harmful relationships at all costs (love addiction)

The issue is not the degree of use or behavior. The underlying issue regarding addiction is that victims of addiction act on the addictive urge even though they don't want to. Impaired control manifests as either impulsivity or compulsivity. You then might engage in the addiction despite the destructive consequences of the addiction, like medical illness, legal difficulties, unemployment, or even divorce. As it progresses, victims spend every waking moment serving the addiction. Work, play, and love all go by the wayside as the victim devotes their time to addicting, and nothing more. This may seem completely illogical from the outside looking in. It is often baffling to others that the victim seems both unable and unwilling to cease their destructive behaviors, no matter how much is at stake or how much they'll lose if they don't.

Many people undergo alterations in thinking, like denying that they have any problems in the first place, or likely minimizing their difficulties. They then lose accountability and blame others for their problems. They become preoccupied, even obsessed, with the addiction. From the inside looking out, victims overvalue the addiction as a positive life solution. They blame the harmful consequences of the addiction on external factors, such as job stress, loneliness, boredom, or relationship conflicts. The addiction plays these mental tricks on people to preserve the addiction. It becomes a self-fulfilling and unbreakable prophecy. Sort of like a merry-go-round that never stops. Victims of addiction go in circles and cannot figure out how they got on the ride in the first place, nor how they'll ever get off it.

There are a number of emotional consequences of addiction. These might include but are not limited to: anxiety, depression, and despair. People become stress-intolerant, often making mountains out of molehills. Where they may have had difficulties experiencing and processing their feelings before, they now become even more impaired and conflicted in their ability to manage negative emotions. The sufferer's emotional life agenda warps to either trying to feel better or to stop feeling worse by addicting.

It is at that point that many people can become extraordinarily self-centered, losing empathy for others and the tremendous negative impact they have on them. The addiction channels the thoughts and efforts of the victim toward feeding the addiction. That is their sole purpose of existence. Addiction poisons the capacity to love. Many experience a profound corruption of character, as they turn to lying, manipulating, stealing, or taking part in other illegal activities.

Does this ring a bell? It is the common path for many who suffer from addiction. This vicious cycle will aggressively eat away at people until they either succumb to the addiction or take the crucial steps to move in the direction of recovery. The good news is that the only thing more powerful than the claws of addiction is the power of recovery. And recovery is the topic of the remainder of this book.

The Hope Found Within Recovery

Recovery is the action or process of regaining possession or control of something stolen or lost. It is also the goal of returning to a normal state of health, mind, or strength. Addiction takes so much away from you, but recovery gives you the tools to take it back. As we discuss and work through the important process of recovery, don't underestimate its great potential and ability to heal even the deepest of wounds and strongest of addictions. Recovery is not a difficult concept to understand, but does call for a great deal of dedication, determination, and help with self-control. Another way to think about recovery is that in addiction, people put relief of distress before self-love. In recovery, self-love comes before relief of distress. People in recovery don't addict because their self-love motivates them not to act on self-destructive urges. People in active addiction do what feels good regardless of what is right. In recovery, people do what's right regardless of urges to feel good through addicting.

The following table lists some psychological, spiritual, and behavioral characteristics of the difference between addiction and recovery:

Table 1. Addiction vs. Recovery

Addiction	Recovery
Disease	Health/healing
Relief seeking	Facing/embracing/dealing
Self-medication	Abstinence
Character disorder	Character transformation
Self-centered	Other-oriented
Thinking disorder/delusional	Intact Reality testing
Poor judgment	Good judgment
Childlike/immature	Mature/centered

Impulsive/obsessive/ compulsive	Thoughtful of consequences
Negative vicious cycle—destructive	Transcendence
Life of deceit	Life of integrity
Dishonesty	Honesty
Taking from others	Giving to others
Relief/self-obsessed	Love
Shame	Remorse
Hopelessness	Hope
Entitlement	Gratitude/appreciation
Isolation/disconnected	Connection
Shame	Pride
Empty	Spiritual
No sense of accountability	Accountable/responsible

The Reality is that you know recovery when you see it. As defined above, you are in recovery when you are healthy, well, living a positive, meaningful life, and contributing while realizing your full potential. Yet guidance on how to achieve this state of recovery is all over the map, from 12-step recovery approaches to cognitive-behavioral approaches to network therapy to psychopharmacology. All of these approaches have merit and can help. Many pathways to recovery exist. The best pathways entail a comprehensive approach to the art of living. Each person's path is unique to him or her and often changes over time as he or she changes.

At its core, recovery is a spiritual process. It is the process of taking a leap of faith that love is a better solution to becoming joyful than addicting. In renunciation, people take their first step in living out of love (starting with self-love) rather than out of fear—including the fear of what will happen if they stop addicting. Recovery helps people to develop harmonious interconnectedness with the world. Recovery takes people from the insanity of addiction to the sanity of love. Recovery marks the death of an old, destructive life and the beginning of a new, productive life.

Yet recovery is work. Only those who put in the effort taste the benefits of recovery. It is a daily process of continual growth until the day you die.

Through recovery, you uncover the truth that life is uncontrollable at times, but manageable throughout. You develop the capacity to both savor and nurture life while skillfully managing distress.

Who wouldn't want that?

The Touchstones of Recovery

The following 12 Touchstones of Recovery encompass a comprehensive approach to recovery that gives you the best chance of living a happy life free of active addiction. In using the word "Touchstone," I refer to a fundamental, essential feature of the complex process of healing from addiction. In these 12 Touchstones, I blend science and spirituality, addressing the biological, psychological, social, and spiritual aspects of recovery. Each of these will play an important role in your journey toward and through recovery. To that end, here are the Touchstones, as well as their fundamental underlying principles:

1. **Work on recovery**
   a) Make recovery your first priority.
   b) Commit to lifelong recovery work.
   c) Develop your recovery skills.
   d) Be wary of complacency.

2. **Create a positive recovery environment**
   a) Attend to your environment.
   b) Minimize external triggers.

3. **Renounce addicting**
   a) Pursue freedom from all addictive substances and behaviors.
   b) Skillfully manage distress and desire.
   c) Let go.

4. **Act with integrity**
   a) Do the next right thing.
   b) Practice honesty.
   c) Put principle before pleasure.

5. Heal

a) Seek professional help.
b) Manage stress.
c) Address trauma.
d) Manage emptiness.

6. Love

a) Refrain from destructiveness.
b) Think before acting.
c) Refrain from obsessing over others' faults.
d) Let go of resentments.
e) Refrain from judging.
f) Cultivate compassion and forgiveness.
g) Let go of shame.
h) Manage anger constructively.

7. Respect Reality

a) Don't expect the world or others to be other than what they are.
b) Don't expect perfection from others or yourself.
c) Change what you can and accept the rest.

8. Grow

a) Learn from the past so you can create a better future.
b) Practice, practice, practice.
c) Use slips and mistakes as opportunities for growth.
d) Pay attention to the feedback of others.
e) Learn from pain.

9. Persevere

a) If you slip, immediately recommit to your recovery.
b) Have faith in yourself and the process of recovery.
c) Practice patience.

10. Develop healthy relationships

a) Develop recovery supports from those with recovery experience and skills.

b) Be assertive and authentic.
c) Associate with those you wish to be like.
d) Sit with your thoughts and feelings and share them with trusted confidants.
e) Don't try to "fix" anyone.
f) Don't isolate.
g) Practice humility and respect.
h) Develop a healthy social network.
i) Do not socialize with anyone who is addicting.
j) When possible, heal damaged relationships by making restitution and amends.

11. Take accountability

a) Take care of yourself so that you can care for others.
b) Live with balance and savor life.
c) Practice positivity.
d) Live blame-free.
e) Manage vulnerabilities.
f) Develop meaning and purpose.
g) Face your fears.
h) Achieve your goals.

12. Cultivate your spirituality

a) Make time for spiritual practice.
b) Cultivate a deeper connection, beyond words, to others and to Reality.
c) Practice mindfulness in all your daily affairs.
d) Don't believe everything you think.
e) Live both for yourself and for something greater than yourself.
f) Live according to a higher set of principles.
g) Keep perspective.
h) See the Sacred in all things and people.
i) Count your blessings.
j) Live life out of love.

The 12 Touchstones all impact and relate to one another. They make up an interactive and interdependent web of the core practices of recovery. For example, you cannot develop loving connections with others without being honest, not hurting others, and acting with integrity. Although they often overlap, each Touchstone speaks to the process of recovery from a particular perspective. This is illustrated in Figure 1.

Figure 1: The Touchstones

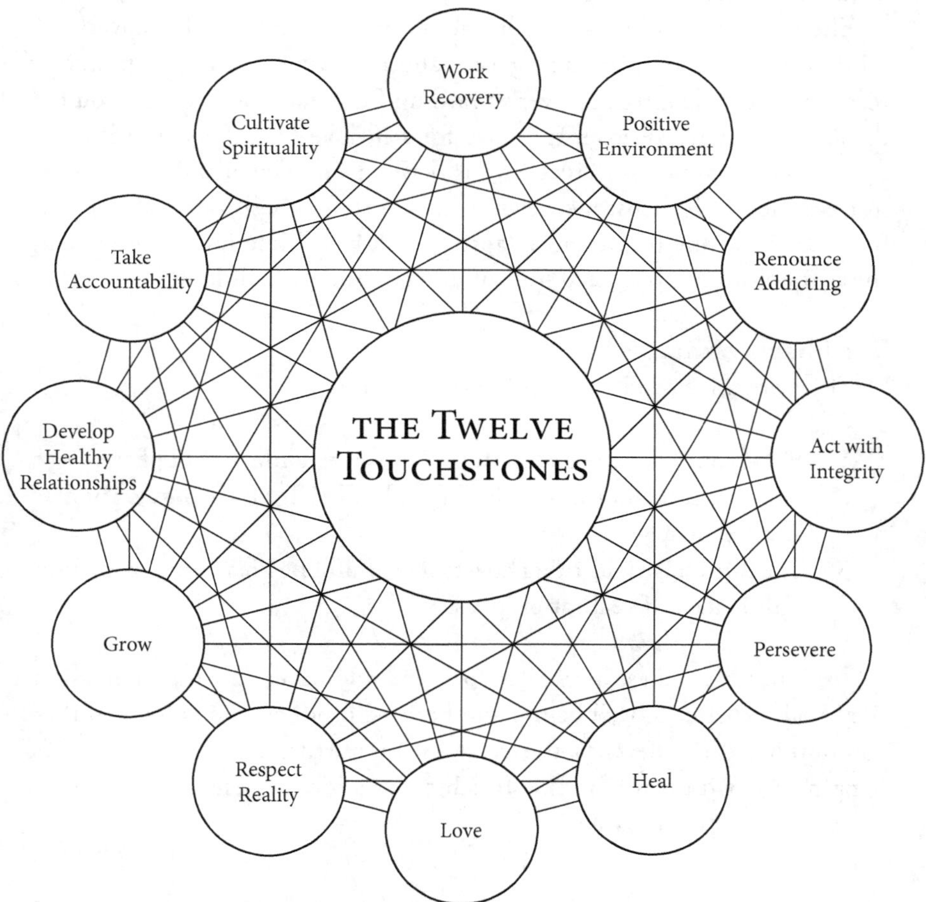

Living according to these Touchstones can provide a life free from addiction. While it does take regular practice and daily effort to live by these Touchstones, they will absolutely help you to skillfully and slowly grow in your ability to live and love. With patience and persistent effort, you will notice a gradual growth in your freedom from addiction and the corresponding enhancement of satisfaction and fulfillment that goes hand in hand. In short, you will experience joy.

The 12 Touchstones are really an interwoven fabric of recovery, all reinforcing and complementing one another. They create a tapestry of recovery that reflects the answer to healing from addiction, which you can distill into one word: love. It is love for self, love for others, and love for life that cures addiction. Since love is both an experience and an action to nurture life, the Touchstones teach you how to manifest the healing power of love in your life to prevent relapsing back into addiction. By practicing these Touchstones, you need not suffer recurrences of addicting.

The Phases of Recovery

There are three overlapping phases of recovery:

1. **First**, you must cease addicting. This is the **renunciation** phase.
2. **Second**, heal and learn to live life skillfully. This is the **integration and repair** stage.
3. The **third** stage is learning how to live a fulfilling life without addiction. This is the **self-realization** phase.

As a result of these processes, people's addictions go into remission; they heal, experience well being, and become productive members of their community. They develop the capacity to nurture and savor life. True happiness is within reach. The Touchstones address these three phases of recovery as shown in Table 2.

Table 2. Phases of Recovery

Phase of Recovery	Relevant Touchstones
Renunciation	Recovery work Positive recovery environment Renounce addicting Act with integrity Cultivate spirituality
Integration and repair	Act with integrity Heal Love Respect Reality Persevere Develop healthy relationships Take accountability Cultivate spirituality
Self-Realization	Grow Cultivate spirituality

During early recovery, the primary focus is on renunciation. Renunciation is the act of refusing or rejecting something, in this case giving up addicting as a way to manage distress. However, people also begin the integration and repair process while considering their personal growth and spirituality. In the middle phase of recovery, people primarily work on integration and repair. In the last phase of recovery, people put more focus on realizing their life vision, purpose, and meaning. They strengthen their ability to live life out of love rather than being ruled by unhealthy fear.

Although describing recovery this way has value, people work on all the Touchstones in all phases of recovery to some degree. The difference is the relative focus on each one, as some Touchstones are more relevant than others in each particular stage.

Recovery Is Loving

George Sand said, "There is only one happiness in this life, to love and be loved." It is within our nature to desire and search for connection and love. Not one of us wants to be alone, destitute, and solitary. We need one another to exist and to evolve. Alone, we stand no chance. That is part of the pain of addiction. You are often alone in your battle to recover, and can find no love when you need it the most. But as you work to reconnect and reengage your life through meaningful and thoughtful acts of love, you'll soon recognize a brilliantly colorful and fulfilling life. The Touchstones outlined in this book will help you accomplish that.

We will now turn to a discussion of each of these Touchstones.

CHAPTER 2

TOUCHSTONE 1: WORK ON RECOVERY

"Whatever you put before your sobriety, you shall surely lose."
—Anonymous

The first Touchstone focuses on making recovery a way of life. It helps you to develop daily disciplines of recovery that in time become your automatic recovery habits. Through doing this, you'll make a strong, single-minded commitment, as your life depends on it. For you to succeed in your recovery, recovery needs to be your first life priority, as everything else depends on it. Commit to a lifetime of intentional recovery work, for recovery is a lifelong process of growth. Develop core recovery skills to stay sober, such as managing cravings and minimizing triggers. Finally, be wary of complacency, as complacency is the shortest path to a recurrence of addicting. This Touchstone will help you do just that.

Make Recovery Your First Priority

It is easy for life to get in the way of recovery. Yet without recovery, you have nothing else. The stresses and demands of work and family often crowd out time for the efforts you'll need to make a full recovery. There might be times where you may feel the need to skip recovery meetings to make more money. A loved one may ask for more of your time. There may be a project that demands your time. You may consider recovery to be less important than other life demands. You may tell yourself you will get back to recovery work "when there is more time." You forget the mantra, "First things first."

Unfortunately, the time for recovery work does not just reappear. You develop new life routines in which your time is then consumed by the many demands and obligations of your life. Recovery work fades into the distance, leaving you vulnerable to the insidious dynamics of addiction that then creep their way back into your life. You may notice you begin to experience irritability, stress, negative thoughts, resentments, or even cravings. You may not even experience these warning signs, but start addicting again, out of the blue. Then you realize, when you are once again at risk of losing everything, that everything else depends on your recovery. Once you focus on the first Touchstone, and see that recovery must come first, you can then have everything else in your life that brings happiness and fulfillment.

Recovery calls for prioritization and balance. Don't take on so much that no time for recovery work remains. A person in strong recovery will even schedule time out from a vacation for prayer, contemplation, recovery readings, journaling, talking to a recovery mentor, or going to a recovery meeting. The same is true in your routine life where time for exercise, a full-time job, childcare, and other family commitments place demands on your time. Say "No" at some point. You must limit your time commitments to a reasonable load that allows for recovery work, if only a few hours a week.

Plan your recovery time. Schedule it. Make time to put in the time. Try as hard as you can to let nothing divert you from your recovery work. Be willing to go to any lengths for your recovery the way you did for your addiction. Make your recovery a daily discipline, a habit, a ritual. When demands on your time increase, cut back and devote more time to recovery, as that is when you most need recovery work.

Tell loved ones that you are doing this for both yourself and them. Explain that with recovery work they are less at risk of losing you to the addiction. If they love you and truly understand addiction, they will support you. Set limits at work. Your boss is not responsible for looking out for you. You are. You will only succeed at work if you make sure work doesn't replace recovery work.

You must make your recovery first to make it last. In the end, you don't want others to say of you, "They gave their almost." It is said that "Half-measures avail us of nothing." Put your full heart into these Touchstones of Recovery. Then you will taste the joy of recovery.

Tips & Tasks

Tip: Make recovery your first priority, as everything else depends on it.

Task*:* Schedule your priorities. First schedule recovery work. Then schedule self-care. Then schedule the rest.

Commit to Lifelong Recovery Work

Thomas Huxley said, "The rung of a ladder was never meant to rest upon, but only to hold a man's foot long enough to enable him to put the other somewhat higher." Stopping addictive behaviors and becoming sober is just the beginning. You work on your recovery not just to get sober, but also to be happy. Like life itself, recovery is a process, not an event. Recovery does not get a day off. If you are not moving away from addiction, you may be moving closer to it. Once you stop turning the handle on the generator that lights your recovery, the light goes out. Recovery is the journey, not the destination. It ends only with life's end. Recovery isn't something you do until you are "better." It is a lifelong way of being, seeing, and doing.

It has been said that: "The biggest room is the room for improvement." Though perfection is unreachable, working a recovery program helps keep you in remission and enhances the richness of your life. If you feed your addiction, it will progress. The same is true for your recovery.

With a commitment to total recovery, the help of others, and grace, you begin the slow process of healing. It can take time, often several years, to achieve a stable foundation of recovery in which you feel a sense of wholeness, integrity, meaning, fulfillment, and serenity. There is a saying that says, "When you walk ten miles into the woods, you have to walk ten miles out." And walk you must, for if you do not, your past will become your future.

When you don't want to do the work, you need recovery the most. You progress in your recovery each day you do not addict and devote yourself to living in harmony with the Whole of which you are a part.

Some people seem to develop out of addiction, sometimes spontaneously, without treatment. For these people vigilance about readdicting is not as much of a concern. For them recovery is more about healing, repair, integration, growth, and self-realization. It is about realizing the Joy of Recovery.

For many, addiction does not go away. It only goes into remission. The best many can hope for is a lifelong practice of seeing the workings of the mind, managing addictive compulsions, and surrendering to what is best for everyone. For many, as soon as they cease their recovery practices, the addiction resurfaces, seeping back into the fabric of their lives. For these people, daily recovery work is a lifelong practice.

Tips & Tasks

Tips: You can stop working your recovery when you die, not before then. Recovery practices include thinking and talking about recovery, going to meetings, getting individual or group therapy, working with a recovery mentor, asking for help, spiritual practices, step work, journaling, and reading recovery literature.

Tasks: Review your recovery plan. Are you doing enough of what's needed? If not, modify your plan. Change your plan as your recovery needs change. Blend discipline and flexibility in your recovery work.

Recovery Rituals and Practices

Those who are successful in their recovery have a suite of recovery practices that keep them "on track." They put their willingness to change into intentional, disciplined daily rituals. This is the work that triggers transformation.

Your "default" mode of being in the world is to addict, with all that goes along with it, including being angry, resentful, fearful, selfish, and dishonest. Use your daily recovery rituals to "clear the way" for your "True Self," your true nature of love, to come forth.

Rituals support recovery. They foster psychological and spiritual growth. Engaging in recovery practices prevents you from falling back into addiction. These practices not only help you grow, they give you the freedom to be who you are and to live out of love.

Some of the most important recovery rituals and practices can include:

Mutual Help Recovery Meetings. These include both in-person and online meetings. Options might include:

1. 12-step meetings
2. Women for Sobriety (WFS), (www.womenforsobriety.org)
3. SMART Recovery (www.smartrecovery.org)
4. In the Rooms (www.intherooms.org)
5. Secular Organizations for Sobriety (SOS), (www.sossobriety.org)
6. LifeRing (www.lifering.org)

7. Refuge Recovery (www.refugerecovery.org)
8. Celebrate Recovery (www.celebraterecovery.com)

Recovery-oriented meetings serve several purposes. They allow people to develop recovery contacts for mutual support, as no one with a severe addiction does recovery alone. Meetings allow people to learn from the wisdom and experience of others. They give you inspiration and hope when you hear how others have succeeded in the face of their disease. Another benefit of mutual help meetings is that they promote self-examination followed by self-expression. This promotes personal growth.

Mutual help meetings can be a very powerful tool for recovery. But, like a chainsaw, one has to be very careful to grab the right end to avoid getting hurt. To use a meeting skillfully:

1. Go early to get to know people.
2. Stay away from the smokers. Associate with members free of all addictive substances and behaviors.
3. Stay late. Only socialize with people who have three or more years of solid recovery.
4. Listen carefully.
5. Identify, but don't compare. Take what's best and leave the rest.

Socializing with those who are fragile in their recovery or who are addicting will likely result in a return to addicting. Some people get cravings when they hear other people's stories. These people need to avoid speaker-discussion meetings if these meetings trigger cravings. By far the most popular and most pervasive of mutual help programs are the 12-step fellowship programs. A full list of options and websites can be found in the resource section in the back of the book.

12-step meetings come in all shapes and sizes. There are speaker-discussion meetings, Big Book meetings, 12-step meetings, women's meetings, LGBT-friendly meetings, and many others. The best strategy for trying on a 12-step meeting for size is to go to 10 or more different meetings to find a few that fit best. You can then focus on the style of meeting that best coincides with your comfort level.

12-step fellowships emphasize gaining power over addiction by surrendering to a higher power to help with sobriety. While many people's higher power is God, it may be anything that helps keep you sober. The proven efficacy of this approach confirms the simple truth that most people, especially those with severe addiction, cannot achieve recovery alone without the help of something outside of themselves.

Some people do not like the religious overtones of 12-step meetings, with their use of the terms "God" and "higher power." Others object to the concept of powerlessness. You do not have to be religious to benefit from 12-step meetings. Your "higher power" is what is outside of you that helps you to stay sober. Your higher power could be important things like your family, your pet, your medication, your sponsor, your therapist, or any other resources. For some, it will be their religion and their experience of a personal deity in their lives. The key with 12-step meetings is to exercise tolerance, live and let live, and take what's best for you while leaving the rest. Chew the meat and spit out the bones. Everyone's recovery path is unique to them.

12-step fellowships are not religious organizations (even atheists can have a higher power). Despite this, some people like neither the spiritual overtones of the 12-steps nor the concept of surrender. For these people, other meeting options exist. Women for Sobriety meetings employ 13 principles to empower women in their recovery.[6]

Smart Recovery focuses on support and self-empowerment in managing cravings by examining the "ABCs" of behavior: Antecedents, Behaviors, and Consequences. Members practice thinking through cravings to the end consequences of acting vs. not acting on them as a way of getting unhooked.

In the Rooms is an online fellowship for those who prefer the anonymity, security, convenience, and accessibility of online meetings vs. in-person meetings.

Secular Organizations for Sobriety and LifeRing both allow for people to come together to discuss their lives. Members give and receive support without the spiritual overtones of the 12-step fellowships.

Refuge Recovery is a Buddhist-based movement that emphasizes meditation and mindfulness as a pathway to freedom from cravings and compulsions. Members support each other in their practice to develop the capacity to sit with urges without needing to act on them.

Celebrate Recovery is a Christian-based recovery program that also leverages sharing and support of members around a common religion. Other religions offer similar recovery support meetings of their own.

No matter your preference or background, there is a mutual help program that can help you through these difficult times and deal with the hardships of addiction as they present themselves.

Journaling. As you work through your recovery plan, writing in a journal brings to the surface what lies just below your awareness. Journaling brings focus and clarity to your life. It allows you to go deeper into the truth of your existence. As you write about your daily experiences, your feelings, dreams, thoughts, and memories, new insights emerge, which you can then share with others. Journaling gives you a safe, private forum in which to work out solutions to your daily dilemmas. You can invoke the "Wise Person" within you, writing about how he or she would solve a particular problem. You will often find yourself amazed at the wisdom you discover within yourself through journaling.

Recovery Mentors. Recovery mentors serve as guides in your growth and transformation. They help you stay sober and navigate the stresses and complexities of life. A good recovery mentor will help you transform your life for the better. Ideal recovery mentors are individuals with extensive sobriety (five years or more) who are free from all addictive substances and behaviors, including smoking. They are older than you are—a parent or older sibling figure. A good recovery mentor is tough, keeping you accountable. They are also kind, showing compassion without judgment. Good recovery mentors are also wise. They give helpful guidance born of their own recovery experience.

You most benefit from your recovery mentor by "getting current"—updating your mentor about all aspects of your life. Do this on a daily or near-daily basis. Be honest and transparent. Prevent shame and self-will from pushing you into secrecy. Tell the truth and then process the truth, resetting emotionally and deepening your understanding of yourself, of others, of how to be in recovery, and of life itself. The 12-step fellowships encourage members to get a recovery mentor called a "sponsor." Other mutual help programs may not offer such a formal arrangement. You can ask someone to serve as a recovery mentor and discuss the nature and structure of the relationship. Many in recovery welcome opportunities to give back. You can also hire a professional recovery coach to serve as a recovery mentor.

Take care to keep the boundaries of the relationship as a formal mentor-mentee relationship. Recovery mentors are not friends or family members; this creates the risk of getting too emotionally entangled in your recovery, causing a loss of objectivity.

Prayer, Meditation, Contemplation, and Mindfulness. In the daily rush of our lives, we all get too caught up in our thinking minds. Many are dominated by the ego, with its concerns for security, inclusion, and power. People sometimes act from a place of fear, insecurity, and lack, alienated from the experience of love. The solution: spend time each day in silence and stillness. This allows you to separate from your thinking mind and have a direct experience of the ground of existence—of Reality. From this, you experience the immediate, present moment, separate from thought, where the sacredness of existence is unobstructed. Though fear and pain may still exist in your mind, you are separated from them, as you see they are not you. You create an opportunity to experience peace, love, gratitude, and a sense of the incredible preciousness and wonder of existence. You might even experience your unity with all that is. You experience the beauty, grace, and miraculousness of life. Whatever "God" is—something inconceivable—you experience in this state of silence and stillness.

Recovery requires a daily grounding in the stillness of your being. You can do this with several techniques:

- Meditation
- Mindfulness
- Yoga
- Contemplative prayer
- Reading sacred texts
- A solitary walk in nature
- Time alone in other quiet places, free of distraction

As we will discuss in the Touchstone on cultivating spirituality, a moment-by-moment practice of mindfulness keeps you rooted in the present moment and out of your thinking head. You benefit from taking several mini-breaks during the day to stop, in silence and stillness, to re-ground yourself in the

Present. This practice is a powerful way of keeping you focused on what is most important in your life—to live a life of love, meaning, and fulfillment. It also helps you to separate from your cravings so you can manage them intelligently.

Recovery Resources. Finally, to supplement your mindfulness and consciousness of your recovery, focus on educating yourself through reading books, watching videos, or listening to podcasts in order to learn from those who have wrestled with the same issues as you. Find books/videos/podcasts that speak to you. Use your journal to write insights you glean from reading and their relevance to your life. Don't just read a book to read it and check it off your list. Read to absorb the wisdom within the pages in such a way that it changes you. Slow down. Allow your reading to transform you.

Adjust your recovery rituals to meet your changing needs. Commit to a daily, disciplined practice, for you must do the work to receive the blessings of recovery.

Now let's shift our attention from recovery activities to the actual implementation of these skillsets into your recovery journey.

First, Develop Your Recovery Skills

With these new resources in place, you can implement them into your recovery program. Whether you choose to focus your energy on a 12-step program, working with a mentor or sponsor, or simply educating yourself through the numerous resources available to you, you have to start somewhere. As you journey along your path to recovery, remain aware of your recovery skills and how exactly you are using them. The first step in developing your recovery skills is knowing what you need to develop. Most people struggle with avoiding the triggers that lead to cravings and in managing cravings once they arise.

You may fear cravings. You may consider cravings to be bad. Cravings are not bad. They are just cravings. It is what you do with cravings that makes them either benign or harmful. Cravings often serve as a signal that your well-being is compromised. You may be hungry, tired, afraid, lonely, bored, empty, or angry. By facing and working through your negative feelings, you learn to resolve and bear distress rather than addictively numb it.

While many things can trigger cravings, in all instances the one common denominator is you. Understand how skillfully you live your life and respond to what happens that is beyond your control. Do you bring on more stress than you can handle? Do you allow yourself enough sleep and relaxation? Do you engage in stressful or abusive relationships? Do you make and maintain loving connections with others? You should not allow yourself to be defined by "people, places, and things" as reasons for addicting. There is always another way.

Then, Manage Your Triggers

Triggers are a normal yet challenging part of your recovery process. So don't be surprised if you experience them. Triggers can be both external and internal. We will discuss managing external triggers of cravings in the Touchstone on creating a positive recovery environment. Minimize triggers, especially in early recovery. You minimize triggers by living life according to the Touchstones.

Internal triggers include negative emotional states (negativity) such as worry, anger, fear, hopelessness, loneliness, self-pity, self-hatred, envy, or boredom. Most people focus more on the negative than the positive, creating "dis-ease" and thus the conditions for a recurrence of addicting. Identify negativity when it arises and do something about it.

Techniques to counter negativity include:

Label thoughts and feelings as just thoughts and feelings you are having. Recognize a negative attitude for what it is—something you can change.

Show appreciation. Say "thank you" to the thought or feeling, asking what purpose it might serve you. Practice unconditional friendliness toward all internal experiences. Don't hold onto them, however. Let them pass.

Inquire and correct. Inquire into the roots of negative thoughts, asking if they are realistic or productive. Counter negative thoughts with more positive, Reality-based thoughts. If someone criticizes you, put whatever truth there might be into a balanced perspective where you appreciate yourself and accept your faults. If self-hatred arises, remind yourself of your immeasurable value despite your imperfections. If you experience non-acceptance of some person or situation, accept the person exactly as they are or the situation just as it is.

Practice gratitude. This rests on the act of intentionally focusing on what is good in your life rather than what is bad.

Talk. Call someone or talk to someone in person. Talk out your feelings.

In doing so, explore how your negativity affects you and shift your attitude to a more balanced, positive perspective. Try to identify any distortions, such as black and white thinking, seeing only the negative in a situation, or taking something personally that is not about you.

Act. Engage in positive, self-soothing, and fun activities. Take good care of yourself. Play. Connect with others for guidance, reassurance, and support. Help someone. If you are bored, do something you enjoy. If you are lonely, pick up the phone and call someone. Reach out. Get something done that will leave you feeling good.

Regroup and recharge. Most negativity is rooted in fear and hopelessness. Get affirmation from affirming people. Reflect on past accomplishments. Notice that even the most "hopeless" people have succeeded in recovery through faithful persistence. Read inspiring spiritual or recovery literature. Remind yourself that failure gives the opportunity to learn and grow. Practice positivity.

Each of these suggestions offers you the opportunity to face your triggers head on. We each have specific experiences that spark emotional challenges. That is simply part of life. But how we manage these issues is by far the most important element of continuing down a positive road to recovery.

Finally, Manage Cravings

As you develop your recovery skills and focus on potential triggers that might occur in the future, you should also remain conscious of cravings that are only natural when dealing with addiction. Managing cravings requires recognizing the first thought of addicting. Look inside to understand what is driving thoughts of addicting. This is the key moment for coping. If you are feeling powerless or helpless, take initiative to assert yourself to resolve your difficulties. Take care of yourself and deal with your problems. Or, you may realize it is best to let go and accept what is beyond your control. These responses are much better than the continued behavior of addicting.

A key technique for managing cravings based on mindfulness practices, borrowed from Pema Chodron,[7] should be a part of everyone's repertoire of craving management skills.

This approach involves four steps, and is referred to as **the 4 R's of craving management**:

1. **Recognize** when you are having cravings.
2. **Resist** acting on the cravings through the use of one or more cravings management techniques.
3. **Relax** into your cravings and inquire into the roots of cravings.
4. **Return** to a state of mindful presence. Do "the next right thing."

These "4 R's" keep people on track and out of trouble. Make it a conscious habit to practice these steps every time you get a craving. With time, you learn to live with your cravings. With practice of the 4 R's, you become free of the attractions and aversions that arise in your mind. Thoughts and feelings arise, thoughts and feelings go. You are here, still, centered in the midst of all this mental turbulence, at peace, on track, untroubled, acting with love and integrity from moment to moment. This takes time as your practice slowly changes your brain. Practice with patience, perseverance, and faith.

But even then, there may be times when cravings seem overbearing and out of control. By far the most important craving management skill people should work to develop in early recovery is to resolve a craving by "talking it out." Many people become lost in their addiction before even asking for help. Learning to use your attachments to those who care for you to manage cravings is one of the ultimate achievements of recovery. Never crave alone.

To ask for help, you have to have a healthy network of recovery supports—people who can help you manage your cravings. One of the first tasks of recovery is to develop this support network, working on the Touchstone "Develop Healthy Relationships."

Asking for help is difficult for many. Many people never experienced stable, safe, close, loving relationships with caregivers when young. No one tuned into them and helped them work through painful experiences and feelings.

Another reason asking for help may be difficult is trauma, especially the trauma of neglect. If you were neglected, growing up emotionally alone, you never developed your innate capacity to connect. If raised in a hurtful environment, you learned both that it was not safe to share yourself with others and that you should expect and accept hurt. If you suffered emotional or physical neglect, you received the message that you were unworthy of love.

Without loving connections while growing up, people enter adolescence and adulthood emotionally crippled and in pain. They feel empty inside, haunted by a never-ending yearning to love and be loved combined with a disabled capacity to do so. They lack the capacity to ask for help because they learned that asking for help wouldn't help. This is not part of their psychological repertoire.

Disabled in loving, victims of abuse and neglect attempt to use others to fill their emptiness or to reinforce their addiction. Because of the disability in loving, they then exploit their relationships to serve the addiction.

Recovery entails reversing this. You humble yourself in the face of your illness and take the courageous step of asking for help when you are most vulnerable. Acknowledge that you are not in control and need help. Though you have never asked before, ask someone to help you.

Asking for help requires mindfully taking a step back from your cravings when they first arise. Realize that you are in trouble. See how you experience the "Forget its," a state in which you don't care and just want the objects of your addictive desires. Note the feeling of not caring about yourself or anyone else. See how you feel nothing and no one can stop you from addicting. When you see the "Forget its," separate yourself from them and ask for help. If you do not, they will sweep you away to temporary gratification, guilt, remorse, destruction, and hopelessness.

Leverage your relationships with recovery supports to get past the craving without addicting. You may struggle with this key recovery skill for two reasons. First, when cravings arise, you have already decided you will addict no matter what. Your self-will is too strong. You do not want to talk to anyone who might talk you out of addicting. You are not yet fully awake. Recognize the first stirrings of cravings. Note, "I am in trouble," and pick up the phone before it's too late.

Second, concerns about your adequacy make asking for help difficult. You consider needing help a weakness. The inability to humbly ask for help is the real weakness. Strong, secure people ask for help.

Practice this skill over and over, until you become adept at it. I often tell patients that this exercise and other recovery practices are like riding a unicycle. You learn by getting on and falling off. With time, you learn to ask for help.

What does "talk out the cravings mean?" It means to note the craving, name it, and talk about the bad things that will happen if you addict, and the good things that will happen if you don't. You can also use your supports to talk about things to do to distract yourself from the craving or other ways to diminish the craving. You may need to be with someone until the craving passes.

Talking out cravings is the most important achievement of early recovery. It is a first step in your ability to "self-regulate"—to use others to manage how you feel. You develop two capacities: to get humble and to get vulnerable. Both capacities will serve you well in life beyond just managing cravings. For additional techniques to combat cravings, refer to the resource section in the back of this book.

Freedom from Addictive Behaviors

Renouncing addictive behaviors does not mean renouncing the behavior. People need to eat, work, exercise, spend money, shop, and use technology devices. While one can commit to celibacy, it is possible to make love while abstaining from addictive sex. Renouncing addictive behaviors entails renouncing the addictive engagement in these behaviors. The agenda shifts from addicting to manage psychological pain to acting to savor and nurture life. You work to live and contribute. You exercise to take care of yourself. You shop and spend money to provide for your material needs. You eat to live. You have sex to give and receive love and sensual pleasure. You do not engage in these behaviors to manage the pain of existence.

Recovery from addictive behaviors requires that:

- You mindfully note your agenda, refraining from the behavior when driven by craving and compulsion to manage pain.
- You manage pain in ways other than engaging in addictive behaviors.

See the automatic, often unconscious ways you manage fear, whether it be masked as anger, anxiety, hurt, or the need to control others. The habitual ways of coping with fear and its derivatives are sometimes called your defensive styles.

Break free of addictive behaviors by identifying feelings of distress, pain, or helplessness. Then respond in more skillful ways. Learn to manage your problems and your emotions. Manage your emotions by:

- Adopting a friendly, accepting attitude toward your feelings
- Dropping negative judgments of yourself and others
- Problem solving
- Practicing positivity. Putting things into their proper perspective
- Honoring what cannot be changed

If you are in a painful situation, first remove yourself if you can. Then engage in problem solving. Problem solving requires several life skills:

- Asserting yourself
- Resisting acting on impulse
- Thinking things through
- Talking it out
- Writing it out
- Gathering information
- Setting limits and maintaining boundaries with others
- Asking for help

Sometimes getting to a safe place where you have space and time either alone or with caring others is all that's needed to soothe yourself and problem solve.

Recovery Maintenance

As you navigate your road to recovery, it is completely normal to feel the stress and temptations to addict yet again. The recurrence of addicting starts before the actual addicting. It starts with allowing the conditions for addiction to arise by living unskillfully or ineffectively managing the inevitable pain of life. You "BUTA"—build up to addict. People lapse every day. We all experience unhelpful feelings and thoughts and behave unskillfully. No one lives life perfectly. We all make mistakes. Things happen, often beyond our control. We experience pain. Often, the return to addicting starts with feeling bad, even before addictive thoughts arise. Or, something else triggers addicting. This is why recovery maintenance requires daily lapse management to take care of yourself and keep yourself on track. This is why you work on your recovery daily.

Be vigilant to detect when you lapse so you can address the lapse before it progresses to addicting. Several red flags signal you are off track. These include but are not limited to:

1. "Stinking thinking," including negative ruminations
2. Destructive emotions
3. Avoidance of accountability; making excuses or blaming others; acting irresponsibly; not following through or keeping commitments
4. Lying or otherwise being dishonest
5. Keeping secrets
6. Isolating or otherwise disengaging from others
7. Breaking the rules or otherwise acting without integrity
8. Boredom
9. Inactivity
10. Losing the healthy fear of a recurrence of addicting; allowing complacency to set in
11. Romancing the addiction; remembering the good times while forgetting the bad

These symptoms indicate you're not right with Life. Correct what's off to get back in alignment with Life. It is important to right the ship when you fall off track. Prevention is crucial to your recovery, but adjusting along the way plays as crucial a role.

Recovery requires a change of lifestyle. Develop a new sober social network. End toxic relationships. It helps in early recovery to get a new phone number or block calls and texts from drug dealers and others who can trigger. Shut down toxic social media sites. You may be lonely in early recovery, with no healthy social supports. If so, develop new, healthy friendships and mature recovery supports. Go to meetings. Make positive connections. Do positive things.

Put up boundaries with harmful people to protect yourself. Maybe you cannot attend a family get-together with a drug-abusing brother or sister. Perhaps the most contact you can have with a judgmental, critical, and unloving parent is to send them a birthday card once a year. Take an inventory of all your relationships. Decide which ones you will end and which ones you will modify to protect yourself. Develop new friendships with people who do not suffer from addiction or people stable in their recoveries.

It can take up to three to five years to establish a stable recovery. Socializing with people with less than this amount of time puts you at risk of returning to addicting.

Many people struggle with shame, low self-esteem, and poorly developed self-care habits. They hate themselves, when they need to love themselves. Self-hatred and poor self-care can trigger cravings and addicting by leading to unnecessary stress. Practice cherishing yourself every day. Commit to caring for yourself as if you were your own child. Avoid chaos, drama, and conflict in your relationships. Live simply and with balance. Claim the right to have your needs met and assert yourself. If you do this, you will reduce the experience of cravings.

Learn to recognize when cravings first arise. Ask yourself what triggered them. Then resolve the root of the craving instead of addicting. Nip cravings in the bud before they take over. Since practice makes perfect, you succeed by practicing your trigger and craving management techniques.

Maintaining your recovery requires living skillfully out of love for yourself and others. Start each day by reflecting on your affirmations and life commitments. Then go forth into your day and put them into action. Practice your recovery rituals daily. If you do these things, you can prevent the recurrence of addicting.

If You Slip . . .

While not inevitable, slips are common, as no one does recovery perfectly. You may have lapses that lead to slips. If you slip, take the following steps:

1. **Admit it and forgive it.** Immediately and gently acknowledge the mistake. It's OK. Be kind to yourself and forgive yourself for being imperfect and having the disease of addiction. Do not beat yourself up. Do not despair or give up. Tell yourself that slips are just mistakes containing a lesson for your growth.
2. **Recommit.** Persist and persevere. Commit to always getting up when you fall. Immediately recommit to your recovery. Call someone right away to get help. Go to a meeting. Throw away the drug/bottle/pack of cigarettes. Get yourself to a safe place. Remove yourself from all triggers.
3. **Tell it.** Don't keep your slip a secret out of guilt or shame, unless

doing so would cause significant harm. Take care to at least be open with your recovery supports.

4. **Investigate it.** What were the triggers? How were you not right with Life? What was the detailed sequence of events that led to your addicting? Process this in your journal, with your therapist, and with your recovery mentor.
5. **Modify.** With your newfound understanding of what went wrong, make corrections to your recovery and life plans. Boost your recovery program. Devise a better way to manage stress and pain. Fix what you are doing wrong as outlined in the Touchstones, whether it be restoring your integrity, simplifying and balancing, taking better care of yourself, asking for help, or repairing damaged relationships.

Develop your recovery skills to secure your recovery. Put into practice plans to manage triggers and cravings. Monitor yourself for the daily lapses that lead to addicting. Correct them. If you slip, recommit and ask for help. Learn from your slip. Modify your recovery plan as needed.

Tips & Tasks

Tips: Secure your recovery by becoming adept at managing cravings, triggers, and the daily lapses that can lead to addicting.

Tasks: Develop craving and trigger management plans. Practice. Modify as needed.

Monitor for the lapses that lead to addicting. Make corrections to how you are living. Modify your recovery plan as needed.

If you slip, recommit, ask for help, learn, and modify your recovery plan.

Be Wary of Complacency

As Anne Lamott says, “You can get the monkey off your back, but the circus never leaves town.” Complacency is a false sense of safety when in danger. For victims of addiction, that danger is readdiction.

Complacency can be lethal for victims of addiction. You may feel as if the monkey has left your back, but he is still there, only quietly sleeping. A drink or a drug is always just an arm's length away, while an addictive act is just one bad decision away. It is important to keep a healthy fear of a recurrence for the rest of your life.

Remember: Addiction May Be Forever

As much as we'd all like to think addiction is just a temporary stage in our lives, addiction changes the brain in ways we only partially understand. It is true that many people "develop out" of addiction and leave their vulnerability to addiction in the past. In vulnerable people, however, addictive substances and behaviors permanently turn on genes associated with craving and loss of control. This is why for some, once you have addiction, you have addiction forever. Addiction may be active or in remission, but your brain is permanently altered. If you return to your addiction and try to control it, you find you have already lost control. While another opportunity for addicting exists, another opportunity for recovery may not. People have a finite number of second chances. Too often, addicting ends up being fatal. Knowing this can help stave off complacency.

No one wants to be "damaged" or "defective." You may be vulnerable to feeling shame about your addiction, feeling you should be free of addiction to be whole. You may link your self-esteem to an unconscious need to be free of imperfections, including addiction. Accept your flawed nature as being part of an unseen perfection. Humbly surrender to the truth of your lifelong vulnerability to addiction. It is said that sobriety is a gift, the price being eternal vigilance.

Remember the "never again" rule for addiction. For most people who have suffered from addiction, once they stop addicting, they can never drink or drug or engage in an addictive behavior again. Doing so too often results in a recurrence of addicting to varying degrees depending on the person. Though you may address the forces that brought you to addiction, you will never stop being vulnerable to the addiction itself if you addict.

Keep the Memory Fresh

Another lure into complacency involves memory. Imagine what it would be like to remember the past traumas of your life with the same intensity of detail and pain as the day they occurred. Fortunately, pain fades with time.

Unfortunately, your memories of addiction's destruction too often fade or even disappear. You forget the intensity of desolation and despair that drove you to recovery. Recovery teaches you how to laugh again, yet you risk forgetting you once cried. You can forget that your worst day in recovery is better than your best day addicting.

Keep the memory fresh. Do this by writing as detailed an autobiography as possible of your days of addiction and keep it in a safe place for reference. Refer to your story of addiction to remind yourself of the truth of your illness. Every day millions of people in recovery tell their story of addiction, recovery, and hope at mutual help meetings around the world. This time-tested practice reminds the audience that addiction is always ready to revisit their lives if they let down their guards.

If you don't keep the memory of addiction fresh, you make yourself vulnerable to its return. Don't lose the "gift of desperation" in recovery. What you forget, you are doomed to repeat.

It is easy to see how someone can addict after 10 years of sobriety. They say, "I'm OK now. I can have just one." They forget that "one is too many and a million are not enough."

Vigilance and Humility

Part of the benefit of daily, lifelong recovery rituals is keeping complacency at bay. Remind yourself daily that you have a vulnerability. See the need for vigilance. Recovery, like gardening, requires constant "weeding" of negative mind states and "fertilization" of what is true, good, and beautiful in your life.

Protect yourself from complacency by practicing humility. Embrace the truth that you are a perfectly imperfect being in a perfectly imperfect world. You are just another beautiful "bozo on the bus." You know you are dis-eased, damaged, and flawed, and accept, with humility, this truth. It is exactly as it should be. You humbly accept this truth while committing yourself to your recovery. In this way, you avoid falling into the trap of complacency and fully dedicate yourself to the first Touchstone: working on your recovery every day.

Tips & Tasks

Tips: Complacency kills, as addiction is forever.

Tasks: Guard against complacency by:

- Writing a biography of your addiction.
- Telling your story to others.
- Guard against shame through humility.
- Working on your recovery every day.

CHAPTER 3

TOUCHSTONE 2: CREATE A POSITIVE RECOVERY ENVIRONMENT

"Environment is of supreme importance. It is greater than will power."
—Paramhansa Yogananda

In the second Touchstone, we will take a look at the foundational importance of managing the many people, places, and things that make up your recovery environment. A positive recovery environment is essential for recovery. If you live in a toxic recovery environment, there is no chance you will stop addicting. In this chapter, we will first discuss the eight characteristics of your environment necessary for recovery. We will then focus on minimizing the many external triggers that bring on addicting.

Tend to Your Environment

Recovery requires a positive environment. If you have a hip fracture, you first need surgery in a hospital, followed by a stay in a rehabilitation facility, followed by ambulation aids in your home. If you have asthma, you may need to have air purifiers in your home.

Recovering from addiction requires a similar approach. Without the proper environment, you are doomed to fail. Many people enter recovery directly from toxic environments. Your family may be riddled with addiction. You may be living among crime and poverty. There may be domestic violence. You may suffer severe job or parental stress. At the extreme, victims of addiction may be homeless, virtually shutting off any hope of recovery.

So to enter recovery, you first have to take toll of your environment. The best practice is to create an "8-S" environment. An 8-S environment is:

1. Safe
2. Supportive
3. Stable
4. Sober
5. Low-stress
6. Structured
7. Supervised
8. Has therapeutic *Sequellae* (consequences)

Let's unpack each of these at greater length:

Safe. To begin, you must feel safe to pursue recovery. Address this as the first order of business in your recovery. Remove any immediate or potential threats to your safety. Once you feel safe, you can work on your recovery. Get help to get safe.

Supportive. We need each other to get by. Just as someone might need a cane to stay upright, you need the support of others to stay in remission. No one does recovery alone. Those supporting you during your recovery actually keep you from isolation. If you have a recovery mentor, "get current" every day. Without shame, share "the truth, the whole truth, and nothing but the truth." Do the same with your trusted intimates, sharing your feelings, both positive and negative. Humbly ask for feedback and direction.

A good recovery support offers honest, critical feedback when you are off track. Yet they will do so without judgment or invoking shame. They may judge your "sins" but will never judge you, the "sinner." Let yourself be held accountable. You need mirrors in your life to reflect to you both the positive and the negative so you can feel good about the positive while focusing on correcting the negative. Support also includes mentoring, guidance, and tutoring on how to live a life of recovery.

Stable. Recovery requires stability, as instability causes stress, which can lead to a recurrence of addicting. You need a stable living situation and work environment. Strive to enter into stable relationships, especially with recovery supports. You need stable life routines. You can't work on your recovery with your life up in the air.

Sober. Recovery requires a change in lifestyle. You change what you do, where you go, and your relationships. You avoid the objects of your addiction. If you don't want to slip, stay away from the slippery places. Remove potential triggers for addicting from your life. This includes people, places, and things that might trigger addicting. It's difficult to end toxic relationships sometimes, especially when those relationships are lifelong in nature. Learn to say to your drug-using "friends" something like:

> "I need to end our contact because I am getting into recovery and can't be around addiction. This is not about you. It's me doing what I need to do for myself. I want you to know I care for you and wish you the best. If you ever get sober and have a few years of recovery under your belt, I hope we can reconnect."

Don't associate with people with less than a few years of recovery. Their fragility can trigger readdicting. Cravings can be infectious.

Low-stress. One of the most common precipitants of addicting is stress. Refer to the section on stress management in the Touchstone on healing. But for now, remember to minimize your stress to protect your recovery.

Structured. We drift without structured, daily routines. Living life skillfully involves balancing discipline with flexibility. You benefit from a daily schedule. This helps give a sense of purpose and meaning. You need reasons to get up in the morning. This creates momentum. Positive routines promote recovery. Examples include a structured recovery program, an exercise program, time with friends and family, time for spiritual practice, etc. Structures not only include your daily commitments to yourself, but also your daily external commitments to others, such as work, childcare, volunteer work, and school. Having these external structures protects you from boredom and keeps you engaged with Life.

Supervised. The mind can be a dangerous place; don't go in there alone. Share your thoughts, feelings, and actions with others. Allow others to supervise you. This provides support and creates accountability. You need to be accountable to recover. Allow yourself to be "supervised." Very early in recovery, this may include living in a residential treatment center and submitting to regular drug screens. It will often mean allowing your recovery mentor oversight of your life and recovery activities so he or she can give feedback and direction. It requires humility to allow yourself to be supervised. It also requires acknowledging you have an illness that can kill you and that you need help.

Supervision can come from many sources. It can come from a spouse, from parents, from other family members, from friends, from therapists, or from recovery mentors. Often, it comes from multiple people. Follow these guidelines in allowing people to supervise you:

1. They should not judge you for suffering from addiction.
2. They should not expect perfection, but should expect commitment, honesty, willingness, and accountability on your part.
3. They should be helpful and supportive. Although they may judge your behavior as helpful or not, they should not judge you.
4. Some should have empathy with the experience of addiction and have strong recovery experience.
5. They should not be so invested in your success or failure that they lose their emotional balance when you make mistakes or addict.

Develop a recovery team. Your team includes loved ones, peer supports, and professionals. Talk to them when you meet with difficulties, including cravings to use. Too many people call their supports after addicting. When you do this, you are not allowing yourself to be supervised or supported.

Supervision takes many forms. If you get a paycheck and spend it on drugs, then supervision of how you spend your money becomes necessary. You may need to sign over your paycheck to someone who can manage your finances until your recovery solidifies.

Supervision in professional treatment or legal settings will usually include drug screening and psychotherapy. Drug screenings hold you accountable, which promotes your recovery. They help you to resist the temptation to cover up drug or alcohol use. They help you stay honest throughout your addiction and recovery. Supervision gives you feedback and direction about your recovery work, your psychological status, your spiritual status, and your relationship status.

Therapeutic Sequellae. Sequellae are usually defined as negative, pathological consequences of a disease. I use the term to refer to any consequence of your behavior. This includes positive consequences because of positive actions and negative consequences because of unskillful actions. The optimal environment for recovery includes both positive and negative consequences that propel growth.

Positive sequellae are rewards you experience when you do the right thing. Negative sequellae are painful consequences of not doing the right thing. Both positive and negative sequellae are powerful tools for change. Recognize the healing power of the pain that drove you to wake up and transform your life. Pain tells you that you are at odds with Reality and need to change. Pain is a gift in disguise.

Others may conspire to shield you from pain by enabling you. One spouse spoke of her willingness to watch her husband die of alcoholism because she did not want to get a divorce and lose his pension and her home. Many parents shield their drug-addicted children in their homes and support their habits out of fear. They try to "control" what is beyond their control. In Reality, they have no control at all.

There is great wisdom in the saying "tough love." To be "tough" is to allow others to experience the painful consequences of addiction, recognizing that pain plus hope is the recipe for change. "Tough" can mean not allowing adult children to live at home if they are using. It can mean insisting they work to support themselves. It can mean limiting a relationship with someone until they are in recovery. Some make parts of a relationship, such as living together, contingent upon recovery. It can include other conditions, such as honesty, fidelity, keeping agreements, pulling one's load, and not harming others. Loved ones should set up conditions for their relationship with you and boundaries to protect them and help you. No one said "tough" would be easy, but it is much better than supporting the addiction over the course of time.

By "love" I mean an unconditional recognition of others as sacred and an unconditional commitment to their well-being. Though people may not live with someone in active addiction, they can still give their unconditional emotional support. They can offer hope. If someone wants guidance, they can offer that. They can offer conditional "rewards," depending on the type of behavior. For example, this may include allowing a loved one to come home as long as they are sober and engaged in recovery.

The challenge is being both "tough" and "loving." Many can be "tough," with judgment and a lack of compassion, or "loving," with enabling. Enabling shields the victim of addiction from the painful consequences of their addiction, allowing them to get "off the hook." Loved ones need to guard against anger, frustration, or hopelessness, preventing these feelings from distorting their actions. When applying or allowing painful consequences, loved ones need to ask if they are helpful to the victim. Above all, they should not abandon. They should maintain an emotional connection whether the victim of addiction is in recovery or not. Coercing people into recovery by threatening them with abandonment is wrong. People caught in the vortex of addiction are suffering. They need and deserve love, combined with accountability for asking for help, choosing recovery, and doing the work.

Realize that you benefit from therapeutic sequellae, both positive and negative in nature. When something painful happens because of your actions, you are tempted to become resentful or even angry. You can feel like a victim, falling into the "poor me's." In and of itself, this leads to a recurrence of addicting, as reflected in the saying, "Poor me, poor me, pour me a drink." What you don't see is your own arrogance in expecting there to be no consequences to your actions. You don't see your entitlement, thinking the world should be different. Humble yourself and realize that you are no different than anyone else.

View pain as a teacher, not an enemy. Don't judge pain as "bad." Pain is pain. Pain is a messenger. It says things are not right and you must fix them. If you vow to learn from your pain and change your behavior, you will heal and grow.

Don't run from "accountable environments" where you experience both positive and negative sequellae of your behavior. Instead, seek out these "tough love" settings. We live in a tough love world. That is good. Work on your recovery to the best of your ability with the help of others, with humility, integrity, and accountability for your actions. Don't allow others to abuse or enable you. "Tough" without "love" and "love" without "tough" don't work.

Tips & Tasks

Tips: Recovery requires an "8-S" environment: safe, supportive, stable, sober, low stress, structured, supervised and possessing therapeutic sequellae, or consequences.

Tasks: Set up an 8-S environment to maximize your chances of success.

Minimize External Triggers

Finally, you have to minimize your external triggers to create a positive recovery environment. While we touched on managing your internal triggers in the first Touchstone, this principle is an important part of creating a safe and sober environment. It is so important that it is useful to identify it as a separate principle, as external triggers can be your downfall, even if you reside in a happy and healthy environment.

External triggers are people, places, things, and situations that awaken cravings.

Common external triggers include drugs, drug paraphernalia, bars, people using, drug dealers, neighborhoods where you got your supply, and places where you addicted.

For example, one common trigger is a call from a dealer. Dealers are predators. Their calls are tests to see if you are vulnerable to addicting. Calls from addicting "friends" can also trigger cravings. Minimize these triggers as much as possible. One common practice is to change your cell phone number, email, and social media sites to make it more difficult for negative influences to contact you.

Conflict, stress, and loss are triggers. Boredom due to a lack of meaningful activities can trigger addicting. Untreated psychiatric and medical illnesses can be a trigger. Minimize these triggers by leading a meaningful and low-stress life and getting professional help.

Jobs that expose you to the object of your addiction can be triggers. If you work in a drug-infested environment, your chances of recovery fall close to zero.

The numbers and types of triggers are many. Although you must work to remove triggers from your life, you cannot protect yourself from all possible people, places, things, and situations. Stress, for example, is unavoidable, no matter how skillful you become at minimizing and managing it. You must learn to manage unavoidable triggers.

Managing External Triggers

As you work through your recovery, the first step to managing external triggers is to mindfully note when you are triggered. Sometimes the trigger can induce a subtle passing negative thought that takes root and grows in your mind, such as self-pity or resentment. You cannot manage triggers if you do not know you are being triggered. Once you note the trigger, tell yourself that you are in trouble and act to protect your recovery.

The second step is to remove yourself from the trigger as fast as possible. If you are at a party or event, excuse yourself. If you see someone on the street, walk the other way. If someone offers you something, say "No" and leave.

Whatever the trigger, call someone as soon as possible to talk out the craving. Exercise one or more of the many craving management techniques discussed in the previous Touchstone on working your recovery and in the appendix. Do what you need to do to minimize external triggers in your life. Become skillful through practice at managing the triggers you cannot avoid.

Creating a safe and sound environment will put you in a great position to successfully journey through your recovery. Addicting is a constant threat, but living in a supportive environment is one of the greatest antidotes to this poison. You should work to be very thoughtful and careful in the manner in which you choose the best environment. A safe environment will better equip you to manage the challenges and triggers as they come. That is the hope and goal of this second Touchstone.

Tips & Tasks

Tips: External triggers threaten your recovery. Minimize your exposure to them and manage the ones you cannot avoid.

Tasks: Identify all the people, places, and situations that trigger you.

Remove these triggers as much as possible.

Develop a trigger management plan to remove yourself from triggers that arise.

Manage cravings that arise using your craving management techniques when triggered.

CHAPTER 4

TOUCHSTONE 3: RENOUNCE ADDICTING

"Every form of addiction is bad, no matter whether the narcotic be alcohol or morphine or idealism."
—Carl Jung

The third Touchstone we will discuss is the extremely important act of renouncing addiction. No one wants to addict. But as you succumb to the powerful claws of addiction, you often find yourself without choice, simply struggling to survive and quench the thirst. This Touchstone first discusses renouncing all addictive substances and addictive behaviors. I will then discuss the skillful management of distress and desire, including addressing the roots of your pain. Finally, I will discuss letting go of the uncontrollable, and replacing addictive grasping with acceptance.

For some, renunciation gets a bad rap. People think of it as deprivation. This could not be further from the truth. Rather than depriving yourself of anything, renunciation is a gift you give yourself. In fact, you get something great in return. It is the act of liberating yourself from compulsively grasping for something you want out of greed, even when the harm outweighs the benefit.

So the question arises: What role does renunciation apply in your journey to recovery? Renunciation is one of the three dimensions of recovery, along with healing and self-realization. Renunciation is the first step of the ensuing process of healing. This is where we begin our process of healing.

Renouncing addicting requires a leap of faith in the healing power of love, as renouncing addicting is an act of self-love. People are often afraid to give up their addictions, fearing the loss of a damaging crutch. Some even believe there is a risk that recovery will make things worse rather than better. People doubt their own capacities as well as the capacities of others to help them. They are afraid to change and lack faith in recovery. As I am sure you can tell, these are mere excuses to continue addicting.

To renounce something hurtful like addicting, people need a combination of the pain that motivates change, the hope that inspires faith, and the help from others. That combination of pain, hope, and help are powerful antidotes to overcome fear and trigger renunciation.

Renouncing addicting is refusing to harm Life if at all possible. We give up acting on compulsions driven by greed or fear when we see that they cause harm. It is central to the joy of healing and recovery. This is because renunciation of harm minimizes the pain we inflict upon ourselves and others through addicting or other destructive behaviors borne of grasping or aversion. It protects against future pain by tending to problems now rather than turning our backs on them.

For those with addiction, I encourage renouncing all addicting as a supreme act of self-love. It sounds easy to say, but is certainly hard in practicality and action. To that end, let's work to answer the following question: how do you develop your capacity for renunciation?

Maintain your faith that loving is the way to joy and make a life commitment to loving. See the harm that grasping and avoiding causes, especially with addicting. Anticipating the suffering, give up a thought or behavior that harms yourself or others by inciting fear, greed, or the impulse to addict. Seeing allows for renunciation of addicting. This is liberating. Seeing frees us to love.

Then, start to cultivate your reverence for Life. To renounce is to cherish and value your life. It is a formal dedication to a no-harm way of being, seeing, and doing. But it doesn't stop there. You have the courage needed to deal with your distress. Manage your pain with love for yourself. Ask for help and take good care of yourself. Make an intentional commitment every day to love—to loving yourself and to helping others. Take the no-harm vow—to not harm yourself or anyone else. Start each day with an intentional commitment to love.

Then practice mindfulness throughout the day. Watch your mind to see when harmful thoughts or feelings arise, including urges to addict. Smile at them and let them go. This is the beginning of renunciation, as our actions flow from our thoughts and feelings.

Gandhi once said, "Renounce and rejoice." Renounce greed and aversion, including when they arise as urges to addict, as you see them arise within you. Then you will be free to devote yourself to the business of enhancing and savoring Life. That is true recovery.

Pursue Freedom from All Addictive Substances and Behaviors

Anne Wilson Schaef said, "You move in your recovery from one addiction to another for two major reasons: first, you have not recognized and treated the underlying addictive process, and second, you have not accurately isolated and focused upon the specific addictions." Renouncing all addicting is an ideal. Some, but not all, attain this ideal. Recovery involves making a daily effort to renounce all addicting as best you can while avoiding "all or nothing" thinking. Do not beat yourself up for not attaining this ideal. Just do your best each day to renounce addicting as best you can.

Most people have more than one addiction. Abstaining from one addictive substance or behavior often leaves people with others. Like in the game "Whack-a-Mole," as soon as one addictive substance or behavior is suppressed another pops up to replace it. Until you address the root of addiction, you will not find the serenity and fulfillment that comes with living a life of love. As Patrick Carnes has said, "Addiction is a relationship, a pathological relationship in which . . . obsession replaces people." This pathological relationship will not end until you renounce addicting in all ways to manage the way you feel.

You want to be open to your experience with complete honesty and non-defensiveness. You cannot be open to the moment if you are addicting.

Yet, refraining from addicting is challenging. It requires concerted effort on all the Touchstones. As Gerald G. May has said: "Addiction is not something you can simply take care of by applying the proper remedy, for it is in the very nature of addiction to feed on your attempts to master it."

Not everyone who renounces one addiction renounces all addicting. The crowds of smokers at AA and NA meetings are a testament to this. Only a portion of people attains total recovery by renouncing all addicting. For many, renunciation is an ongoing process rather than a one-time event. Although conventional wisdom says to give up one addictive substance or behavior at a time, many people succeed by ceasing addicting altogether, including with cigarettes. Though difficult, this may lead to greater success rates.

You may find it easier to let go of one addictive behavior or substance at a time. This works if you do it. Too many people become complacent when they have ceased their most destructive addictive substances or behaviors while continuing others. You have not then changed your fundamental way of living.

Tips & Tasks

Tips: Addicting hurts you and prevents you from developing healthier ways to manage pain.

Addiction can be to addictive substances or behaviors.

Total recovery entails renouncing all addictive substances and behaviors.

Tasks: Renounce addicting in all ways. Practice your craving and trigger management techniques.

Note when you are distressed, and address your pain through problem solving, acceptance, and the practice of positivity.

Benefits of Renouncing

There are immeasurable benefits of a commitment to total recovery. You'll find authentic happiness, peace, and fulfillment free of addiction. No longer a slave to addiction, you at last find freedom.

With this in mind, commit to pursuing freedom by attending to your pain. Renounce addicting to manage the way you feel. When you do this, several important things happen to your recovery:

1. You feel a renewed sense of safety. Everything is clear. There are no gray zones. It is black and white. You simply abstain from addicting.
2. You notice your cravings subside. You feel more stable. Living in recovery becomes more sustainable.
3. Living requires less work, as you don't have to invest effort into attempting to manage cravings, compulsions, and negative consequences. You are less distracted, more focused, and more productive.

4. Life becomes much more satisfying, as you experience true freedom and lack of impairment. Guilt fades as life becomes more coherent. You can bask in the satisfying feeling of doing the right thing. You are living according to your conscience.
5. Self-efficacy grows, meaning that you have control over your actions and your life. You feel more empowered. With empowerment, you become accountable for your life.
6. With no addictive outlet for managing stress and pain, you are forced to cope with life on life's terms. Problem solving improves. You take better care of yourself. You explore your feelings, share them, learn to bear them, and put them into perspective.

With time, you realize that recovery delivers everything addiction promised, but did not deliver. You realize that your problems have non-addictive solutions. If you recover, you will find you become as good as you thought you were when you were immersed in addiction.

Skillfully Manage Distress and Desire

Because of instinctive drives, we grasp for pleasure and push away pain. This is natural. Yet we are more than other mammals. We are human. We have a spiritual nature as well as an animal nature. We can love, experience wonder, grace, beauty, oneness, and a sense that we are part of something greater than ourselves. We can experience a sense of purpose. We have creative and artistic drives. We can experience deep empathy and connection with others and enjoy loving and being loved. We can differentiate gratification from fulfillment, seeing that one is transient and the other can last a lifetime. We also have the human capacity to derive meaning from our experiences. Herein lies our salvation. If you can positively reframe distress and desire as valuable messages and give them meaning, then you can achieve freedom from addiction.

The following steps will help you to reframe your distress and desire:

This too shall pass. To begin with, remind yourself that all experience is impermanent, just as everything is impermanent. When you are feeling good, savor your experience, knowing that it will pass. Let go when good times pass, without grasping. Without grasping, there is no suffering. When you are in pain, remember that this will pass as well, especially with skillful living. Work to reduce your distress as much as possible and accept what cannot be avoided. Practice hope and gratitude for your many blessings. Acceptance takes the suffering out of distress.

Pain can be a gift. While pain may have no merit, it can also be a gift. The painful consequences of unskillful actions teach you how to live in harmony with the world if you only look and listen. Then you will see and hear. Many understand karmic pain, in retrospect, as the source of their salvation. Their despair awakened them into recovery. Some pains can be alleviated. Some cannot. For those that cannot be eased, you have no option but to accept and bear your pain and search for a way to make sense of it. Acceptance is the key. You ground yourself in the realization that this Universe is sacred and that what happens is sacred, even senseless pain. With profound humility, you accept what you cannot change. With this act, suffering ceases. So, managing distress comes down to skillful action along with acceptance of what is beyond your control.

Positivity over pain. The problem for those suffering from addiction is that they are vulnerable to problem solving with an addiction to manage distress. This is a dead-end road that only multiplies pain tenfold. Just as you do not grasp for pleasure, you do not addict to avoid distress, but instead face it head on. Just as you say "Thank you" to life's pleasures, so you also say "Thank you" to the distress that helps you learn and grow. With positivity, you look for opportunities in the middle of hard times. You value pain as a helpful messenger telling you that something needs to be corrected through skillful action or transformed through acceptance. When you renounce addicting to manage pain, you will look back and realize that your distress forced you to grow. Your greatest pains bring your greatest strengths when you address them without addicting.

Each of these coping mechanisms should help you deflect and redirect the pain you might experience while addicting. If and when you do experience substantial pain, these can help you shift your consciousness and look at things in a different way.

Healing Comes from the Heart

To heal from painful emotions, embrace your awareness with your heart, and not just with your head. Welcome whatever arises, no matter how painful or unacceptable it may be. Don't judge experiences as "good" or "bad." Refrain from judging others or the world (Reality) as "good" or "bad." Cultivate a universal friendliness and inquiring attitude toward your experience. When you do this, you realize that, while distress is inevitable, suffering is optional, as suffering springs from your judgments and attitudes.

Suffering comes when you judge what is happening as "wrong" or "bad" and fail to accept what you cannot change. Suffering comes when you are caught in the illusion that you can control something you cannot.

Negative emotions don't go away forever merely by naming them, accepting them, and saying "Yes" to them. They continue to arise. What changes is your ability to relate to them in a friendlier manner and to release yourself from their grip. That is the shift from negativity to positivity. Instead, you respond in a more loving, intelligent, and compassionate way. Your pain may still be there, but you have the freedom to respond with love. You need only to name and accept your pain, whether it be shame, grief, fear, hurt, or anger. Seeing and naming your anger, for example, allows you to respect others even as you express your anger with kindness. Repressing your suffering perpetuates and compounds your suffering. This is avoidable pain.

Craving Pleasurable Experiences

Cravings for pleasurable experiences bring on another form of suffering. Many might argue that cravings create as much distress, if not more, than painful emotions. They bore into your mind. You feel possessed by them. They even intrude into your dreams. They leave you feeling haunted. Their intensity and persistence can make it seem impossible to not act on them. This is where your management of your impulses becomes subtle and requires mindfulness.

For example, when you eat, is it because of hunger, or because of the pleasurable taste of the food? Can you savor the pleasurable sensations of eating and yet stop when you are full, without a compulsion to keep on eating solely for the pleasure of eating? When you make love, can you do so intending to give and receive love while enjoying the pleasure of sex? Or are you using your partner solely to satisfy a compulsive sexual craving? Can you engage in recreational and creative activities without a sense of compulsive grasping? Can you keep it light? Can you let go when things don't go "your way"? Can you have fun without having to have fun? If so, then you are free and you do not suffer as conditions beyond your control unfold.

By freeing yourself of your compulsions and aversions, you experience the truth that distress is inevitable, but suffering is optional. Let go of compulsive self-will, which imprisons you more than the bars of a true prison. Practice a light, friendly acceptance of your emotions, cravings, and compulsions. If you sit with them, seeing them for what they are, the strength of your vision will show that they only bring enslavement and suffering. Then you will be free.

Tips & Tasks

Tips: Recovery entails learning to manage distress and desire.

Distress and desire are inevitable. Suffering is optional.

You achieve freedom from addicting though a combination of awareness and acceptance.

Managing pain effectively reduces the vulnerability to addiction; recovery entails good pain management.

Tasks: Practice mindfulness, letting go, and acceptance of all experience. Change what you can.

Look within, with the help of others. Come to understand your pain. Access therapy, the support of others, and your spiritual practices to heal your pain.

Renounce self-hatred. Commit to loving yourself and others.

Let Go

Frustration, resentments, fear, and negativity poison recovery. You must learn to let go to prevent addicting. We are born with instinctual drives for power and control. These are evolutionarily adaptive. We have a remarkable capacity, unlike any other animal, for manipulating and controlling our environment. . . to a degree. Likewise, we have an unprecedented capacity for collaboration. Because of these drives and capacities, humans have adapted to virtually every niche on earth and have built intricate civilizations. We have worked to control our environments and all that goes on around us.

Yet much is beyond your control. You cannot control the weather, solar flares, or asteroids. You cannot avoid death and decline, aging, distress, or disease. You cannot eliminate impermanence. Despite your powers to control, Life is largely unmanageable. With civilization comes interdependence. Everyday events beyond your control, such as terrorist attacks or the oil cartels' manipulation of oil prices, affect you. When you look closely, you see you have limited control over most circumstances.

Although you can manipulate others to get what you want, you have little control over others. If you are a dictator, you might force others to submit to your will through fear, but you cannot dictate others' thoughts and feelings. You cannot make someone love you or satisfy all your desires when you want them satisfied. You cannot change others.

From the truth of limited control comes the dictum, "Change what you can and accept the rest." Don't be passive or resigned to fate. Working to change things often makes things better. Effective problem solving is the most potent antidote for most troubles. Yet have the wisdom to recognize and accept what you cannot change. Then let go. Let go of your desire for Reality to be what it's not.

The True Power of Letting Go

How do you let go? First, you have to see the cost of wanting to change what cannot be changed. See your suffering from grasping. Notice that grasping is like holding on to a red-hot iron rod that sears your skin. Your pain tells you that you are not in alignment with Reality. People, places, and circumstances are as they are. Just breathe, let go, and accept.

Letting go is an act of humility. You acknowledge that you are not "God." You surrender to the fact that the Universe will not change to meet your expectations. Come into alignment with Reality.

This can be harder when it comes to letting go of resentments. Resentments are an attempt to control by objecting. You may resent people and conditions that do not line up with your expectations. You resent difficult events, such as illness, death, or unemployment. You resent because people, places, and things aren't what you want.

Through letting go, you allow for reverence of the miraculous gift of existence. Even death becomes your friend as you see the essential nature of impermanence and let go of your resentment of mortality. Without impermanence, you wouldn't exist. Life requires death. Letting go of immortality, you value your sacred, impermanent life all the more.

Letting go of the uncontrollable is the path to freedom from anxiety. Look into your fears. Notice your non-acceptance of risk, harm, and loss. While valuable for survival, untempered anxiety is too much of a good thing. Anxiety and fear may serve you well if you are leaning too far over a 100-story building, or if you are swimming with sharks. The problem is the fundamental, underlying lack of acceptance of the inevitability of harm and loss. You will eventually lose everything, including your life. You will suffer insult and injury, illness and disability, and innumerable other traumas, no matter how skillfully you live. When you let go of your need to control the uncontrollable, your anxiety recedes. Peace ensues from acceptance. Acceptance begets serenity. Letting go is the most powerful of all anxiety remedies—more powerful than any pill.

Finally, let go of regrets and past traumas. The past is also beyond your control. What's done is done. You can't change the past. Don't look back with regret. Look back with a commitment to acting skillfully with love today. You can only act in the present to influence the future. Ask yourself what you can learn from the mistakes you have made. Transform your pain into wisdom and compassion. Wisdom arises when you allow yourself to learn from the past. Compassion arises from understanding our common suffering and imperfections. You are not alone in having suffered from mistakes and the harmful actions of others. Know that loving yourself means letting go of the past to live in the Present with love.

In the End, It's All Your Choice

So when you are in difficult circumstances, you have choices. That is important to remember. While you might be limited in your control of certain things, you always retain complete control over your attitude and your choices. You often have the ability to remove yourself from toxic situations. You can engage in surrendered action to hopefully change your situation if possible. Act positively, knowing karma is on your side in the long run, while accepting that there are no guarantees. Part of your hope should rest in the comfort of choice.

Since you can only control the little you can, channel your efforts into positive activities that enhance your life and the lives of others. Remember, the saying is "Keep your side of the street clean." Commit to doing your best and accepting the rest. Letting go doesn't mean you stop controlling what you can. Actions have consequences. Karma exists. What goes around comes around tenfold, often later, in unforeseen ways. If you stay positive, act positive, and let go of the rest, then you are doing what you can. This will help you renounce addicting and find alignment with the third Touchstone.

Tips & Tasks

Tips: Grasping for the impossible creates resentment, fear, negativity, and frustration. These feelings fuel addicting.

Suffering subsides by humbly honoring Reality and letting go of what cannot be changed. As suffering subsides, so does addictivity.

Tasks: Change what you can. Accept the rest.

Let go of what you cannot change to avoid the resentments, fear, negativity, and frustrations that fuel addicting.

Let go by humbly honoring Reality.

CHAPTER 5

TOUCHSTONE 4: ACT WITH INTEGRITY

Integrity involves acting in accordance with your morals, values, and ethics. When you have integrity, you'll then experience harmony between your experiences, thoughts, feelings, and actions. Integrity starts with the notion that you know what is right. It is the act of understanding the rules and committing to following them. You then follow through. People with integrity walk their talk. They are trustworthy and reliable.

To that end, this Touchstone on integrity has three sections. The first section discusses doing the next right thing. You'll then find a section on honesty, as dishonesty with yourself and others is an inherent part of addiction. Finally, we will review the essential recovery skill of putting principle before destructive pleasure. As we journey through each of these, you'll find yourself better grounded and more connected to building a life filled with integrity.

Do the Next Right Thing

Mahatma Gandhi said, "Happiness is when what you think, what you say, and what you do are in harmony." A fundamental human challenge is to do what is right in the face of urges to do otherwise. To do that, we should first have a basic understanding of the difference and distinctions between acting through instincts and acting based on morals. Trouble arises when our instinctive urges conflict with a higher set of moral principles and values. We live in a complex and highly interdependent civilization. Acting without a moral compass damages the Whole.

That said, our collective prosperity requires that we live according to principles such as honesty, mutuality, and collaboration. Ideally, socialization teaches people to manage raw impulses to meet needs while not harming anyone in the process. This is not easy. Everyone struggles with fear, greed, and a desire to exploit or even harm others if it will bring benefit. This can be very subtle, such as when you secretly judge others to feel better about yourself.

Part of being human is submitting your will to what is best. Integrity comes from being part of something greater than just yourself. Note that Life is sacred and miraculous. Experience the beauty and grace of Life that goes along with tragedy and suffering. Make the ultimate commitment to devote your life to the service of something greater than your own selfish needs. Live by a set of higher moral principles and values regardless of your selfish urges. With integrity, you transcend to the pinnacle of enlightened self-interest in which you see that the ultimate selfishness is to be selfless. Because you are an interdependent part of the whole of Life, serving Life serves you. You serve Life that Life might sustain you. This becomes the spiritual moral star that directs your life journey.

Fear vs. Love

To act with integrity is to act with love. To act out of fear alone means that your ego, and not you, is in charge. People enter this world with a tension between fear and love. Moral growth entails resolving this tension for yourself. Moving from fear to love means you serve the greater good. Recovery involves transitioning from being ruled by fear to being informed by fear while acting with love.

What may appear as love may in fact be ego in disguise, as when you give expecting something in return. As T.S. Eliot wrote, "The last temptation is the greatest treason: to do the right deed for the wrong reason." Make a choice. Do you allow your ego to manage your life, or do you harness your ego in the service of Love? Why do you live? Do you live only for your own self-gratification, or do you live to sustain yourself so that you can contribute? This is the fundamental spiritual question that underlies your commitment to a life of integrity.

Some cast this dialectic between ego and love as the tension between good and evil. Note the story of two wolves:

> One evening an old Cherokee told his grandson about a battle that goes on inside people. He said, "My son, the battle is between two

> 'wolves' inside all people. One is evil. It is anger, envy, jealousy, sorrow, regret, greed, arrogance, self-pity, guilt, resentment, inferiority, lies, false pride, superiority, and ego. The other is good. It is joy, peace, love, hope, serenity, humility, kindness, benevolence, empathy, generosity, truth, compassion, and faith." The grandson thought about it for a minute and then asked his grandfather, "Which wolf wins?" The old Cherokee simply replied, "The one you feed."

Your commitment to doing the right thing regardless of impulses to do otherwise brings good not only to the world, but also to you. The Law of Karma dictates that you reap what you sow. Love begets love, just as evil begets evil. How you conduct yourself determines how your life unfolds. There is a Persian saying that, "As you move, so God responds." By acting with integrity, you strengthen your spiritual muscles and become strong in character. You shape your fate.

I want you to realize the fulfillment than comes from loving. Love leads to a life without remorse or regrets. You have nothing to regret if you do nothing that causes regret. Your esteem-able acts build your self-esteem, reducing the tendency to fuel feelings of shame. See that who you are is far more important than what you accomplish. Shift your sense of gratification from what you get to who you are. As Henry Ward Beecher said, "He is rich or poor according to what he is, not according to what he has." Living according to this principle, you can look back on your life with minimal regrets, knowing you made the world a better place and left a legacy of love.

Building Character Creates Integrity

Integrity is the manifestation of good character. Alfred Armand Montapert summed it up when he said: "Reputation is what folks think you are. Personality is what you seem to be. Character is what you really are." Your character determines your destiny. A strong character will bring goodness to your life and the lives of others.

Your true character comes out when you are under stress, or as Dr. Dyer says, character is "What comes out of you when you are squeezed." Martin Luther King Jr. once said, a bit more eloquently and from a more sociopolitical perspective, "The ultimate measure of a man is not where he stands in moments of comfort and convenience, but where he stands at times of challenge and controversy." Being in the midst of "challenge and controversy" or being "squeezed" triggers egoic drives for survival. If you are operating under a paradigm of fear, then your ego will color your character. If you are operating under a higher paradigm of love, integrity will direct your actions with an abiding faith that all will be well if you but do well. Addiction challenges both of these.

Do the next right thing for the sake of doing the right thing. Accept that you have little control over the outcomes of your actions and act with integrity simply because it's the right thing to do. As Abraham Lincoln said, "I am not bound to win, but I am bound to be true. I am not bound to succeed, but I am bound to live up to what light I have." Remember, in the end, you have to live with yourself. You want to go to bed each night and sleep without regrets and go into your final sleep at the end of your life with no regrets. You do this by acting with integrity.

To have integrity, walk your talk. Benjamin Franklin once said, "Well done is better than well said." Actions speak louder than words. When acting with integrity, no discrepancy exists between what you do and what you say. Be honest, consistent, reliable, and accountable. Take responsibility for your actions and the consequences of your actions on others. Be trustworthy. Remember that consistency in the small things makes the biggest difference. When your insides match your outsides, you know you are in good recovery.

See what is best from moment to moment. You cannot do the "next right thing" if your mind is clouded in self-delusion. Knowing the truth requires opening your heart and mind to what Reality has to say. Gandhi spoke of this as "listening to the still, small voice within." This is the voice of your conscience.

Virtually no one acts with perfect love and integrity at all times. Commit to a life of integrity, but realize you will not practice integrity perfectly all the time. You just have to do the best you can and make a conscious effort to move in the right direction. As one victim of alcoholism said, "Trying is what got me drunk; doing is what keeps me sober." Recovery requires acting with integrity, as acting without integrity causes tremendous stress, which triggers addicting. Integrity protects your recovery.

Tips & Tasks

Tips: Having integrity means doing the next right thing regardless of urges to do otherwise.

Integrity arises out of a commitment to loving the whole of Life of which you are a part.

The ultimate of selfishness is selflessness.

You know what is right by getting still and listening closely to your conscience.

Acting with integrity is in your best interest. If you put bad out into the world, bad comes back to you. If you put good out into the world, good comes back.

Acting with integrity reduces stress, guilt, and shame, which reduces the risk of readdiction.

Tasks: Write down your moral principles and values. In doing so, determine what is best for both you and others.

Commit your life to serving the whole of Life of which you are a part.

Do the next right thing, moment to moment.

Get still and listen closely to your conscience. Let it tell you what is best for you to do.

Practice Honesty

Gary King said, "There is no such thing as an inconsequential lie." Lies and dishonesty are a difficult part of addiction. Honesty is so important to recovery it deserves special emphasis. It is a cornerstone of integrity. Everyone lies. The person who says "I have never lied" is not telling the truth. People lie out of guilt, shame, fear, or to get what they want. At the end of the day, it is hard to say who dishonesty harms more—you or others. It destroys trust and poisons relationships. Dishonesty leaves people separated and disconnected. As Renee Bledsoe has said:

> The Light is more than some abstract, unknowable energy force. Light is Truth. If Light is Truth, then darkness must be lies. Each and every lie you tell to yourself and others casts the shadow of separation upon you. Every time even the most minor deception is revealed and the truth is made known, you are reunited with the Light. So, let there be Light. Those are the words by which you can create your own magnificent world.

This is why a commitment to rigorous transparency and honesty is so critical to your recovery. You cannot have authentic connection and mutuality with others under the veil of deceit.

Integrity requires rigorous honesty in all your affairs. This is very difficult in early recovery, for addiction compels you to develop a way of being that depends upon deceit for survival. It was a crucial coping mechanism to protect your Master, the addiction. To give it up feels both unfamiliar and frightening. It takes a leap of faith to share your feelings and actions with others and hope others help and not harm you. Many fear judgment if they return to addicting. People fear rejection. They fear the painful consequences of their behavior and feel an overwhelming urge to lie to protect themselves from these consequences. See that recovery means "facing the music" of your unskillful actions. The painful consequences of your unskillful behavior are part of the healing process of recovery. No matter the case, you must intentionally practice honesty to break this default way of acting.

Lying to protect an addiction can be a core survival need if you do not see other ways of dealing with your helplessness. When caught in the grips of addiction, the addiction rules. Attempts by others to block your addictive behavior can then bring out frustration, rage, and deceit. Honesty helps to free you from the shackles of addiction.

As you enter recovery, renounce even the smallest lies. Lying only adds fuel to the fire of your guilt, shame, and remorse. You may lie in a rationalized attempt to "protect" loved ones from the painful truth of your addiction. This only creates separation when you need connection. When people discover the lie, it shatters trust and incites hurt and anger in the ones you have deceived. This multiplies the shame that led to lying.

Committing to honesty is a courageous act born of the insight that it's what's best. Accept the consequences of your actions. Don't lie out of fear of what will happen to you. Be honest. This builds trust and connection with others. Do it to decrease your own shame, guilt, and remorse. Let the Golden Rule guide you; you don't want others to lie to you.

Practicing Intelligent Honesty

Developing a daily practice of honesty requires diligence. At first, you may lie about the smallest things. When this happens, correct yourself at once. Become mindful of everything you say, monitoring your words for their truthfulness and the underlying intentions that drive what you say. Ask yourself, are you speaking truthfully? Be very honest with yourself about why you are saying what you are saying. Is it to make yourself look good—to impress others? Is it to evoke sympathy in others? What is your true intent? Do you speak to serve yourself only, or to serve the greater good? It takes time to learn to be honest with yourself and with others. Honesty develops with patience, practice, and perseverance.

When telling the truth, take care to not cause unnecessary harm. Truth spoken without compassion is a weapon. Ask yourself if telling the truth is necessary for the greater good. If so, then speak the truth with tact, care and kindness.

Wake up every morning and commit to being honest for the day. Choose right over convenient. Don't hide, manipulate, or otherwise deceive to enhance yourself or to shield yourself from the just consequences of your actions. Make this challenging practice a central part of your daily psycho-spiritual practice.

Tips & Tasks

Tips: Dishonesty hurts everyone.

Recovery requires honesty and transparency. Honesty builds trust and reduces guilt and shame.

Tasks: Practice meticulous honesty. Monitor yourself. Correct any untruths immediately.

Take care to not be unnecessarily hurtful.

Put Principle Before Pleasure

Thomas Jackson said, "I like liquor—its taste and its effects–and that is just the reason why I never drink it." The principle in this section is the principle of love. Recovery means replacing pleasure to treat pain with the fulfillment of love. Savor pleasure when it comes, but don't use it to manage pain.

Addicting out of desire is a disguised form of relief from pain. Why would you feel a compulsion for destructive pleasure if you felt fulfilled? You may say to yourself you addict for fun. Really, life feels boring, tedious, or unfulfilling, or you otherwise feel a vague "dis-ease" or lack in your life.

It is not to say that pleasure is a bad thing. Everyone engages in pleasurable activities like playing, eating, or having sex. If these activities enhance your life, or at least harm no one, then pleasure for pleasure's sake is not a problem. Pleasure is actually a gift. Pleasure is one way the Universe rewards us for right action. Renounce pursuing pleasure to manage pain. If you are living life correctly, including enjoying the moment-by-moment experience of existence, then pleasure will be abundant—you need not seek it through addiction to relieve your pain.

Many people can have an occasional drink or drug, enjoy themselves, and go on with their lives with no compulsion to continue using and with no adverse consequences. They lack addictive vulnerability to these substances. It is only when a compulsion arises to pursue pleasure to manage pain to the detriment of yourself and others that you violate the principle of love. Putting the pursuit of pleasure before love causes tremendous suffering for yourself and others. It creates a warehouse of regrets. In the end, you will not look back and savor how many times you addicted.

To commit yourself to the principle of love over pleasure requires that you surrender to the dictates of your conscience. The quality of your recovery is proportional to your submission of your will to your conscience. When you submit, you win. You don't have to like it. Just do it. Commit to doing the next right thing for a lifetime.

Francis C. Kelley said, "Convictions are the mainsprings of action, the driving powers of life. What a man lives are his convictions." The principle of love over pleasure requires that you free yourself from yourself. When your pursuit of pleasure to manage pain at all costs enslaves you, you suffer from the karmic consequences of your destructive behavior. Put love before pleasure.

Integrity is crucial to both your recovery and success as an individual and active member of society. We all want to be thought of as morally fit and honest in what we say and what we do. If you are dealing with addiction, you will find a distinct battle between two parts of your mind. One part will tell you that addicting is wrong, but the other part craves the alcohol, drugs, or addictive behaviors. You then stand in the middle of two very powerful forces. But as you welcome honesty into your life, and work to build your integrity, you can then continue on your path to recovery by doing the next right thing, moment by moment.

Tips & Tasks

Tips: Principle before pleasure means acting with love, savoring pleasure when it comes, but never pursuing pleasure at a cost to anyone.

Principle before pleasure includes not addicting to feel better.

Putting the pursuit of pleasure to relieve pain before love causes tremendous suffering for yourself and others.

Tasks: Put love before pleasure, seeing that this is the path to happiness.

Savor pleasure when it comes. Have fun. But let love for yourself and others be your primary life agenda.

Manage urges to addict with pleasure to alleviate pain by practicing the Touchstones.

CHAPTER 6

TOUCHSTONE 5: HEAL

The fifth Touchstone focuses on the important aspects of healing. Healing entails:

- Getting professional help if needed
- Practicing good self-care
- Facing difficulties head-on
- Learning to switch from living out of a sense of lack to living out of a sense of love

This Touchstone addresses each of these components. I start by discussing treatment. A section on stress management follows. The next section addresses trauma. Finally, I will teach you how to manage the emptiness that drives so many people to addict.

Seek Professional Help

Psychiatric illnesses, including mood disorders, anxiety disorders, and attention deficit hyperactivity disorder (ADHD), often fuel addiction. Trauma engenders self-hatred, fear, anger, and emptiness. Psychic suffering from mental illness, stress, and trauma beget addiction. Treating these conditions helps diminish cravings for the objects of addiction that ease psychological pain. Therapy helps people manage the pain that fuels addiction. Without addiction, you face pain head-on. It is important for you to find effective ways to manage pain or you will experience an overwhelming urge to return to addicting. Sobriety is a start, but not the end. Sobriety is necessary, but not sufficient. Go beyond mere abstinence to addressing the biological, psychological, social, and spiritual roots of your suffering so you need not addict.

Addiction Psychotherapy

One of the most valuable and helpful ways to fight addiction is through psychotherapy. Addiction treatments vary in modalities, strategies, and intensities. Treatment should match your needs at a given moment in time and phase of recovery. No matter the case, good treatment starts with comprehensive medical and psychiatric evaluations to determine your impairments and recovery needs.

A skilled clinician can assess your needs and help you to choose the interventions and services you receive. The addiction treatment field is fraught with ideology and dogma, such as the irrational belief that you are not "sober" if you take medications to treat your addiction. Be wary of clinicians and others who make ideological proclamations about what treatment should be with no evidence base to support their beliefs. Good clinicians use evidence-based treatments, including cognitive-behavioral therapy, 12-step facilitation, motivational therapy, dialectical behavioral therapy, psychodynamic therapy, and interpersonal therapy. Many clinicians use a combination of these approaches. You are unique, so the best suite of interventions for you will also be unique. As you heal and grow, your needs will change over time. Therefore, the nature of your treatment will need to change along the way. Work with a clinician who understands both your needs and preferences and works to provide individualized treatment.

Individual Therapy

Individual therapy provides a forum to work through your obstacles to recovery on a one-on-one basis. You receive individual coaching and support in a safe, confidential setting. Individual therapists should not just teach basic recovery skills. They should address the psychological roots of your addiction. These roots can include a need to self-medicate:

- Feelings of boredom, lack of meaning, hopelessness, emptiness, and loneliness
- Feelings of helplessness and frustration
- Negative emotions such as depression, anger, anxiety, and shame

Addiction therapy can help you learn new ways to soothe yourself. You learn how to have fun, to do something you enjoy, to write your feelings in a journal, to obtain others' support. You might practice going for long walks, or talking to a loved one. You learn to soothe yourself without destroying yourself at the same time. When therapy helps you notice your unconscious self-hatred, you gain the ability to manage it, rather than letting it manage you. With the trauma work discussed below, you develop a sense of wholeness and goodness. Then you need not destroy yourself.

For many, addiction stems from a need to self-medicate feelings of helplessness. People suffer from the illusion they should be in control of their lives and should be able to control what happens. If you examine this belief, you see it's not true in many aspects of your life. You see you can't control what others do or say. Frustration and helplessness arise when Reality doesn't go your way. Rather than addicting to soothe yourself during times of helpless frustration, practice seeing how little control you have. Practice acceptance as a way of dissolving your helplessness rather than dissolving your helplessness in addiction.

Despite your helplessness and ultimate lack of control, you can empower and assert yourself to maximize the chances you achieve the outcomes you want. Acceptance does not mean passive resignation to external forces. Work to change what you can and accept the rest. Apply creativity, problem solving, and hard work to improve your life. Fight, if you must, to protect yourself. Assert yourself and set up boundaries with those who are harmful. Do this with love, care, and compassion. Don't infect the world with anger.

Dr. Lance Dodes, an analyst who writes about addiction and helplessness, talks about identifying the "Key Moments" in your life where you feel helpless followed by an urge to use.[8] Examples include someone rejecting you, when work becomes oppressive, or when someone is hurtful. In therapy, you work to identify these "Helplessness Triggers" and think of ways to deal with them other than addicting. See your addiction as a psychological mechanism to cope with conflict and avoid painful feelings. Develop an awareness for your feelings of lack of control and learn to anticipate helplessness-inducing situations. Then problem solve, accept the situation, or both.

With good therapy, you can develop insight into the connections between present "Helplessness Triggers" and early childhood experiences where you felt a similar sense of helplessness. Feelings of helplessness in the present often stem from the similar situations you had with parents and other childhood caregivers. Childhood experiences can make you see others and the world according to how you experienced it in the past. You re-experience the helplessness and dependence from when you were truly helpless and dependent upon the love and good graces of your caregivers. Clinicians call these developmentally programed ways of seeing the world, understanding the feelings, motives, and actions of others, and of experiencing yourself "schemas." If you were blessed with loving parents, you developed healthy, realistic schemas of yourself and others. You feel empowered to take care of yourself. You have the interpersonal skills to protect yourself, assert yourself to get your needs met, and to ask for help and support when necessary.

If you grow up with trauma or neglect, your schemas become twisted. You misperceive others, fail to protect yourself, and fail to assert yourself. This leaves you vulnerable to experiencing helplessness. With treatment, you develop an understanding of your relational vulnerabilities and then develop the interpersonal skills needed to manage them. You realize that your relationships, although imperfect and sometimes hurtful, are manageable. You can reduce your helplessness to that which is beyond your control. You become a perfectly imperfect person who can love perfectly imperfect people and take care of yourself.

Ideally, treatment for your difficulties will integrate addiction treatment, trauma therapy, and treatment for your psychological problems. We speak of "dual competent" therapists who can help you with both your addiction and your other psychological problems. Too many clinicians with no training in addiction "chop up" treatment by sending you away for addiction treatment. You are much better off working with a dual-competent therapist who folds addiction treatment into your therapy instead of carving it out.

Group Therapy

Many benefit more from group therapy than individual therapy. This is especially true if you have difficulty developing healthy relationships and then using these relationships to stay sober. In a group setting, you can re-program old ways of relating to others that are unskillful or destructive. You can receive feedback from others in a safe setting, under the group therapist's supervision. You can work through conflicts and distortions to learn new ways of feeling and behaving in your relationships. With time, you learn how to safely love and be loved. Since no one does recovery alone, this development allows you to create the loving and supportive social and recovery network needed to stay sober, thrive, and prosper. Group therapy can be difficult emotional work. Yet with patience and persistence, you experience an emotional transformation that makes it worth it.

Your recovery program extends beyond the therapy office into every aspect of your life. You will need more than an hour a week of therapy to recover. You may need the support of mutual help meetings. You may benefit from online recovery forums. A sponsor or other recovery mentor can provide seven-days-a-week, 24-hour support when you are in danger of addicting. Checking in with a recovery mentor daily to "get current" helps you live your life intelligently and skillfully while maintaining emotional balance. A sponsor can also guide you through the process of emotional and relational transformation as you work the 12-Steps.

Engage in mutual-help meetings carefully to avoid being hurt. Meetings, sponsors, and other recovery supports are "tools" you must learn to use skillfully. Some hook up with unsafe people. Some develop romantic relationships with a partner who is in early recovery and too unstable to be in a healthy relationship. A good clinician will coach you on how to use meetings and recovery supports. They might recommend only associating with people with three to five years of recovery and avoiding romantic relationships when in early recovery. Your therapist can coach you in picking the right sponsor—someone with strong recovery experience, a parent or older sibling figure, who is tough, kind, experienced in recovery, and wise as a result of their lived recovery experience.

No matter the case, you do have to practice abstinence from impulsive action. This is a core component of meditation and a thoughtful life. Abstinence gives you the opportunity to think of more productive and intelligent responses to difficulties. With time and practice, you learn better ways to manage vulnerabilities. You heal your vulnerabilities by acting in healing ways.

A critical skill in recovery is learning to avoid and manage negative emotional states that trigger addicting. Addicting starts long before the first drink, drug, or addictive act. Practice getting current with therapists, mentors, and other recovery supports to resolve negative states before they trigger addicting. A good addiction clinician will help you not expect perfection in your recovery. You learn to accept that you will make mistakes. You reframe slips, mistakes, and even full-blown addicting as opportunities to learn, renounce shame and guilt, and commit to grow from your mistakes.

A good addiction therapist will take a comprehensive, multidimensional approach to help you build your recovery skills and transform your life. Your therapy should help you develop the recovery skills shown in the following table by leveraging the right Touchstones.

Table 3: Recovery Skills and Their Relevant Touchstones

Recovery Skill	Relevant Touchstones
Develop a recovery routine Cope with cravings to neutralize them without addicting Manage slips and addicting	Work on recovery Renounce addicting Persevere
Cultivate supports	Create a positive recovery environment Develop healthy relationships
Minimize and manage triggers: people, places, things, situations, and negative emotional states	Create a positive recovery environment Heal Respect Reality
Practice living with integrity	Act with integrity Persevere
Manage stress to keep it at an optimal level	Heal
Make positive lifestyle changes	Create a positive recovery environment Heal Love Take accountability Develop healthy relationships Grow Persevere
Live life on life's terms	Respect Reality Take accountability

Your therapist should take an active role to coach you in your recovery. They should provide education, support, encouragement, and feedback. Becoming adept at recovery requires practice over a lifetime, under the guidance and direction of your therapist and others with lived recovery experience.

Addiction Psychopharmacology

We are fortunate to live in a time when several medications exist that help promote abstinence and recovery. Medication should supplement your treatment regimen, rather than simply replace it.

Controversy exists regarding medications to treat addiction. Many people in recovery consider those who take methadone or buprenorphine, which are very effective opioid-type medications used to treat opioid use disorder, as not being "sober." Often, these people who are judging the recovery of those on buprenorphine or methadone are themselves using a nicotine patch to overcome their nicotine addiction. The irony is obvious. Some judge non-smokers on buprenorphine as not being "sober," while they simultaneously destroy themselves by smoking. Who's in "total recovery" and who's not?

The fact is that medications to treat addiction can mean the difference between life and death, or recovery and despair. As wonderful as the 12-step fellowships are, they only help a minority of the victims of addiction. Psychotherapy is sometimes not enough. People vary in the severity of their compulsions and cravings and in their recovery skills. People's recovery supports vary. It isn't realistic to cling to an arbitrary ideology that those taking medications are not in recovery. Embrace whatever works, including medications, in treating this lethal disease. If medications help you to reclaim your life, deliver you from cravings, and give you a recovery foundation, then the good may outweigh the risks.

However, addiction psychopharmacology is a double-edged sword. Unskillful prescribing or use can cause more harm than good. One risk of medications is that they can make people feel cured. They come to believe they no longer suffer from addiction. Medications can invite complacency. Some people then come off their medications and promptly return to addicting, sometimes with fatal consequences.

By delivering you from the torture of addiction, medications can take away the life-saving "gift of desperation." Desperation motivates you to engage in daily recovery practices and rituals. Medications should empower you to develop your recovery skills and supports, not remove the need to work on your recovery. Recovery activities, just like regular exercise and a good diet, should be a part of your daily lifestyle whether you take medications or not. A good prescriber will insist that their patients take part in a recovery program that both appeals to them and is effective. Medications don't substitute for recovery work.

As with all medications, medications to treat addiction have risks and side effects. Both the prescriber and the patient must balance the benefits against the risks and costs.

The Food and Drug Administration (FDA) has approved several medications to treat various addictive substances based on research studies that establish both safety and efficacy. Clinicians look to the literature for information about the efficacy and safety of non-FDA approved medications. Though FDA approval is a factor to consider in prescribing and taking a medication, it's not always a deciding factor. Evidence-based research remains the cornerstone of good clinical practice. You can find a list of these medications, their descriptions, and potential benefits in the resource section of this book. No matter the case, make sure you rely upon a doctor to make the best recommendations for you. Self-medicating is both dangerous and counter-productive.

Tips & Tasks

Tips: Holistic healing entails attending to the biological, psychological, relational, occupational, recreational, and spiritual aspects of life.

Treatments include medical care, psychiatric care and spiritual care.

Contemporary addiction treatment sometimes includes addiction psychopharmacology.

Tasks: Get treatment from compassionate and competent providers.

Avoid ideologues. Work with clinicians who give evidence-based treatment that meets both your needs and preferences.

Address all areas of impairment and distress.

Get help to live life with a balance of work, love, and play.

Managing Your Stress

Once you choose the right therapy for your addiction, you should then shift your attention to focusing on those areas of your life that can impact your recovery. One of the largest threats is stress. Stress is part of life. You promote your healing from medical and psychiatric illnesses, including the illness of addiction, by learning to manage stress. "Optimal" stress helps stimulate and activate you to live a productive and meaningful life. Without some stress, life becomes empty and lacking in meaningful engagement.

However, excessive stress results in suffering and reduces productivity. Too much stress damages the brain and body. Stress also triggers cravings to addict, resulting in slips or recurrences of addicting.

You experience stress when you feel threatened or frustrated. Stress is the experience of the ego when survival drives are blocked. This can happen when:

- Someone threatens you.
- You are hungry and cannot get food.
- You encounter barriers to achieving your goals.
- You're alone, alienated, and lonely.
- You have too much to do.
- You have a conflict with someone.
- You don't have enough money to live.
- You are physically ill, or have loved ones that are ill.

Happy events, such as getting married, getting a promotion, having a baby, or buying a house, might also cause stress. To that end, almost any significant life change can create stress.

There are many causes of stress. Stress is a signal that your survival, comfort, or prosperity might be threatened. Several cognitive, behavioral, and spiritual techniques can help you manage your stress. These include:

- Becoming aware
- Getting support
- Setting realistic expectations
- Solving problems

- Prioritizing, planning, and pacing
- Engaging in surrendered action
- Relaxing, releasing, and resetting
- Taking care
- Taking perspective
- Balancing work, love, and play

Let's now discuss each of these techniques.

Becoming Aware

The first step in effective stress management is to be aware of your stress and its causes. This requires mindfulness. Ask, "What's going on?" You know you are stressed when you realize you are worried, angry, irritable, depressed, or distracted. You may feel stress in your body as pain, muscle stiffness, stomach or bowel problems, or problems sleeping.

When you experience any of these uncomfortable emotions or physical symptoms, stop, pause, and reflect on why you are feeling this way. What are the root causes? Are you hungry, angry, lonely, or tired (HALT)? Have you not been taking care of yourself? Are you setting limits on others' requests of you? Are you taking too much on? Are you balancing work, love, and play? If you ask yourself and stop to see what arises in you, the answers will almost always appear.

It helps to keep a daily journal. Write about your thoughts and feelings, your problems, challenges, and difficulties. This helps you realize what's going on. This is a great technique for becoming aware not only of your stress, but of how you are managing or mismanaging it.

Denying or disregarding your stress only perpetuates it. Knowing you have a problem is the first step in addressing it. With understanding of what is happening, you can then put into play other stress management techniques. You can organize yourself to take effective action to manage the stresses you have pinpointed.

Getting Support

People who manage stress well ask for help from others. They seek out people who are healthy, positive, loving, and wise. No one should worry or suffer alone. There is a saying that a problem shared is a problem halved. It is amazing how just talking through a problem with others can bring peace and clarity.

Many people with a history of trauma, abuse, neglect, and addiction have developed toxic social networks with people who are also addicted or otherwise impaired. An essential task of recovery is to develop a new social network of happy, healthy, functional, loving friends. Connect with family members and relatives who are happy, healthy, functional, and loving. One of the main reasons you may readdict under stress is that you do not have a healthy social network upon which you can rely.

The opposite of developing a healthy social network is maintaining a toxic social network. Though very difficult, reduce your stress by no longer socializing with your old "friends" who addict. Say to a friend who calls you to get together to addict something like: "I'm in recovery now, so I can't expose myself to my addiction. This is not personal. I care about you. I want to reconnect with you someday after we both have a few years of solid sobriety and recovery."

Avoid harmful relationships. If you can't end a toxic relationship, such as with a child or parent, set up strong boundaries that protect you. You cannot afford to sacrifice your own well-being for the sake of a relationship.

To someone who is abusive, neglectful, or otherwise harmful to you, ask for what you need. Then see what you get. People may change how they treat you if you calmly and kindly point out to them their hurtful behavior. Tell them what they need to stop or start doing. If this does not work, protect yourself by limiting or even eliminating your contact with them. You may say nothing to them. If necessary, say something like:

"I need to stop:

- Seeing you
- Talking to you in person
- Spending time with you

because our relationship is harmful to me in the following ways . . ."

Don't argue with hurtful people. They may:

- Be unaware of their behavior

- Be mentally ill
- Deny their behavior due to an inability to be accountable for their actions
- Have a set of values that condones their harmful behavior

Your intention is not to seek justice or validation, as this may never come. You only want to limit or end contact with harmful people.

Other important sources of help are your recovery mentors and therapists. One reason a recovery mentor is so helpful is that you have someone there, 24/7. You can ask for support in times of need, whether it be to get help with managing cravings or dealing with your problems. An ideal therapist is not only available during sessions, but is available between sessions when you have an urgent need for support and guidance. Since building a healthy social network takes time, skill, and practice, your therapists and recovery mentors support you as you create such a network.

Setting Realistic Expectations

Succeed by nurturing your passions and skills. Stress comes from doing what you're not good at or don't enjoy. Set realistic expectations for yourself regarding what you can do well and what you cannot.

Expect imperfection. No one does life perfectly. Mistakes are part of life. In fact, expect to make mistakes, knowing you learn and grow through your mistakes. Expecting yourself to be perfect is unrealistic.

Solving Problems

Effective problem solving stands as one of the most effective stress management techniques. You face problems and challenges daily. Your problems may be biological, such as dealing with illness or disability; psychological, such as mental illness; relational, including family, work, and other social relationships; or occupational. Get what you want if you can. Avoid what you don't want. Doing this will decrease stress. If you are unemployed and get a job, stress over money will recede. If you end an abusive relationship or assert yourself to stop the abuse, relational stress will diminish. If you get effective treatment for a medical illness, you will have less biological stress.

The problems of life are many. Fortunately, solutions are just as many.

When you are feeling confused, trapped, afraid, lost, or conflicted, share your dilemmas with wise, trusted intimates and get professional help. Meditation, contemplation, journaling, and reflection help. Often, the solutions to problems come in moments of stillness when fully focused on the present moment. Insights arise out of "thoughtlessness." Dream work can help. Keeping a dream journal by your bed and writing any dreams you remember when you wake up helps to capture dreams. You can then ask yourself, "What is this dream saying?" Exploring your dreams with others can lead to insights that show you how to solve problems.

Effective problem solving involves taking effective action. Worrying about a problem does not solve the problem. Worry only causes suffering. Taking care of problems is far better than worrying about them.

Prioritizing, Planning, and Pacing

Managing stress requires organization, planning, and time management.

You reduce stress by scheduling your priorities. Recovery comes first as your highest priority. Next is self-care, including exercise, rest, love, play, and treatment. You must be good to do good. Cultivating your vitality makes you more effective in all aspects of your life.

Tasks come in four categories:

1. Urgent and important
2. Urgent but not important
3. Not urgent but important
4. Not urgent and not important

Prioritize your efforts, knowing you can't do it all, by first tackling the problems that are both urgent and important. Next, take care of urgent but unimportant problems you can't avoid. Address urgent issues so you can spend most of your time on the important, but non-urgent tasks. Delay non-urgent and unimportant issues to those rare times when you have addressed other, higher priority tasks.

Part of prioritization is deciding how much you can take on and letting go of projects and tasks that are less important. You can't do everything you might want to do. Ask yourself if what you're doing gives you meaning and helps you fulfill your key life goals. Abandon activities beyond these. You can do one to three things well, or several things poorly. Staying true to your key life goals and values helps you keep your life manageable.

Prioritization includes the prioritization of others' requests. Most people want to help others. Sometimes, however, you may please others for the wrong reasons. The wrong reasons include:

- Fear of another person's anger, rejection, or criticism
- A belief that if you please someone, they will like or love you more

Significant life accomplishments need planning. By scheduling your priorities, you create a plan. To be efficient, plan your days and weeks ahead of time. Break down large projects into small tasks. Sequence them in their proper order. Then tackle them one at a time.

Be both disciplined and flexible in your planning. You may encounter important tasks you can address the moment they arise. Examples include paying a bill, scheduling an activity, making a reservation, or completing paperwork. Efficient people do these tasks when they arise. They don't procrastinate. Procrastination leads to more things to do. When important tasks come up, "do it now" if possible. Following the "do it now" rule unclutters your mind and shrinks your daily agenda down to a manageable size.

Rome wasn't built in a day. Most worthwhile accomplishments take time, persistence, patience, and pacing. Get more done with less stress by pacing yourself. Take breaks. Keep routines. Set aside enough time every day for rest, relaxation, love, play, and exercise. Carve out time for silence and stillness, even if just 10 minutes twice a day. By pacing yourself, you preserve a healthy balance between work, love, and play.

Engaging in Surrendered Action

You create unnecessary suffering for yourself when you act while expecting a specific outcome. You may ask your partner to clean up after himself or herself, expecting they will comply. When they do not, you become annoyed. You forget you have no control over others' actions. You may give wise advice, then feel disappointed when people don't follow your advice. There is a difference between hoping for vs. expecting a certain outcome. With others, ask for what you want. See what you get. Then do what's best for yourself.

Focus on what you can control. Do what you can. Hope for a positive outcome while letting go of expectations of what will happen. Do your best and accept the outcome.

Practice surrendered action, moment by moment. By surrendering the outcome, you stay positive. You avoid frustration, anger, and hopelessness. With repetition of surrendered action, you will persist, improvise, adapt, and often overcome.

Relaxing, Releasing, and Resetting

We've all heard the term, "blow off steam." Several relaxation techniques help you do this. Many find massage, saunas, steam baths, and hot tubs relaxing.

Deep breathing and muscle relaxation exercises are much less expensive and are always available. Sometimes just taking five slow, deep breaths can help to release stress. The "dive response" is another powerful relaxation technique. When stressed, put your face in ice water for 30 seconds. This stimulates a natural parasympathetic surge that calms the body.

Meditation, yoga, prayer, contemplation, Qigong, and Tai Chi are all proven techniques for promoting relaxation. Exercise also reduces stress and promotes relaxation.

Getting outside in nature, in the sun, and being around plants all help to calm. Going for a long walk often helps. Bringing plants and pets into your home and workplace can leave you feeling calmer and less stressed. Other soothing activities include listening to music, reading a good book, taking a bath, lighting scented candles, and playing with a pet. These are just a few examples. There are many others.

Getting away from a stressful situation to regroup and reset helps to manage stress. Don't say or do anything when angry. Take a "time out" when upset. Count to 10 before impulsively speaking out of anger and making matters worse.

Dealing with stress often takes time to figure things out, get a proper perspective, and develop an action plan, often with the help of your trusted intimates.

We all need down time. Scheduling time to "hang out" helps to reduce stress and regroup.

Take in and appreciate your surroundings. Savor the simple miracle of consciousness. Become fully present to this moment, in all its richness. This gets you out of your head so you can relax, reset, and regain a healthy perspective.

Taking Care

Good self-care is a foundational part of a low-stress life. Self-care involves optimizing your biological, psychological, social, and spiritual well-being. Taking care of yourself involves:

1. Eating healthy
2. Getting plenty of sleep and rest
3. Abstaining from addictive substances and behaviors
4. Keeping regular routines
5. Getting regular exercise
6. Getting from and giving to others
7. Taking part in community
8. Pursuing your passions
9. Making time, in solitude, silence, and stillness, for prayer, meditation, contemplation, or reflection
10. Keeping a balance of work, love, and play

These are all integral pieces to your overall health and happiness. There is no perfect recipe, and each person is different. You might find one type of self-care more important than another. Choose best for you and remember that each of these will make a difference in your ability to care for yourself.

Taking Perspective

Stay positive during tough times. Even in the darkest of times, keep your hope that this too shall pass. Reassure yourself that you will survive, thrive, and prosper as long as you act skillfully. People who handle stress well see the glass as half full, rather than half empty.

Observe your thoughts mindfully. Notice positive, hopeful, optimistic thoughts, and negative, pessimistic thoughts. Negative self-talk increases stress by promoting a sense of inadequacy and hopelessness. A good practice for promoting positivity is to write out realistic, self-empowering, positive thoughts. Examples include:

- "I can do this."
- "Everything is going to work out."
- "Things aren't that bad—they could be much worse."
- "No matter what, things are as they should be."
- "I am blessed."

Attitude is everything. When faced with hardship, you have a choice. You can choose to:

- Be grateful for what you have.
- Have hope.
- Look for opportunities for learning, growth, and change in the midst of difficulty.
- Consider all life events, whether painful or pleasurable, as teachers.
- Cultivate understanding, acceptance, and forgiveness.

You are in charge of both how you perceive your situation and how you respond.

Cultivating gratitude helps to cope with stress. It helps to make a list of things you are grateful for. Reviewing your list when things aren't going your way helps to stay appreciative, positive, and hopeful. If you are grateful to others, let them know. This is a simple act that helps everyone feel better.

One way of getting a balanced perspective on a stressful situation is to imagine how you would feel if you were on your deathbed. See that, ultimately, all that matters is who you loved and how you lived. It matters less what you have, as in the end you lose everything. Power, prestige, and position shrink to their proper importance. In the end, these mean nothing. This puts everything into perspective. Perspective taking lightens the heart and energizes the soul. Practice perspective taking to reduce stress and the risk of readdicting.

Balancing Love, Work, and Play

A balanced life entails proper proportions of work, love, and play. Balance helps you realize your purpose in life: to nurture and savor life. Loving and being loved give connection, support, and the deep fulfillment of nurturing others. Work fulfills the need to contribute and provides resources to survive. Play involves activities that restore and rejuvenate. Let's unpack each one at length.

Love

I discuss love in more detail in the Touchstone on Love. What follows is a synopsis related to stress management. It is crucial to both love and be loved. We need each other to get by. Loving and being loved fulfills our deepest human need and allows us to stay on track while navigating the challenges of living. Just as virtually no one practices recovery alone, so most people need love, support, understanding, affirmation, validation, and help. Civilization would not exist were it not for the intricate matrix of an incomprehensible number of interdependencies based on loving and being loved.

Loving and being loved requires some key relational skills:

1. Being able to enhance and maintain your well-being and vitality so you can devote yourself to the care of others and of Life itself
2. Practicing understanding, compassion, acceptance of others, and non-judgment of others' *personhoods* (as opposed to their *actions*)
3. Knowing we are imperfect and vulnerable to hurtful and selfish behavior, you love while protecting yourself from being harmed
4. Astutely assessing others' characters and intentions
5. Trusting trustworthy people in the ways they can be trusted
6. Connecting with others
7. Treating others with unconditional love, care, and respect

It is cliché to say you must first love yourself before you can love others. Yet it's true. The first step of recovery is to love yourself. If you cherished yourself as you cherish a baby, you would do nothing to harm yourself, including addicting. If you are self-destructive or self-neglectful, you suffer and become obsessed with your suffering. Then you treat others as you treat yourself, sometimes despite your best intentions.

Loving enhances the well-being of Life. To love yourself is to enhance your own well-being. To love another, you must feel whole and fulfilled. This requires loving yourself and enhancing your sense of wholeness and value.

Everyone needs your care and support. You cannot give this without understanding, acceptance, compassion, and non-judgment. Failure to achieve these qualities of mind has a direct effect on your actions, causing others to feel devalued and judged. By developing these qualities of mind, you enable yourself to show care and kindness to others, even when they are destructive. Not that you do not set limits, assert yourself, and create boundaries to protect yourself; it is just that you protect yourself while maintaining an attitude of loving-kindness. This can require a lifetime of practice. With practice, however, this capacity grows.

Understanding the roots of another person's unskillful behavior, which always stems ultimately from fear, creates the internal conditions for compassion to arise. Understanding comes from listening to others, asking questions, and observing closely. Learn not to judge others by reminding yourself that we are all imperfect. See that if you were in their shoes, you would act as they acted. People are as they are. You cannot change others; others need to change themselves. Accept others, with their quirks, foibles, and their evil (evil being anything that harms Life). We are as we are and can't be otherwise.

Armed with compassion, acceptance, and non-judgment of others' personhoods, protect yourself from other people's hurtful behavior. Stay clear to sustain your love and care. In the extreme, when fighting for your life, you might harm another while maintaining a loving heart.

If others who you trusted in the past hurt you, you will have difficulty trusting other people, out of fear they will hurt you too. Learning to trust intelligently requires seeing others clearly. You can always trust another to do what they feel is in their best interest. Not everyone understands that to treat others with respect and care is in their best interest. Not everyone understands that if you do good, good comes back to you, and if you do bad, bad comes back to you. A minority understand that the ultimate selfish act is selflessness. Learn to assess others' character and motives.

Note when people manipulate, exploit, or harm you. Many do what's right for the wrong reasons. They act for self-gain alone. They don't do what's right because it's right. Clear seeing helps you decide who you can trust, and what you can trust them for. Recognize the true friend. Those who "have your back." Those who don't cause harm. Take small steps of trusting. Test the waters. See who is trustworthy. As you see others accurately, you cultivate the courage to trust.

To build love, healthy relationships require communication. The most important skill of communication is the ability to stop what you are doing, pay close attention to what another person is saying, and listen. Then mirror back to them what you have heard for correction and confirmation, your intent being to make sure the other person feels understood.

By helping another to feel understood, you create the conditions for them to be more receptive to what you have to say. Take care in your speech to make "I" statements, avoiding blame and criticism. These are both communication stoppers. It's one thing to say, "When you don't clean up after yourself, I feel annoyed, and wish you wouldn't leave messes for me to clean." It's another to say, "You're an inconsiderate slob." If you voice your feelings and preferences with care and respect, you will stand a better chance of getting care and respect back. Help others to understand you by not causing them to feel judged, hurt, or afraid, as these emotions lead to defensiveness and anger.

Everyone deserves your care and respect because they are sacred human beings, apart from their actions. Everyone is of infinite value and worth. By seeing others as sacred, you cement your commitment to unconditional care and respect regardless of how hurt, frustrated, or angry you may feel. You commit yourself to being respectful and loving because that is who you are, regardless of another person's destructive behavior.

These relational skills take effort and practice to develop, with the help of your therapist, recovery mentor, spiritual advisor, family, and/or friends. You do not learn these skills on your own. Healing and growth require humility, and the ability to both ask for help and accept feedback. If you devote yourself to the practice of loving and being loved, with the help of others, you will enhance your relationship skills over time.

Work

Work gives people sustenance, stimulation, meaning, and purpose. It provides the material resources needed to survive. Work gives a sense of value according to the value you give others. It gives a channel for living for something greater than yourself. Any work can be rewarding with the proper attitude. It's in how you approach work and the meaning you give to work. Work can be a calling, not just a means to a paycheck. You can experience even the most menial of tasks as a sacred opportunity to serve. Any work can be a vehicle for exercising creativity.

Work can be an addiction. People engaged in work addictively do so to compensate for feelings of fear and inadequacy. Work gives a sense of worth through contributing. This differs from your unconditional inherent worthiness. Victims of work addiction recover by attending to their trauma and fear, gaining a sense of inherent wholeness and value apart from work. Then they can balance work, love, and play.

If work is difficult, ask for help. Vocational counselors and vocational rehabilitation services exist. Opportunities to volunteer abound. Sheltered vocational workshops provide opportunities for those with various disabilities to learn job skills. The resources and opportunities are there. All it takes is the will to ask for help.

Play

Children can teach the value of play to those who have forgotten it. Your vitality requires fun, pleasure, joy, time away from your routines, novelty, time to do less and be more, down time, and physical activity. Play might be anything that provides these. Play is something pleasurable you do for its own sake, where the act is more important than the outcome. Good play engages you. You lose yourself in it. It takes you out of time. The purposelessness of play actually serves your human need to savor Life for Life itself. Play is a great way to relieve stress. It enhances your social well-being, helping you connect with others. Play helps you to laugh. The more you laugh, the less stress you feel. Laughter brightens your mood and energizes you.

We all need breaks from the seriousness of Life. Play is non-serious. There is no purpose other than to have fun. We need "time-outs" from the stresses of survival. The time-outs that play provides restore us. Play renews us. It keeps us from becoming dull. Play keeps us young at heart and energetic. It may even prolong our lives!

Play fuels creativity and enhances mood. Ironically, it can actually help you solve problems by taking you away from these problems for a while. When you play with others, you deepen and heal your relationships. Couples need to make regular time to play with each other. This deepens and revitalizes intimacy. The same is true with friends. The possibilities of play are endless:

- Reading for fun
- Playing a sport
- Engaging in a hobby
- Solving puzzles
- Going to the movies
- Listening to music
- Practicing an art; taking an art class
- Going to parties and entertaining
- Going to museums and performances
- Joking, telling stories
- Going to comedy shows
- Playing board and card games
- Going on outings and trips
- Visiting new places; sightseeing; exploring
- Playing video games
- Playing with children
- Joining a singing group
- Going out with friends to sporting events, to go bowling, to play miniature golf, or some other fun group activity

Play is active, not passive. It is not zoning out in front of the TV or taking a nap, although rest is very important if you are tired. Play engages you. Don't make play anything more than play. If you get too competitive, the purpose of winning takes over. If you practice an art as play, allow yourself to just enjoy yourself without focusing on perfection.

Just as you budget time for work and love, budget time for play. Take advantage of opportunities to play that arise, such as joking with strangers while waiting in line at the grocery store. Make time every day for a little play. Make time each week for a special outing or activity. Mix it up, adding novelty and variety to your play. This breaks up the routines that can become ruts. Play also serves as a powerful antidote to cravings.

Work, love, and play,
In healthy portions,
Every day.

Tips & Tasks

Tips: Stress is a normal part of life. Stress occurs when we are frustrated or threatened.

Too little stress may cause apathy. Optimal stress makes for a productive and meaningful life.

Multiple effective stress management techniques exist.

Tasks: Become aware of your stresses.

Practice the stress management techniques in this section to optimize your stress.

Chapter 14

Address Trauma

Trauma is almost universal among those suffering from addiction. When it comes to healing, you must address any past trauma you've experienced. An unknown author said, "It can be very painful to confront your woundedness and trauma. Yet it is even more painful not to, for what you avoid ultimately controls you." Trauma can leave people with lifelong psychological wounds. Survivors can experience a sense of worthlessness. They may lack a solid sense of themselves or feel they are bad, unworthy, or defective. They can also feel very insecure and can lack confidence; they don't feel safe in their skins. If you have suffered trauma, you may have a lack of meaning or purpose. You may struggle with emotional instability, including anger, irritability, anxiety, emptiness, and depression. You may experience being out of control of your actions when stressed or emotionally aroused, impulsively acting in ways that hurt others or yourself.

Trauma takes many forms during childhood. It comes as *abuse,* family *dysfunction*, and *neglect.* Felitti and Anda delineate the prevalence of the following childhood traumas from their many years studying Adverse Childhood Experiences:[9]

Abuse

1. Emotional—recurrent threats, humiliation (11%)
2. Physical—beating, not spanking (28%)
3. Contact sexual abuse (28% women, 16% men, 22% overall)

Dysfunction

1. Mother treated violently (13%)
2. Household member was alcoholic or drug user (27%)
3. Household member was imprisoned (6%)
4. Household member was chronically depressed, suicidal, mentally ill, or in a psychiatric hospital (17%)
5. Not raised by both biological parents (23%)

Neglect

1. Physical (10%)
2. Emotional (15%)

Of all these childhood traumas, neglect may be the most damaging. As Asa Don Brown once said, "Trauma does not have to occur by abuse alone."

The trauma of neglect can take the form of physical neglect, emotional neglect, or both. Neglect deprives you of the critical developmental opportunity to experience being loved and cared for, safely, by someone to whom you can turn when you are in distress. Since your caregivers didn't love you, you enter adulthood with a yearning to be loved combined with a conviction, often unconscious, that you are unworthy of love. You then seek the love of people who cannot love. You do this to correct the deficits in love from your childhood, while unconsciously proving to yourself your unlovability. Children often grow up to choose mates like their parents, for that is all they know.

With neglect, not only do you fail to learn how to be loved, you fail to learn how to love others and yourself. When times are rough and you are hurting, you lack the capacity to use loving relationships to feel better. Thus, you may addict to feel better.

Trauma creates lifelong damaging consequences. The more traumas you have experienced, the more likely you are to suffer one or more of these consequences. Besides an increased prevalence of addiction among those who have suffered trauma, we also see increased incidences of:

- Depression
- Suicidality
- Antidepressant use
- Hallucinations
- Amnesia for childhood
- Unexplained somatic symptoms
- Fibromyalgia and chronic pain
- Smoking
- Obesity
- Sexual promiscuity
- Criminality
- Cardiovascular disease
- Hepatitis
- Emphysema
- Shortened lifespans

The more trauma you experience, the more impaired your social relationships will be, and the more difficulty you will have being successful at work. People with trauma histories have more absenteeism, financial difficulties, and serious work problems. If you suffer the traumas of neglect or abuse, you might develop very different understandings of yourself and others. You learn that:

- You are defective, and unworthy of love.
- You deserve abuse and neglect.
- All you can hope to receive from others is neglect or abuse.
- You cannot trust others.
- The world is both unsafe and cruel.
- You are on your own.

You may have learned to survive through manipulation, as you cannot experience true loving mutuality. Instead, you expect others to exploit, manipulate, and abuse you. You then manipulate, exploit, and abuse others.

Victims of trauma experience many negative emotions, including:

- Helplessness and powerlessness
- Alienation
- Emptiness
- Hurt
- Anger
- Bitterness
- Resentment
- Irritability
- Self-hatred

When abuse or neglect occurs repeatedly over a long time, these feelings become part of the fabric of your being. Just as fish swim in water, you swim in the ocean of your being, your experience contaminated by your trauma. Trauma damages spirituality. You then find it difficult to get "high" on life.

This is where addiction comes in. People addict to numb pain. Trauma survivors suffer. Sooner or later they discover something that takes the pain away and may even give them pleasure. The possibilities are many; anything that numbs, gives a semblance of joy, or distracts people from their pain will do.

You will continue to be vulnerable to addiction until you get to the roots of your pain and heal. This requires trauma work, ideally with a professional trained and experienced in treating trauma.

Healing from Trauma

To fully heal, you have to recover from the trauma you've experienced in your life. Be the author of your own recovery, with the help and guidance of a trauma expert. While you need a therapist, you also need to act as your own co-therapist in your healing. You intuitively know what treatment will work best. Your success in treatment correlates with your role in your treatment.

Benefitting from treatment requires humility and acceptance of your trauma. Surrender to the need for help and let go of the illusion of omnipotence. Renounce "pseudo autonomy," where you need no one's help because you are strong enough to help yourself. This feeling of not needing anyone is a sign of weakness and insecurity. It is the secure person who knows when they need help and can ask for it. Take charge of your life, but let others help.

Yet be clear-eyed. See the capacity of even those who love you to hurt you, as you know your own capacity to hurt others. Knowing people's destructive potentials, take responsibility for protecting yourself through boundaries and assertiveness, while keeping an open, loving heart for those who share your human predicament. Try to strike that tenuous balance between interdependence and autonomy, staying true to yourself while leaning on others and letting others lean on you.

Healing from trauma requires passing through five stages:

1. Safety and stabilization. The first step is to stabilize your life enough so you can bear the painful emotions that arise when you begin trauma work. You create a foundation for healing. This means first making yourself safe and achieving a sense of stability. Establish a safe environment for healing and recovery. Stop hurting yourself, whether through addicting or through other self-destructive behaviors. Surround yourself with safe, supportive, trustworthy people who care about you.

The key goal of trauma work is to reestablish a basic sense of safety, security, and self-confidence. Trauma therapists utilize a variety of mind-body practices to address the hypervigilance and dissociation that occur with severe trauma. One technique is called Eye Movement Desensitization and Reprocessing (EMDR). There are many more. A discussion of all these practices is beyond the scope of this book. Explore these techniques in greater detail with your trauma therapist.

Once you are feeling safe and secure, you can begin the next step in your healing from trauma.

2. Remembrance and mourning. The second step is optional, as some peoples' traumas are so severe that to share them would be too overwhelming. It is possible to recover from trauma without talking about the trauma. For some, first creating a sense of strength, safety, and confidence being in the world allows for some capacity to go through a remembrance and mourning process.

For those whose traumas are not too destabilizing to discuss, the next step in the healing process is to share your trauma, learning to bear the pain. Do this with a therapist and with wise, trusted friends. Share the pain of your trauma and the confusing emotions that go with trauma. Share your hurt, your anger, your fear, your guilt, your yearnings, and even your love, if this is the case, for those who hurt you. With the help of your therapist and others, receive validation of what you endured. Affirm that what happened was wrong, and that it was not your fault. Come to accept the confusing and contradictory kaleidoscope of feelings that your traumas create. This work requires strength and courage to feel your pain fully, in all its forms. Rumi once said, "If you desire healing, let yourself fall ill. Let yourself fall ill." You must cease avoiding your pain by addicting and let yourself "fall ill." Feel the pain, cry, and grieve. In the process, you learn to bear it.

Through journal work and talking, share your trauma with yourself and others. With repetition and practice, you develop the capacity to tell your story with regulated feelings. Mourn the losses resulting from trauma. Mourn the loss of trust and the experience of love and security. Mourn the loss of critical opportunities for loving relationships, education, or a career. Mourn the loss of a sense of wholeness, healthy self-esteem, a sense of purpose, and a spiritual connection to a loving Life force.

Facing your pain requires patience and perseverance. Just as you cannot rush the healing of a broken bone, so you cannot rush mourning. Know that the pain you experience while grieving leads eventually to peace and acceptance. Patiently stick with the process. Once you have fully embraced and shared your pain with others, you are ready to put what happened in perspective.

3. Perspective taking. See how your traumas affected you and still affect you now. With time, see that self-hatred and lack of self-love are the bitter fruits of your traumas. Understand how your traumas give rise to destructive emotions such as anger, depression, anxiety, and urges to addict. See how trauma damaged your ability to love and be loved. Note how you attach to people who are not good for you. Recognize how difficult it is to make loving, stable, secure, mutual attachments to people who can love you in healthy ways. Though you may have been a victim before, see that you orchestrate your own life. You are no longer a victim. Recognize you perpetuate your trauma by acting out the unconscious schemas you learned as a child, often before you could talk. These include deep, emotionally-charged convictions such as "I am unlovable," or, "I can't count on anyone," or, "People will hurt me if I get too close to them."

Putting your trauma into perspective is both emotional and intellectual. Intellectually, realize that your trauma is not your fault. See the randomness of Nature, with some not having the best luck. It is not personal to you; many are born into traumatic situations. Life is not fair. We are imperfect and do destructive things, often because of trauma, or just because we are human, and thus vulnerable to selfishness and anger. See that abuse and neglect are signs of other people's impairments and are thus not your fault or something you deserved.

Emotionally, work through hurt and anger. Cultivate acceptance and forgiveness—of both yourself, others, and of the world itself. Experience the love and grace of this world, which now helps you to heal. Develop hope you can live a happy and meaningful life. Experience a deepening of gratitude for what good you have received, despite the traumas you have endured. Discover a new appreciation for the simple gift of conscious existence. Finally, focus outward on others, with love, while focusing less on your own trauma. At this stage, it's time to emotionally move on. As China Miéville once said, "A scar is a healing. After injury, a scar is what makes you whole."

Taking perspective is hard work, requiring both intellectual and emotional effort. It is not something that happens overnight, but rather takes place over time, and continues to evolve and deepen throughout your life.

4. Reconnection and integration. As you make peace with yourself, with others, and with what happened, your new, outward perspective allows you to reconnect with Life. You develop meaningful relationships. You develop the capacity to truly love and allow yourself to be loved. Your new perspective allows you to create a new story of your life that gives your life a new definition. Reintegration with Life allows you to develop a life cause, a mission, or a new purpose.

5. Tending to your spirituality. Finally, your recovery from trauma involves healing your spirituality. Through your deepening connections, you experience a greater sense of oneness with all that is. Your life becomes filled with a sense of meaning, with peace, acceptance, and serenity, and with love and gratitude. I will discuss this in detail in the Touchstone on cultivating spirituality.

How you address your pain and trauma today determines how your life will unfold. It determines your future. You can't change what happened, but you can choose to heal. Learn to let your trauma not influence or define you. Let go, move on, and be happy. Let your trauma teach compassion, acceptance and forgiveness. Gail Caldwell once said, "I know now that we never get over great losses; we absorb them, and they carve us into different, often kinder, creatures." If you heal from your trauma, your greatest pains can be your greatest gifts.

Tips & Tasks

Tips: Trauma is common among sufferers of addiction.

The trauma of neglect may be the most damaging of all traumas.

Trauma causes biological, psychological, social and spiritual damage.

Healing from trauma is essential for fully healing from addiction.

There are five stages of healing from trauma.

Tasks: Take charge of your healing. Make healing from trauma a priority.

Work with a trauma specialist.

Work sequentially through the five stages of healing from trauma.

Manage Emptiness

Marguerite Duras said, "Alcohol doesn't console, it doesn't fill up anyone's psychological gaps. All it replaces is the lack of God." Far too many of people grow into adulthood with a pervasive feeling of emptiness, born of a lack of self-love. This may be due to physical or emotional neglect while growing up, or other childhood traumas. Genetics also play a role, as some people are more resilient. They grow up amid adversity and emerge into adulthood with an intact sense of self—feeling intrinsically whole, good, and worthy. Growing up emotionally alone, with no close attachments to others who understood and valued you, who responded helpfully to your distress, can lead to a feeling of emptiness. It is a feeling of alienation, of emotional disconnection with the rest of humanity. In your empty, emotional isolation from others, you feel un-whole. Neglect damages your sense of self-worth. You feel unlovable because you do not love yourself. Just as others may have abandoned you, so you now abandon yourself.

Everyone has a core human need to feel whole. The craving for drugs, alcohol, and other objects of addiction is equivalent, on a low level, to the spiritual thirst for wholeness and a sense of union with Life. Until you develop non-addictive ways of filling your emptiness, you will be vulnerable to readdicting and cross addiction, addicting to numb the painful emptiness within. Since addiction takes on a God-like quality in your misguided belief that it will bring salvation, it drowns out your spirituality. Getting high on drugs, sex, food, or thrills, or any other addictive behavior, prevents you from getting high on Life. Addiction prevents authentic wholeness or connection.

Healing is an important part of your journey to overcome addiction and remain clean. The path to addiction often leads right back to the tremendous pain and suffering you've experienced. Early childhood trauma can impact you for your entire life. But as you learn to heal, you learn to refocus the negative of the past to the positive of the present. You replace dark with light. Sadness with happiness. Emptiness with fullness. The only antidote for emptiness, born of a lack of self-love, is love. Love fills you and makes you whole. Love fills the emptiness. Love yourself. Give generous, unconditional love to others, expecting nothing in return. We will discuss this further in the next Touchstone on love.

Tips & Tasks

Tips: Neglect breeds emptiness.

Emptiness springs from a lack of self- love and loving connection.

Emptiness feeds addiction.

Emptiness recedes with the intentional practice of loving yourself and others.

Tasks: Adopt a daily practice of loving yourself and others as discussed in the Touchstone on Love.

CHAPTER 7

TOUCHSTONE 6: LOVE

What Is Love?

Love is more than just an emotion. It is action taken for the well-being of everyone. It is a thousand small and daily acts of kindness. Love is acting without expecting anything in return. Otherwise, your love is barter. Love is something you freely give away.

The great Sufi poet Hafiz once wrote:

Even after all this time
The sun never says to the earth,
"You owe me."
Look what happens with
A love like that,
It lights the whole sky.

The sun shows how to love to give light and life for love's sake alone. To Love is to embrace a way of being, seeing, and doing that both respects and nurtures Life. Loving is easy when you are feeling affectionate, warm, and caring. Loving is more difficult when you're feeling angry or hurt. It is these moments that test love. Recovery involves learning to love yourself and others regardless of any negative or destructive emotions because loving is simply the right thing to do. The sixth Touchstone along your road to recovery is love. Only when you allow in the light of love can you turn from the darkness of addiction, anger, resentment, and pain. I start this Touchstone by discussing self-love, love of all of Life, and the commitment to no-harm living. I then discuss the practices of respecting others' autonomy, letting go of resentments, refraining from judging others, cultivating compassion and forgiveness, and letting go of shame. I then touch on anger management. I conclude with reflections on the sacredness of Life.

Self-Love

Authentic recovery from addiction is impossible when you hate yourself. The solution to addiction is self-love. Self-love is the foundation of recovery. If you truly cherished yourself, would you do anything to harm yourself, including addicting? When you realize you are an amazing creation of the Universe, your attitude toward yourself is one of reverence and gratitude. Seeing the truth of your infinite value and preciousness, you cherish yourself the way you cherish a young child. This means you take good care of yourself. You do not addict or otherwise harm yourself.

Accordingly, the first step of recovery is to stop hating yourself. Hatred is a very destructive mental habit. If you hate yourself, how can you possibly heal or improve yourself? Change begins with reverent self-acceptance.

You do this by replacing hate with love. How? By practicing some of the following healing habits all day, every day, and for the rest of your life.

1. Remind yourself of the truth of your sacredness. Since you are sacred, love yourself unconditionally.
2. Practice radical self-acceptance and self-forgiveness. Accept and forgive your faults, flaws, deficiencies, failures, mistakes, and your diseases and disabilities, including the illness of addiction. Realize you can be no other way. You are beautiful and imperfect, like everyone else.
3. Appreciate your gifts and achievements.
4. Dissolve self-hatred. When negative, judgmental emotions arise, mindfully note them. Lovingly thank them for arising in your consciousness. Then replace them with an opposite, more realistic, positive thought of valuing, appreciation, acceptance, and gratitude. Show yourself deep compassion for your suffering.
5. Care for yourself:
   - Get sober. Renounce all addicting.
   - Ensure your safety and secure your basic needs.

- Remove yourself from destructive people, places, and things.
- Take accountability for your life.
- Face your self-hatred with kindness, acceptance, and forgiveness, made easier by taking ownership of your destructive actions.
- Surround yourself with loving people.
- Eat right, get plenty of sleep, rest, and exercise regularly.
- Take time for yourself.
- Simplify and balance your life; minimize stress.
- Work on recovery every day.
- Get the help needed to treat medical and mental illnesses and to heal from trauma.
- Have fun. Play.
- Lovingly connect with others. In doing so, assert yourself and set boundaries as needed. Practice honesty, care, humility, and respect. Act with integrity. Forgive others as you have forgiven yourself. Appreciate others' gifts and good fortune rather than comparing yourself enviously to them.
- Give both yourself and others the love you want. Fill your emptiness with your own love.
- Pursue your passions.

With this practice, your life agenda transforms from negative self-preoccupation to constructive engagement with Life. Your self-love is the fundamental act of recovery. Self-love also enables you to love others. With time, the loving light of acceptance dissolves hatred. You shift from feeling un-whole to experiencing "imperfect wholeness." You stop abandoning yourself, as others may have done in the past. You commit to your life. You name, claim, and tame your vulnerabilities while appreciating your basic, innate goodness.

However, it requires action to fill the emptiness within. Develop a daily discipline of nurturing both your life and the lives of others. This is the purpose of a life of love. Tend to the garden of your life with a thousand daily acts of kindness—to yourself and others. If a thought arises to do something kind for someone, do it. Love others without conditions or expectation.

Loving Life

To love is to love all of Life. You are part of the one great web of Life. Once you experience your incredible interconnectedness with others and your interdependence upon others, you realize life is not just about you. Life is about Life. To be in harmony with Life, be about Life. Loving all of Life requires that you recognize and renounce self-centeredness. Add to your daily intentional practices a regular reflection on those around you.

Healing your emptiness means embarking on a program of generosity. Give to others. Giving is one of the most useful practices to take you from negative self-preoccupation to the fullness of Love. One practice involves giving something to someone every day for 29 days. This practice involves forgetting your preoccupations and worries. Though you still care for your needs, you also forget yourself in the giving. In the end, you feel rejuvenated, energized, and full of joy. You discover that giving is a gift to yourself.

This is why love is a "selfish program." Acting with love in all your daily affairs not only heals your emptiness, it brings you straight into the joyful fullness of Life.

Tips & Tasks

Tips: Loving means enhancing life—yours and others'.

Loving others requires first loving yourself.

Tasks: Develop a daily intentional practice of self-love. Remember your sacredness. Practice self-acceptance and self-forgiveness. Appreciate your gifts and achievements. Dissolve self-hatred. Take good care of yourself.

With a foundation of self-love, make it your life agenda to love.

Refrain from Destructiveness

Learn to act out of love by first making a vow of no harm—to others or yourself. This means renouncing addicting and entering total recovery. It also means eliminating toxic people, places, and things from your life. Engage with life-promoting rather than life-destroying forces.

The practice of no harm is all about managing destructive emotions. Everyone experiences destructive emotions. The difference between a destructive life and a constructive life lies in how you manage destructive impulses. There are many types of destructive impulses. Addictive impulses are one of these. Your first no-harm act is to renounce addicting.

A second common destructive impulse is anger. When you feel anger, you experience an urge to hurt. Hurting others never makes things better, only worse. Anger begets anger. Hurt begets hurt. To act on your angry impulses not only harms others, but yourself, as we are all part of one interconnected web of Life. What goes around comes around. To harm others is to harm yourself.

Anger arises out of failed expectations. Each of us has expectations about how things "should" be. When the world does not meet with your expectations, anger arises. Before anger, there is hurt, frustration, or disappointment. Someone has let you down or hurt you. Someone has not done as you wished. You have lost something. The world isn't to your liking.

A third destructive emotion is fear. Fear is the root emotion from which all other destructive emotions arise. Recovery involves transitioning from being fear-enslaved to being fear-informed. Fear can be healthy when it mobilizes you to protect yourself. Fear becomes destructive when it stops you from taking effective action. When paralyzed by fear, you cannot do what's necessary to prevent harm from befalling you or others. Fear, such as a fear of failure, or a fear of being alone, can make it difficult to improve your situation. Like an ostrich with its head in the sand, you make things worse when you do not deal with the problems you face. Read the section on facing your fears in the Touchstone on accountability to learn how to manage fear.

Fear and its derivatives, including anger and addictive desire, make up the emotions that cause you to harm others or yourself. With patience and persistent practice, you will learn to manage these destructive emotions intelligently, rather than letting them wreak havoc in your life.

Tips & Tasks

Tips: Loving requires taking a personal life vow to not harm yourself or others. This is a Life mandate. It is in your best interest.

Desire, anger, and fear drive most destructive behavior.

Tasks: Take the "No Harm" vow. Vow to cherish yourself and others unconditionally.

Work your recovery to counter addictive desire.

Practice humility and acceptance to counter anger.

Practice surrendered action to counter fear.

Don't Obsess over Others' Wrongs or Faults

Focusing on the flaws of others is a negative, destructive behavior for several reasons. First, it takes your focus off your own faults, which is your first order of business. You lose your humility and cease to grow when you shift your attention from your own vulnerabilities to the unskillful behaviors of others.

Second, thinking about others' faults only stirs up resentment and self-righteousness. It snuffs out compassion. It hardens you into an emotionally insensitive shell that suffocates your humanity. Without compassion, you stray from your purpose of loving.

Third, you cross a boundary when you try to control others. Just as you dislike others criticizing you, so others dislike it when you criticize them. While you have every right to do what you can to stop others from hurting or exploiting you, you are not in charge of the way others run their lives. You have enough running your life. Live by the saying, "Live and let live," cultivating your acceptance and understanding of others. Don't critique or control others unless you are their boss, supervisor, parent, caregiver, or someone is asking you for feedback. Otherwise, this is not your place.

Fourth, focusing on flaws blots out the ability to appreciate people's gifts and virtues, leading to negatively balanced appraisals of others. Appreciation of others' humanity suffers.

Focus on ensuring your side of the street is clean. Ironically, as you take accountability for your actions, making amends to others along the way, your non-defensive behavior and accountability encourages others to be less defensive and more accountable. People don't need to be defensive if you're not attacking them. When you drop the weapons of blame and judgment, others feel safe with you. If you do not attack others, they will be less likely to attack you. This allows for mutual safety, connection, and intimacy. By focusing on yourself and letting others tend to their own lives as they see fit, you create the conditions for love to flow.

Tips & Tasks

Tips: Focusing on other's faults deflects you from attending to your recovery, cultivates negativity, resentment, and self-righteousness, and distorts your balanced appreciation of others.

Tasks: With some exceptions, don't attempt to control others. Ask for what you need. Be assertive and set limits as needed.

Focus on cleaning up your side of the street.

Let Go of Resentments

Resentments arise from failed expectations. You expect people or situations to differ from what they are. You expect things to be as you want them, as if you were God. People shouldn't be hurtful, neglectful, or deceitful. People should be loving, considerate, generous, and kind. But this is not Reality. People are not always loving, considerate, or kind. People, including you, can be hurtful, neglectful, and deceitful. You're picking a fight with Reality when you expect Reality to differ from what it is. When you do this, Reality always wins. Whenever you feel hurt, disappointed, resentful, or even angry, identify the unrealistic expectations that fuel your suffering. You will see you abandoned your mandate to honor what is.

Resentments destroy. There is a saying that "hatred destroys the hater." The bitterness of resentments consumes your joy. When you tighten the noose of resentment around someone's neck, you choke yourself. Resentment makes people spiritually ill. You suffer, and in your suffering, you cause suffering for others. Too many then descend into a world in which they forget everything except their grudges.

When you let others anger you, they conquer you. You lose touch with the goodness of Life. For some, even the smallest of "mis-expectations" cause resentment. If you become resentful over petty matters, what does that make you?

By releasing your resentments, you set yourself free to love. Several techniques exist to let go of resentments:

1. Imagine the person you resent as a child. See that they were once innocent. Reflect on the fact that no one chooses their genes, their character, their parents, or their environment growing up. See that if you were they, you would have acted exactly as they did.
2. Reflect on the harm you have done to others. Acknowledge your own ego, which wants to control Life, including others, to your own advantage, without regard for the well-being of others. See that everyone struggles with this trait. Recognize that everyone manages their egos imperfectly. No one is invulnerable to harming others.
3. As you consider another person's harmful behavior, contemplate the role of their disease, their ignorance, or their situation in their actions.
4. Pray for the person who has harmed you. This invites forgiveness.
5. Give something to the person you resent. Do something for them.
6. Accept what has happened and move on. Accept people as they are and Reality as it is—a perfectly imperfect Universe that only seems imperfect from your limited point of view. Accept, while still holding others accountable for their actions.
7. Assert yourself—do what you must to protect yourself from harm and to improve your situation. Remember that love requires boundaries. Different people need more or less boundaries, depending upon how intimate you are with them and how destructive they might be. Put up proper boundaries so you can love without being harmed.
8. Remember the sacredness of all things. All people are sacred and deserving of your utmost respect.
9. Let go of injured pride. It was never about you in the first place. Practice patience, tolerance, and equanimity. Respond with love and

care from a place of mindful calm and tranquility. Treat others with respect and care because you are a respectful and caring person.

10. See all that Life brings you not as reward, harm, or punishment, but as an opportunity for growth, liberation, and a deepening of your humility.
11. Contemplate on the fact that resentment only hurts you. As the saying goes, "It is like taking a poison and hoping the other person dies." If your mind ruminates on resentments and grievances, observe the impact this has on your well-being. Does it bring joy, or does it bring pain? Are resentments helpful to you, or hurtful? There is a saying that "time wasted in getting even can never be used for getting ahead."

Resolving resentments allows for forgiveness. Forgiveness relieves you of your pain. It is truly a gift to yourself. Resentments fuel addiction. When you let go, you drop a painful psychic load of negativity. Less pain leaves you more secure in your recovery.

Tips & Tasks

Tips: Resentments poison you and others.

Releasing resentments sets you free to love.

Tasks: List all your resentments. Then use the various techniques in this section to resolve them. Make this a lifelong practice.

Do Not Judge

Someone once said, "An addict can lie in the gutter, and yet still look down on other people." We have no right to judge others, just as others have no right to judge us. Everyone experiences negative emotions and thoughts and behaves unskillfully. While you may judge another's actions as being destructive or unskillful, that is far different from judging who they are. You may pass judgment on the sin, but not the sinner. That is off limits. Instead, hold others accountable for their actions while maintaining compassion, goodwill, and respect in your heart. This fosters love.

To cultivate non-judgment, note that we don't decide what to think or feel. Thinking and feeling naturally happen. Thoughts and feelings then drive behavior. Much of our behavior is automatic, neurologically predetermined even before we are aware of it. We can only hold ourselves accountable for the actions we consciously will out of our capacity for free will.

Second, note that at our core we are the same. We are pure, empty Awareness. This pure Awareness is perfect, sacred, unchanging, and complete. Thus, we are all perfect, sacred, unchanging, and complete, apart from the constant changes in thoughts, feelings, understandings, actions, and our physical form. The sacred light of Awareness shines in each of us. This is beyond judgment.

Third, recognize the impact of grace and circumstance. When the impulse to judge others arises, see that you would have acted exactly as they did if you had their genes and life experiences. This understanding invites compassion. It also helps you to let go of judging yourself for your own unskillful behavior. You simply do the best you can. It can be no other way. All we can do is learn from this moment to improve the next moment.

Finally, stop condemning yourself for who you are. Compassion begins with you and then flows outward to others. Judging others for who they are is destructive. When you notice your mind judging, see it as a destructive habit and gently let it go.

Tips & Tasks

Tips: Who we are is beyond judgment.

All we can judge is others' behavior.

Tasks: When judgment arises, reflect on this passage and gently let judgment go.

Cultivate Compassion and Forgiveness

We do not willfully forgive or be compassionate. These are feelings that flow through us from beyond us. Authentic compassion arises within you of its own accord. Forgiveness happens. All we can do is cultivate the conditions for forgiveness and compassion to arise within us. How do you cultivate compassion and forgiveness?

First, strive to understand the people involved. Understand their experience. What were they feeling and thinking? What were their beliefs? What destructive forces might have overtaken them? This requires thoughtful investigation. Too often our minds jump to negative conclusions about others before we have fully investigated the situation. Be mindful of "contempt prior to investigation."

If someone has harmed you, begin the process of inquiry by talking to them, but only if safe to do so. Ask about their feelings and the reasons why they acted as they did. Through inquiry, you gain a deeper understanding of their worldview and what drove them to act as they did. While you may not agree with what they did, you at least understand the roots of their unskillful behavior.

Once you have listened, you might share the impact of their actions on you. If relationship repair is a desirable goal, then letting the other person know of your experience can help you to release your own hurt feelings. Avoid criticizing, judging, blaming, or accusing. This will only bring on defensiveness. Instead, invite understanding of your experience, just as you have sought to understand theirs. You might say, "When you did A, I felt B." For example, "When you lied to me, I felt hurt and angry, and lost my sense of safety and trust in you." Or, "When you attack me, I feel hurt and defensive, because I don't feel you perceive me in a fair and balanced way." You can follow this feedback with a request for different behavior in the future. For example, "Please be honest with me," or, "Let me know how what I do affects you, but please stop attacking my character."

By sharing your pain with your offender, you invite them to acknowledge their wrongdoing. If they can express their understanding of your harm, and express remorse and an intention to not harm you again, then forgiveness is easier.

Sometimes you cannot, or should not, talk to your perpetrator. It may not be possible, or it may not be safe. Then do one of two things. First, talk about what happened with someone, asking them to help you understand why the offender may have acted as they did. This is particularly helpful if the person you talk to knows the offender or is aware of the situation. Second, reflect, in silence and stillness, on the other person. Put yourself in their shoes. Reflect on their suffering and limitations.

Understanding begets compassion and forgiveness. See that hurtful behavior often comes from a place of hurting. By understanding others' suffering or ignorance, you experience compassion.

Cultivate compassion and forgiveness by wishing for your offender's well-being. Some call this the practice of "loving kindness." Reflect on the suffering and unskillful behavior of others, and wish for an end to their suffering. There is a saying, "If someone hurts you, pray for the bastard." This practice consciously flips your mind from wishing for someone's harm to wishing for their healing. As you wish for their healing, you promote your own healing. Remember that love begets love. Remember also that loving others is loving yourself.

Facilitate forgiveness by noting that forgiveness is for your benefit. Letting go of resentments has a direct positive effect on your well-being and thus your recovery. Take your time, as the process of forgiveness takes time. You may have to work on forgiving someone several times before forgiveness comes.

Tips & Tasks

Tips: Understanding breeds compassion and forgiveness.

Forgiveness is a gift to yourself.

Tasks: Practice the techniques for letting go of resentments to cultivate compassion and forgiveness. Wish for your offenders' well-being.

The Toxicity of Shame

Oscar Wilde said, "Every saint has a past and every sinner has a future." Where there is addiction, there is shame. When you lose control of your actions and behave destructively, you feel bad about yourself. Doing bad things makes you feel you are bad. Your compulsive, self-destructive behavior tells you there is something wrong with you. You conclude that you are bad, and not just sick in a bad way. Shame is not conducive to love. In fact, it poisons it.

Shame is guilt taken to an extreme. While guilt says, "What I did was bad," shame says, "I am bad." With shame, you pass judgment on who you are, rather than on your actions. While guilt can stimulate you to reflect on the consequences of what you have done, shame blocks reflection altogether. When filled with shame, you can't learn and grow. Because of this, shame only perpetuates active addiction and prevents healing.

While guilt creates an inner pain that can motivate change, protracted guilt and remorse can harm. When you focus too much on past mistakes, you stop thinking about the future and how to behave differently based upon what you have learned. Forgive yourself for being human and move on. Look at the past, but don't stare. It is impossible to love yourself or others when filled with shame.

Shame perpetuates addicting by creating a compulsion to both harm and soothe yourself. You harm yourself to punish yourself. You punish yourself out of shame by addicting, which then only perpetuates your shame. In this way, shame creates a vicious cycle.

Shame poisons your recovery. You are not a bad person becoming good, but a sick person becoming well. Shame deflects your recovery efforts from achieving peace, happiness, and fulfillment, to becoming "a better person," because you feel you are not good enough just as you are. In this way, shame robs your recovery of its serenity. In your recovery, be mindful of "Worthiness Projects," in which the agenda of your actions is to bolster your self-worth to neutralize shame. Even recovery can become a worthiness project. You do not recover to become "worthy," but to realize happiness and fulfillment.

Shame arises from a lack of acceptance of mistakes, failures, and imperfections. Letting go of the shame of imperfection allows you to recover. From the outside looking in, perfectionism is the outward face of shame. Expecting yourself to be perfect implies you are not good enough just as you are. Perfectionism is thus a psychic cancer that eats away at your intrinsic sense of goodness and wholeness. Those seeking human perfection need to move to a different Universe, for they will not find it in this one. Imperfection is part of the perfection of the Universe. We are all perfectly imperfect.

Few see that imperfections are a blessing. Even addiction can be a blessing, as it forces people to grow and become whole. Some of the most beautiful people are in recovery. Those in recovery are gifted. Groucho Marx once wisely quipped, "Blessed are the cracked, for they shall let the light in." Shame snuffs out love. When you live out of shame, you feel unlovable, and thus live in such a way that makes it difficult for others to love you.

Healing from Shame

Finding true love requires healing. And you cannot heal until you accept, with humility, your flaws and imperfections, including the fact of your addiction. Shame about your addiction will only keep you trapped in it. Carl Jung once said, "Condemnation does not liberate. It only oppresses." Accept the Reality of your addiction without shame. To heal from shame, first see and accept it. Once seen and accepted, you can let it go.

Through acceptance of your shame, you avoid becoming ashamed of being ashamed. Someone once said, "I've been beating up on myself so much I feel like hitting myself." This is toxic non-acceptance of shame.

Healing from shame involves re-parenting yourself. It requires feeling grief and pain. Allow yourself to feel the pain you have carried with you all your life. Embrace your pain not as something bad or destructive, but as something natural and necessary. Hold your shame within the larger crucible of your vast, loving Awareness. See that you are not the deficient self you feel you are.

You are the Awareness of the feelings, thoughts, convictions, and experience of your deficiency. That larger Awareness can hold your deficiency in its loving presence, freeing you of its toxicity. Mindfulness is the key. When you pause and name your shame, you separate yourself from it. This frees you from compulsively acting out your sense of unworthiness. You then experience shame as simply a painful experience. It is not who you are and has no bearing on your value or worth. It is just the illusion of unworthiness.

In healing shame, practice being your own best friend. Love yourself unconditionally, apart from your talents or achievements, solely for the fact of your sacred existence. Healing from shame means traveling from your head to your heart. This is the longest and most challenging of journeys. By intentionally loving yourself, you begin to feel miraculously worthy and whole. It is then that you can forget about your self-worth and go forth and give others the same love you have given to yourself.

Tips & Tasks

Tips: Shame results from a failure to recognize your inherent worth apart from what you do. You are not your mistakes and failings.

Shame perpetuates addiction.

Recovery requires the dissolution of shame.

Tasks: Accept your flaws.

Base your self-worth on the bare fact of your miraculous existence as a living being.

Face your pain. Feel it to heal it.

Take responsibility for loving yourself unconditionally.

Managing Anger

Aristotle said, "Anyone can become angry, that is easy . . . but to be angry with the right person, to the right degree, at the right time, for the right purpose, and in the right way . . . this is not easy." We have already touched on not acting on destructive emotions. Anger is one of the emotions that, if not managed skillfully, can result in great harm to yourself and others. Acting impulsively on anger almost always leads to regret.

Anger is a normal, healthy emotion. Acknowledge and accept anger. Don't suppress it. We naturally feel anger when others mistreat, wrong, or violate us. Anger becomes destructive when you are angry too often, for too long, and too intensely, and you are hurtful. Anger is destructive when it results in violence—either violent acts or violent speech.

Unmanaged anger also damages your relationships and career. Many a divorce has resulted from out-of-control anger. Since anger begets anger, and violence begets violence, your acting out your anger can cause angry and violent reactions from others. Our prisons are full of people who have acted on their anger. Every day, people die because of anger-driven violence.

Perhaps the worst anger is justifiable anger. If someone has harmed you, then your sense of being justified in how you feel can seduce you into feeling your resulting anger-driven actions are proper. This is never true. Acting destructively out of anger is never justified.

Anger is beneficial if you manage it skillfully. It can motivate you to protect yourself and others and to improve your situation, as when you constructively address an injustice. To be constructive, however, first metabolize your anger. Transform it into a commitment to make things better, with care and respect for everyone. Anger only becomes useful once channeled into positive action.

Several myths exist about anger. One is that it is good to vent your anger. While it is good to express and process your feelings, it is never helpful to rant. This only makes matters worse, as it disturbs others and makes your anger worse. You might believe that you are helpless to control your anger. This is not true; everyone can learn to resolve anger if they practice the right techniques.

Some people may feel their anger empowers them and increases their respect. In fact, people respect you less when you are emotionally out of control. Instead, you earn respect and cooperation by first being respectful yourself.

Finally, it is not good to suppress your anger, as this causes stress. Suppressed anger then leaks out involuntarily as passive aggressive acts, such as when you withhold attention or fail to do something for someone. Feel and resolve your anger so you can act constructively and find a path to love.

Techniques for Resolving Anger

It takes effort and practice to learn how to resolve anger. But you can do it. The reason why it is so tremendously important to manage your anger is that anger is the single greatest enemy of love. It is extremely hard to be both angry and loving. One is poison, the other the antidote. You may feel you are helpless in the face of rage, but this is not true. With practice, the techniques that follow can empower you to master your anger, so that it no longer masters you.

The first step in managing anger is to know you're angry. Tune in to your feelings and bodily sensations. This requires mindfulness. Ask yourself, "What is happening?" You may notice muscle tension, heart racing, sweating, knots in your stomach, or rapid breathing. Too many people lash out impulsively because they don't notice they are angry.

The second step in learning to resolve anger is exploring the reasons behind your anger. You do this by asking, "What are the thoughts, beliefs, feelings, and expectations behind my anger?" There are three ways to do this:

1. Meditatively ask this question of yourself, in silence, free of distraction, and see what arises. Insight often comes by asking the question and then watching the thoughts that arise.
2. Journal. Writing about what angers you can provoke a flood of feelings and thoughts.
3. Explore the roots of your anger by talking through the situation, your thoughts, and your feelings, with someone else. Talk to good listeners who can ask you the right questions to explore your underlying thoughts, beliefs, feelings, and expectations.

We are rarely angry for the reasons we think. Behind anger there is always hurt or frustration. Behind hurt or frustration there is fear about our well-being. These feelings always arise from failed expectations. We all want to feel cared for, secure, in control, and respected. The problem is expecting these things, as the world does not revolve around our expectations.

Ask yourself, "What am I really angry about?" You discover it's not what you thought. If someone stands you up for an event, for example, you may first believe you are angry for being inconvenienced. Looking within, however, may reveal that you are hurt because you feel unvalued or disregarded. Then you can look at your expectation that people should always be considerate with you and keep their commitments to you. You then see it's the unrealistic expectation that is really fueling your anger. Anger never results from the situation; it arises from your reaction to that situation.

Once you've identified the feelings and failed expectations driving your anger, identify the thoughts that go along with your feelings. These thoughts are always dysfunctional. You may have strict beliefs about how things should be and how people should behave. These "shoulds" and "musts" result in destructive "musterbation," in which you torture both yourself and others. Notice your rigid thinking for what it is—not Reality—and let it go. The world is much more "gray" than black and white.

Another type of dysfunctional thinking is to jump to negative conclusions before you know all the facts. As mentioned previously, this is called "contempt prior to investigation." It is common to assume bad intentions of others, only to learn this was not the case. You have just wasted minutes, hours, days, or even years stewing on a negative belief that was not true.

Yet another cognitive mistake is to overgeneralize. You may believe that people always do this or never do that. But this isn't true. Making negative, unrealistic generalizations fuels anger and resentment.

You may see only the negative things that people do or the negative aspects of a situation. Your perception is not balanced. You don't recognize both the good and the bad.

Perhaps the most common thinking mistake that results in anger is "victim thinking." Victims put all the blame on others and fail to see their own role in bringing about their misfortune. This distortion results from a failure to take accountability for your own actions or lack of action. Harm often comes to us because we put ourselves in risky situations or fail to protect ourselves when others are hurtful. When you take accountability for your own role, your anger and resentment toward others subsides.

The third step in managing anger is to get safe and sane, so you don't act out destructively. Practice ways of reducing anger in the moment and making yourself and others safe. Techniques for getting safe and sane include:

1. Recommit to the "no-harm" vow. Resolve within to not act out destructively, regardless of how much you want to lash out and hurt others.
2. Take a time out. When you feel you are about to lose control, walk away until you've cooled down. If in the midst of a fight, say something like, "I love you, but right now I'm feeling I'm on the verge of doing or saying something hurtful. I'm going to leave to cool down. I'll return and we can discuss this further once I've gotten a better grip on myself."
3. Breath and count. Take three slow, deep breaths, or slowly count to ten. Give yourself a mental time out to relax and recover. Recognize what is going on and get some mental distance so you can respond intelligently rather than react destructively.
4. Meditate. Become present. Watch angry feelings and negative thoughts like clouds, passing in the sky of your Awareness. Differentiate the thoughts and feelings from your Awareness. This gives you the distance needed to become free of the grip of destructive urges.
5. Work out. Exercise relieves stress and tension. If done mindfully, you can empty your mind for new insights to arise.
6. Soothe yourself. Listening to music, taking a bath, or getting a massage can help you to relax. A yoga session is another effective way to ground and center yourself.
7. Take perspective. How important is this problem, really? Is it worth getting angry about? What impact is my anger having on my day? Am I possibly making a mountain out of a molehill?
8. Talk it out. Talk through your anger with someone supportive and wise. Be careful, however, to not rant against the person who upset you. When talking to someone else, keep the focus on two things: trying to understand the other person—why they did what they did, and trying to understand your own reaction. What are you really angry about? What are the feelings that lie beneath your anger? What are your unrealistic expectations?
9. "QTIP" it. "Quit taking it personally." Reflect on the truth that others' actions spring from their own realities. It is ultimately never about you.
10. Think before speaking. Never speak impulsively, venting your angry

feelings in an accusatory or critical way. Instead, think, think, think before speaking. Insure what you say is both necessary and improves the situation.

11. Investigate. Inquire into the suffering of the other. Try to imagine what pain they felt that caused them to act as they did. This will help to transform anger into compassion.
12. Practice loving kindness. Engage in a loving kindness meditation or prayer: "May I be happy, at peace, and free of suffering. May you be happy, at peace, and free of suffering." Repeat this over and over. Still the mind by letting go of distracting thoughts. Return again and again to the meaning, spirit, and intention of this meditation. With repetition, the mind quiets into a state of loving acceptance of what is and a spirit of goodwill arises.
13. Get help. "Anger Management" therapies, both individual and group, help many learn to manage anger. Some find their loss of control when they get angry occurs even after practicing various anger management and anger resolution techniques. This is usually due to some sort of neuropsychiatric disorder, such as ADHD, Intermittent Explosive Disorder, a mood disorder, or some personality disorders. When this is the case, medications exist that can help calm the storm. For these people, psychopharmacology combined with psychotherapy provides the best results.

Once you have regained a calm, cool, collected, and compassionate state of mind, you can assert yourself to correct wrongs and make things better. Assertiveness is non-hostile, non-blaming, and non-confrontational. You express yourself with respect and care for the other person.

While wanting to express yourself, also strive to understand. Not only share your experience, but ask about the other's experience. Listen deeply and non-judgmentally.

When addressing a conflict, focus on the present. It is not helpful to bring up issues from the past that cannot be changed. Focus on what can be done to improve the situation.

Humor can help greatly to resolve anger. Seeing something funny or ironic in a situation can help everyone to feel less threatened. Humor can ease tension. Be careful, however, to not be sarcastic, as sarcasm is hurtful. We all function better when we feel safe and relaxed.

Through assertive communication, both parties may acknowledge a dilemma, issue, or problem. Once this occurs, the opportunity for reconciliation arises. Problem solving can occur. If possible, identify possible solutions to a problem. Search for solutions that optimize the benefits for everyone, not just you. Rather than being upset over a friend's showing up late, for example, agree to an earlier meeting time to accommodate for your friend's difficulties with time management. It is never helpful to demand that a person change a fault that is beyond their ability or willingness to change.

Recognize that we all have different viewpoints. It is harmful to a relationship to think your point of view is the best and only proper point of view. Worse yet is to judge the other person as bad or wrong for their point of view. This behavior poisons a relationship, as no one likes to be judged or invalidated. If the relationship with the offender is a priority, you may decide to let go of your need to be right and accept that you can't make people behave or believe as you like. This is when it's best to agree to disagree.

Lastly, as we have already discussed, cultivate the conditions for forgiveness to occur. Holding grudges hurts everyone, especially yourself.

Learning to resolve anger is a skill that takes time and practice to master. Be patient with yourself and persist in your practice of the techniques in this section to learn how to manage your anger so it no longer manages you. The finish line for managing your anger is cherishing the world and the people around you. As you progress toward that target, you'll find love around each and every corner. Consider how you treat something you cherish. Think of how a parent cherishes his or her child. It is with the greatest of love, care, and respect. Once you come to your own reverence for the lives of others and for yourself, you treat yourself and others as a parent treats his or her child. You treat all of Life with love, care, and respect. This is what it means to treat yourself and others as sacred.

There are literally thousands and thousands of quotes, clichés, movies, narratives, songs, and writings about love. But when it comes to addiction and recovery, the truth is that love plays a crucial, if not pivotal, role. Anything is possible with love and the support of those that love you. That is why loving plays such a tremendous role in your journey to recovery. Use this Touchstone to remain connected and motivated to heal and overcome the darkness of addiction.

Tips & Tasks

Tips: Anger is a normal emotion. It can be good or bad depending on how we manage it.

Lashing out destructively out of anger hurts everyone.

Tasks: Practice the techniques in this section to learn to manage anger constructively.

CHAPTER 8

TOUCHSTONE 7: RESPECT REALITY

Having a run-in with Reality is a common trigger for readdicting. In this section, we discuss the importance of humbly respecting Reality to secure and then maintain continued sobriety.

Whether you feel so or not, the Universe is perfect just as it is, with all its randomness, injustice, evil, death, decay, and destruction. However, we perceive the Universe to be imperfect only from our limited, self-concerned perspective. In our self-obsession, we forget that Life is not about us, but about the larger Life of which we are a part. We are only agents of Life. Life is both personal with respect to our lives, but also impersonal with respect to Life itself.

For example, imagine Life without death. If it weren't for the constant recycling of Life in a Reality of constant change, Life would not exist. We would not exist. From the very beginning, the first self-replicating life forms would have multiplied to the point of unsustainability. We exist because of untold trillions upon trillions of mutations over the past four to five billion years, because of death, orderly disorder, and randomness. We owe our very existence to the seeming "imperfection" of Nature.

How can Reality be other than as it is? The answer is that it cannot. It is logically impossible for things to be other than exactly as they are. The phrase, "What is, is," is profoundly true.

A mysterious life force (which some call God) infuses Reality. When you rant against Reality, you are picking a fight with "God." Remember the insightful words of Byron Katie, "When you fight Reality, you always lose; but only one hundred percent of the time." For those suffering from addiction, "losing" often means readdicting.

Although pain and distress are inevitable, acceptance makes suffering optional. Accept, and suffering disappears. Practice acceptance by saying "Yes," kindly and gently, moment by moment, to what is. No matter your pain, maintain a genuine attitude of friendliness. Learn to say, "Thank you, I have no complaints," with gratitude, even in the darkest of times.

However, distinguish between acceptance of this moment and working to improve the next moment. Preserving and enhancing Life is your life mandate. The real issue is your attitude. Is your attitude one of non-acceptance, which causes suffering and readdicting, or is it one of acceptance, even while you work to make things better? The secret to serenity is accepting "What Is." You don't have to make things "wrong" to make them better. Acceptance lightens your load. It reduces stress and makes life easier. Acceptance gives you the courage to face things just as they are. Now you can deal with things more effectively, without the negativity and anger that drive addicting. The following sections discuss unrealistic expectations, with a special focus on perfectionism, concluding with a discussion of surrendered action.

Don't Expect the World or Others to Be Other than What They Are . . . The "I want what I want now" instinct can cause us to disregard the needs and rights of others. It can destroy our humility and respect for Life apart from ourselves, leading to grandiose entitlement, disregard, and destructiveness. People become objects to serve our needs rather than sacred fellow beings.

We can speak of "functional" and "dysfunctional" entitlement. To be functional, couple your entitlement to your survival and well-being with humility, regard, and respect for others. Keep yourself "right-sized" regarding your importance vs. the importance of all of Life. Both are equally important. Functional entitlement stimulates us to assert ourselves to get our needs met, hoping for a better future, while accepting things are as they are in this moment. You are entitled to do what you can to take care of yourself. You are not entitled, however, to expect people, places, or things to be different from exactly how they are. Nor are you entitled to disregard or harm others.

Functional entitlement entails hope, not expectations. Hope, but don't expect. When you pair hope with acceptance, you become right with Life.

The slogans "Easy does it" and "Live and let live" come into play for dropping expectations. These wise sayings imply living an expectation-free life. Rather than trying to become master of a Universe beyond your control, we become humble servants of Reality, our true Master, not the other way around. Dropping expectations involves humility and acceptance. Grandiose entitlement gives way to hope. We stop our ego-maniacal dictating to others that they must meet our demands and be exactly as we command them to be. Keep in mind that respecting others in this moment is part of respecting Reality. Work to influence others for the better, but do so with acceptance of who they are.

Tips & Tasks

Tips: You have a right to ask for what you need.

Destructive entitlement includes expecting others to be other than what they are. This leads to resentments, which poison recovery.

Tasks: Ask for what you need, see what you get, and act accordingly.

Balance your entitlement to safety, comfort, and security with a respect for other's rights to the same.

Replace unrealistic expectations with acceptance and hope.

Don't Expect Perfection from Others or Yourself . . .

Perfection is unreal. Perfection does not exist. As Janelle Jalbert says in *Triangulating Bliss*, "Perfection is pure-fiction." It contradicts Nature. Perfection is an ideal. It is not real. Those who compulsively pursue the unattainable goal of perfection are victims of the disease of perfectionism. Although it is good to reach for the stars, perfectionists forget that no one can touch them. The only perfection that exists is the perfection of imperfection.

Demanding perfection of yourself and others is futile. It only causes stress, bitterness, and disappointment. The more you try to be perfect, the more you fail. No matter how hard you try to live your ideals, you will always be who you are in each moment. When you don't settle for doing your best, you abandon who you are.

Respecting Reality includes respecting imperfection as part of a greater, hidden perfection. Live your life respecting and accepting the imperfection of things. Doing so will decrease your stress and promote your recovery.

Honoring Who You Are

Trying to be perfect is not respectful of the Reality of who you are. Perfectionism robs people of wholeness and fulfillment, for how can you feel whole if you do not accept who you are? Perfectionism is an indicator of damage to your self-esteem. Perfectionists feel unworthy and incomplete just being who they are. By accepting only the perfect, you accept nothing.

Perfectionism robs your authenticity. You become fake, unable to experience and acknowledge that which you find unpleasant within you. You believe no one will love you just as you are. As a faker, you attract fakers. Unable to be authentic, you become unable to have authentic relationships. Perfectionism thus delivers you into an idealized, unreal world, causing anxiety, depression, and exhaustion as you spend wasted time denying what you cannot accept within yourself. Unable to own the bad and ugly within, you seek things from outside yourself for relief. This includes your addiction.

If we are to work toward sobriety, we have to honor who we are, with all the good and all the bad. Don't mandate impossible perfection from yourself and others. Instead, pursue your ideals. Reach for the stars, but don't forget you will never touch them. Your goal is excellence in what you say and do, not perfection. Just be the best you can be.

How do you heal from the disease of perfectionism? The first step is clarity. See how destructive perfectionism is. With seeing, you are free to let it go, just as you would stop eating a food that makes you sick. See your fear—the fear that others will not love you if you be yourself. With investigation, you see that this fear is unfounded—that the reverse is true; people love you more when you are real, not perfect. Seeing this, let go of your fear.

Letting go of perfection improves your relationships. You now love others for who they are, despite of and because of their flaws. You no longer measure yourself and others according to perfection, but according to your heart. The good in others, not their talents, matters most. Accepting people for who they are makes you more attractive to others. When you share your weaknesses, you invite others to drop their burden of perfection. This creates the opportunity to develop meaningful and rewarding relationships with those who, with your invitation, can be real with you.

Just as there is no perfection in life, so there is no perfection in recovery. No one does recovery perfectly. Accept and expect this in your recovery. You will make mistakes. You may slip or even readdict. Hope for the best, but prepare for less than that. Accept the imperfection of recovery as a part of healing.

Realizing your best self is realizing the imperfect best you can be. Healing from perfectionism means honoring who you are, with both your light and dark sides, and honoring the perfect imperfection of all things.

It is your mistakes and foolishness that give you the gift of humility, which allows you to be human, just like everyone else. This adds to your attractiveness, making others attracted to you, rather than to an inauthentic façade.

Tips & Tasks

Tips: Perfection is unreal.

Perfectionism springs from a lack of love. It poisons all of life. It fuels readdiction.

We are all perfect in our imperfection.

Tasks: Honor yourself and others just as you and they are.

Drop the pursuit of perfection. Pursue instead doing and being the best you can.

Replace mandates with ideals to guide you.

In the End: Change What You Can and Accept the Rest

Theologian and Ethicist Reinhold Niebuhr famously wrote the following, which most of us know as "The Serenity Prayer:"

God grant me the serenity
to accept the things I cannot change;
courage to change the things I can;
and wisdom to know the difference.

Living one day at a time;
enjoying one moment at a time;
accepting hardships as the pathway to peace;
taking, as He did, this sinful world

as it is, not as I would have it;
trusting that He will make all things right
if I surrender to His Will;
that I may be reasonably happy in this life
and supremely happy with Him
forever in the next.
Amen.

This prayer motivates us to explore acceptance and surrendered action. We have touched on dropping unrealistic expectations, including that you and others should be perfect. We see that acceptance entails respecting Reality. Changing what you can is not about changing this moment, but the next. We act in a thousand ways every day to modify Reality to our benefit and the benefit of others.

But our control is limited. We can change only what we can change. We can't change other people. We can influence others, and even manipulate them to bring about a certain outcome, but ultimately, we have no control. People will do what they will do.

Similarly, we can influence the world, such as when we plant seeds and water them to grow food. Yet we have no absolute control, as the weather or disease could still destroy our crop. So it is with all of your life. Our actions do have an impact. There is much we can change; this book is about making changes to improve your life. Yet ultimately, Life will happen as Life will happen.

That said, you often have no choice but to surrender action to the circumstances occurring around you. Surrendered action means to do what you can, but surrender your expectation of a particular outcome. You may *hope for*, but not *expect from*. All that is certain is that nothing is certain. To expect is to cross over a line to a place you should not be. You are not the whole of Reality, but a very small part. Make plans, but don't plan the outcome.

Once you have changed what you can, accept the rest. Practice acceptance of this moment, asking only what you might do to improve upon it. Do this with respect for this moment, no matter how difficult.

Although events beyond our control may harm us, we are not complete victims, for we always have the freedom to respond positively to every situation. It is not our circumstances that define our experience, but the ways we respond to these circumstances. What happens within you is more important than what happens outside of you. Each of us can change our attitude. We can say "Yes" to this moment. We can respond positively, rather than negatively. Rather than seeking strength in fighting what is, find strength in working with what is. Your friendly acceptance of even the hardest of times empowers you to make positive changes. With positivity, you derive some good from the worst of times. Positive acceptance leads to positive consequences.

Enjoy the relief of acceptance. Suddenly the weight of the world is off your shoulders. Don't make yourself responsible for what you cannot control. Realize that it was useless to worry about things you could not change. Now you can at last lighten up. With acceptance and letting go, you find peace in the midst of the storm. Savor life just as it is. Acceptance promotes your recovery by promoting positivity. Non-acceptance produces negativity, which then leads to cravings and readdiction. The more positive you are, the stronger your recovery will be.

Remember that Reality is partly something you create, and partly something that happens to you. Maintain a reverent attitude toward Reality to protect your recovery.

Tips & Tasks

Tips: Changing what you can starts with accepting this moment.

Positivity leads to positive outcomes.

While right action brings positive results, nothing is guaranteed.

Acceptance leads to serenity.

Tasks: Accept this moment to potitively change the next.

Plan, but don't plan the outcome. Hope, but don't expect.

CHAPTER 9

TOUCHSTONE 8: GROW

Learning and growth are not journeys you ever complete. They are a lifelong process. You never become. You are always becoming. Everyone is a dynamic process, not a static object. There is no arriving. To that end, the eighth Touchstone focuses on the constant and extremely important process of growing and evolving.

So long as you are developing and growing, you will keep yourself busy and connected to the world around you. This singular action can help you maintain perspective and remain healthy. When we stop growing, we stop being fully human. Be careful not to become complacent and self-satisfied. The risk of readdicting is always close behind you and increases when you lose your love and vigor for growing.

Happiness, peace, serenity, and fulfillment are qualities of mind you can achieve in your recovery. But you will not achieve them 100% of the time. Cultivate these states of mind, just as you might cultivate a garden. When you stop working on yourself, you stagnate. This is why growth is one of the 12 Touchstones of Recovery.

Learning and growth entail several components. One of these components is learning from both the past and present. Another is befriending your mistakes as gifts for growth. Others include seeking the feedback of those around you, and embracing pain as an invaluable teacher.

Learn from the Past and Present

It is important to recognize that every moment is an opportunity to learn. Be a student of life in your recovery. Each day when you wake up, reflect on what you can learn from yesterday and what you can learn today. To learn from the past, however, confront and overcome your shame. We gain some of the greatest insight and growth from our past experiences—even the bad ones. Often, those in recovery look at both the past and present difficulties in their lives with an attitude of shame. By doing so, you avoid accountability for your actions and deprive yourself of the opportunity to learn. Either you are a hopeless "loser" who has no chance of learning and changing, or your problems are the faults of others. You then become a helpless victim of a cruel, insensitive, and unjust world.

In either case, you have no empathy for the harm you cause to others. You are disconnected, isolated, and ultimately alone. There is no mutuality in your relationships. There is no opportunity to learn from others about the impact your behavior has on them. The shame/blame cycle prevents you from seeing and taking accountability for your behavior so you can change.

When you suffer from shame, you might then try to cover up your feeling of inadequacy through achievement or through self-delusions of how unique and special you are. You judge others' imperfections as a way of avoiding looking at your own imperfections. By judging others and blaming them for your difficulties, you don't have to face the pain of your shame. It is remarkable, even when in recovery, how people lose their empathy and compassion for the imperfections and struggles of others. Their quickness to judge others reveals that they still feel defective. This is a step back, not a step forward.

Shame prevents belonging, respect, love, and connection. You can't be present to right the wrongs you have caused. You can't attend to the hurt you have inflicted. You're absorbed in your hopelessness and self-hatred. It not only harms you, but it leaves others feeling disregarded, abandoned, and unloved. Shame prevents you from opening your heart to those you love. Immersed in a state of shame, you cannot learn.

Promoting Learning

Developing the capacity to learn from mistakes means confronting shame head on. When shame arises, don't squash it by blaming others. Don't sink into the despair of hopelessness about yourself. Instead, affirm your immeasurable value. The question of your worth is a false question. The true questions are how to heal, how to learn from your mistakes, how to live and love skillfully, and how to live sober.

Learning from the past means taking accountability for your actions. You're responsible for what you did or didn't do. Reclaim your power. You are no longer helpless, for although you may have no control over the world, you have control over your own actions. Move beyond yourself to take stock of the impact you have had on others. Dedicate yourself to changing your unskillful and hurtful behaviors.

When you reclaim your power, you can then engage in constructive problem solving. You can ask yourself, "What happened?" Be very honest with yourself and be courageous enough to see and acknowledge your own unskillful behavior. Listen carefully to what others say. Learn and understand what happened from those around you who observed or were affected by your behavior. This is growth in its purest form.

Looking deeply means looking at several things. One is dissecting the sequence of events, or triggers, that occurred prior to or during your unskillful behavior. If you look honestly, you see that your troubles began brewing long before a crisis, slip, or episode of addicting occurred.

Once you see the chain of events that led to your "misactions," see the underlying thoughts and beliefs. One belief might have been, "Addicting is the only thing that is going to help right now." Another belief might be, "I can't trust others to help me," or, "I won't get my needs met unless I lie." Process these thoughts with others. Ask yourself if these thoughts are true, and how you know for sure they are true.

Next, examine the underlying feelings that go along with your thoughts—either before, after, or with your thoughts. These can be cravings, or feelings of anger, resentment, hopelessness, fear, or loneliness.

Finally, understand and acknowledge everything you did because of the thoughts and feelings you had.

Once you have a good understanding of the sequence of events, and the way your thoughts and feelings drove your actions, note the consequences of your actions. This requires empathy, without shame, for yourself and others. Acknowledge the damage you have done and the suffering you have caused.

Think of this process as the ABC process of analysis of your behavior. "A" stands for antecedents, or the events that occurred that triggered destructive thoughts and feelings. This includes the "people, places, and things" that you encounter in your daily life along with your beliefs and feelings. "B" stands for your behaviors, and "C" stands for the consequences of your behaviors.

The key to learning from the past is to learn how to respond more skillfully to what you perceive (people, places, and things) and experience (thoughts, beliefs, feelings). Then, correct unrealistic beliefs. Once you have a more realistic set of beliefs and expectations, manage your internal discomfort, your painful feelings, in non-destructive ways. Soothe yourself non-addictively. Get the support of others. Identify better ways of responding when you encounter similar events and experience similar feelings.

There are many lessons to learn through this process. They can be found in these Touchstones of recovery. Learning transforms the past from a source of great pain and hopelessness to an invaluable and necessary teacher. It is up to you to decide whether the past is your ally or your enemy. If you make the past your ally, you are not only growing, but moving farther and farther away from readdicting.

Empowered with a deep understanding of your mistakes and having taken the shackles of shame off, you experience your heart opening. The suffering you have caused others becomes your first priority. You put empathy before ego. You right the wrongs you have done. With insight and understanding, you see more clearly and take one more step closer to freedom in your actions. Seeing is freeing. You end the cycle of repetition without the resolution that enslaved you and gain the ability to give up old, destructive habits.

Tips & Tasks

Tips: We grow when we learn from the past and present. This promotes recovery.

Shame prevents learning and growth.

Tasks: Promote learning and growth by dropping shame and taking accountability for your actions.

Analyze the events, thoughts and feelings that drove you to act unskillfully. Correct your attitude and perceptions. Figure out better ways to respond to similar situations in the future.

Practice, Practice, Practice

Mahatma Gandhi said, “You cannot, in a moment, get rid of habits of a lifetime.” Your daily program of recovery is a life practice. So is growth.

Although practice does not make perfect, it makes progress. There is no progress without practice. As it takes about 10,000 hours of practice to master an instrument, so it takes thousands of hours over a lifetime to approach mastery of recovery.

The good news is that practice leads to success. Recovery works for those who work it. If you want something you've never had, do something you've never done. That something is the practice of recovery. Nothing of great value, including your recovery, comes without sustained effort. Nothing of great value comes easy. Growth does not happen overnight or in the blink of an eye. The fact is that recovery is difficult, with the path filled with obstacles and detours. Value the difficulties of recovery, for the greater the difficulty, the greater the growth that comes from practice. The adversity and distress you encounter during your healing from addiction only serves to make you better. You need only practice the skills of recovery.

The enemy of change is fear. Fear keeps you from trying. If you succumb to fear, you will stop growing and learning. Since practice is simply trying something over and over again, fear prevents practice. To recover, overcome fear. We will discuss overcoming fear in the Touchstone on accountability.

Practice also requires motivation. The consistent practice of recovery requires consistent motivation. Since motivation is a state and not a trait, work to maintain your motivation. Do this by remembering the pain you were in and keeping in mind your vision of recovery, with the joy that recovery brings. When you're in a constant uphill struggle, remind yourself of the view at the top. Motivate yourself by reminding yourself that the greater the difficulty, the greater the value of what you achieve through practice. Continuous motivation leads to continuous effort, which leads to your realizing the full potentials of recovery.

Practice recovery by doing what's needed because it's the right thing to do, regardless of how you feel. This may mean staying away from people who trigger you to use even though you want to be with them. Ask for help when you have cravings even though you don't want to and would rather use. Practice doing the right thing, over and over again. If you do what's right, the feelings will follow. This is why people say, "Bring the body and the mind will follow." Take part in meetings and/or treatment. Practicing recovery requires "acting as if" it were real until it becomes real. These practices are indicative of growth.

Practice your recovery with the support of others. As Anita Johnson says:[10]

> Very slowly and carefully, you let go of the log and practice floating. When you start to sink, you grab back on. Then you let go of the log and practice treading water, and when you get tired, hold on once again. After a while, you practice swimming around the log once, twice, ten times, twenty times, a hundred times, until you gain the strength and confidence you need to swim to shore. Only then do you completely let go of the log.

The only difference is that, in recovery, you always keep a "log" close by in case you need it, for nobody swims the seas of recovery without support.

Make it a lifetime project to practice the Touchstones. With practice, you will gradually taste the fruits of recovery. It may not be today or tomorrow, but eventually things get better. You will look back with gratitude on your years of effort, seeing that your efforts gave you the gift of your life. With practice, you become like Emile Coue, who wrote, "Every day, in every way, I am getting better and better." In short, you are growing.

Tips & Tasks

Tips: Recovery is a complex process that requires practicing the Touchstones over a lifetime.

Tasks: As you read this book, make a list of all the tasks from each Touchstone that you need to practice. Then go about an intentional practice of these tasks over a lifetime. Focus from week to week on the skill that seems most relevant at the time.

Use Mistakes and Failures as Opportunities for Learning and Growth

Part of growth is failure and mistakes. That is not just normal, it is absolute. Michael Jordan, arguably the greatest professional basketball player of all time, said:

> I have missed more than 9000 shots in my career. I have lost almost 300 games. On 26 occasions, I have been entrusted to take the game winning shot . . . and missed. And I have failed over and over and over again in my life. And that is why . . . I succeed.

Then there is the great salesman Dale Carnegie, who reminds us: "The successful man will profit from his mistakes and try again in a different way." What can we take away from these two thoughtful quotes? No one is perfect and everyone experiences failure. The same is true when it comes to recovery. Rarely does someone succeed at recovery the first time. No one succeeds all the time. Mistakes and failures are a Reality of recovery and of life. If you make no mistakes, you make nothing.

Failure is underrated. It is only through failure that you grow and gain wisdom. Sometimes failure is final, the only lesson being the humble acceptance of our limitations. Usually, however, failure comes with an opportunity to improve, so long as you adjust your performance accordingly. Great people are great because of the wisdom they gained from their failures. So it is with you. Failure is your pathway to greatness. Your greatest disappointments, if dealt with properly, lead to your greatest successes.

Failure is the most powerful of teachers. They say experience is having made every mistake at least twice. It is through failure that you gain the experience of successful recovery. Failure is success in disguise. Failure also gives you humility. This keeps you "right-sized" with respect to others. Failure protects you from arrogance.

The pain of failure is a gift, for it motivates you to change. Without pain, there would be no transformation. Helen Keller knew the value of pain when she wrote, "Only through the experience of trial and suffering can the soul be strengthened, vision cleared, ambition inspired, and success achieved." She understood growth as much as anyone.

Recovery means taking risks. The one mistake you can make is to be afraid of making mistakes. You are much better off trying and failing than not trying, for through learning from your mistakes, you succeed in your recovery. So, welcome failure and pain as honored guests and not with shame. Shame has no place in recovery, only in addicting. When failure arrives at your doorstep, keep shame out. That way, failure can teach you without distractions.

The practice of recovery is a practice of problem solving when you fail. This is how you reap the benefits of failure. You achieve by overcoming obstacles. Start fresh, strengthened by the lessons you have learned. If you had a recurrence of addiction when you went into a bar with friends, stop going into bars. Grow from your mistakes. Focus not on how far you fell, but on how far you can bounce back. Growth is utilizing failure as a silver lining opportunity to rebuild stronger than ever.

Mistakes and failures in recovery often come as slips and episodes of addicting. Although you work to avoid these, welcome them when they occur, for what else constructive can you do? Slips and readdiction are often part of the process of recovery. They are merely messengers telling you that you have something to learn about how to live a life free from the bonds of addiction. Don't "kill" the messenger. Let your slips and episodes of addicting serve you.

Tips & Tasks

Tips: Mistakes and failures contain the seeds for learning and growth.

Tasks: When you look back, learn back. Embrace mistakes and failures, including slips and episodes of readdiction. Use the lessons learned to change your behavior.

Seek the Feedback of Others

We are partially blind without the eyes of others. We grow the most if we allow others into our garden. You need others to know yourself. Part of us is unknown to us, but is clear to others. Because of this, others can teach you about yourself, helping you to become more self-aware. Invite and welcome the feedback of others. Their input will help you to stay on track and to grow. An open mind is key to recovery.

Taking in feedback can be difficult, as no one likes to hear about their unknown foolishness. This leaves us feeling "em-bare-assed." Being open to feedback requires humility and self-acceptance of your imperfection. This is hard. As Doug Larson said, "To err is human; to admit it, superhuman." Yet as difficult as humility can be, it is essential.

Inviting the feedback of others requires a willingness to be uncomfortable and to be comfortable with your discomfort. Humility gives you this ability. As we discussed, we cultivate our humility by accepting our imperfect selves. Self-acceptance takes the edge off painful feedback, enabling you to learn from others.

Some have an inborn inability to be honest with themselves or take feedback. They lack humility. They simply cannot see and admit their flaws. They fall into falseness and blame rather than taking in the feedback of others. They cannot learn from their mistakes because they are so busy denying them. Their terror of being flawed, or their refusal to take ownership of their actions leaves them unable to learn and grow. Their defensiveness and dishonesty doom them. These unfortunate souls would rather die than learn anything about themselves. And this is exactly what happens.

There is a balance between openness and cautiousness when taking the feedback of others. There is a difference between people telling you what you did and the impact it had and telling you who you are and why. Be open to the former and cautious about the latter. People's ideas about you can be spot on, but not always. The perceptions of people are often skewed and inaccurate. Exercise cautious openness to the feedback of others, being careful not to fall into defensiveness if you hear something painful, but true.

Learning requires listening. Listening leads to learning. And both lead to growth. As someone once said, "Never miss a chance to shut up." This allows you to listen. Listen carefully to what people say to you, feeding back your understanding to them and asking for clarifications. If you are busy talking, you will only learn what you already know.

We come to know ourselves through our relationships with others, but only if these relationships are authentic. Just as you must speak the truth of your experience (with tact), invite others to share the truth of their experience. With this, you grow in self-awareness.

Tips & Tasks

Tips: We cannot fully know ourselves without the feedback of others.

Tasks: Invite the feedback of others. Listen carefully to what they have to say. Humbly acknowledge what rings true. Use feedback to self-correct.

Learn from Pain

No one wants to experience pain. But just like failure, pain can become a tremendous learning opportunity and occasion for growth. When you respond to it correctly, pain can also be the greatest of gifts. Pain catalyzes change. Though cliché, there is truth to the saying, "No pain, no gain."

Nature designed you stay the same if everything is going well in your life. To change could be disastrous. Nature seems to agree with the maxim, "If it ain't broke, don't fix it." We are creatures of habit, only changing when the pain of changing is less than the pain of continuing the way we are going. The pain of living to serve your addiction is Nature's way of helping you to wake up to the Reality that this way of living does not work. Addicting hurts. This is exactly as it should be. Pain teaches what not to do.

Yet recovery, especially in the early stages when you are deep in the wreckage of your addiction, is also painful. Just as pain exists before sobriety, pain persists until you find serenity. By facing, enduring, and learning from your pain, you transform it.

Avoiding your pain only prolongs it. Although the pain of addiction is necessary for change, the pain of avoiding your pain is not. Avoid future pain by facing the pain you have now and learning from it. It is important that those who love you also realize the value of pain. This form of acceptance will aid in your development and growth. Parents and spouses often provide for their loved ones who cannot provide for themselves because of addiction. By shielding victims of addiction from the painful consequences of their addictive acts, others inadvertently perpetuate the addiction by removing half of the hope-pain equation. By shielding you from pain, those who enable you prolong and multiply your pain as the addiction progresses. This is why it is so critical for loved ones to provide unconditional love and support while not shielding those suffering from addiction from the consequences of their actions.

Benjamin Franklin said, "Without continual growth and progress, such words as improvement, achievement, and success have no meaning." The eighth Touchstone is about growth. Strive each day to examine yourself and others to deepen your understanding. Work to live to the best of your capacities while working to expand them through continued effort and practice.

You risk your recovery when you stop growing. Adaptation to a constantly changing world through growth is essential for survival. It is also a tremendous ally in your efforts to not fall back into addicting.

Tips & Tasks

Tips: Pain is an invaluable teacher.

Tasks: Face and embrace your pain. Don't run from it. Learn from it what not to do. Make the changes your pain tells you to make.

CHAPTER 10

TOUCHSTONE 9: PERSEVERE

Sometimes life can seem so unbearable you just want to give up. Hopelessness washes over you. You feel your pain is too great to bear. That is when you must focus on the ninth Touchstone—perseverance.

When you find yourself feeling down and out, you are in a dangerous position. Readdicting is just around the corner. If recovery seems impossible, why try? Better to numb yourself in addiction since there's no other option—or so your mind thinks. Some of us feel overwhelmed by the "F-its." This is a poisonous state in which one wants to feel better now through addicting, regardless of the consequences. There is a complete abandonment of any care for one's long term well-being.

When you feel you can't take another step, you have to revive your strength and conviction to carry on. Do this through several recovery techniques discussed in this Touchstone. No matter how dark or difficult the day, persevere to your fullest extent.

Recovery requires persistence. As Christopher Morley says, "The big shots are only the little shots who keep shooting." When you fail, and feel like a loser, remember that a winner is a loser who kept trying over and over again. Greatness comes from not giving up, but from getting up. As the Japanese proverb goes, "Fall seven times, stand up eight." Through perseverance, you will achieve greatness. When you feel like you're going through hell, keep going. This is perseverance. The first section discusses slip management. A section on faith then follows. Finally, I conclude this chapter by exploring the virtue of patience in recovery.

If You Slip, Immediately Recommit to Your Recovery

Slips are setbacks filled with the secrets of success. Recovery takes time. It can take two to three years to heal from the damage of addiction. It can take more than a lifetime to achieve full psychological, social, and spiritual health, as described in these Touchstones. Persistently practice the art of recovery. Put in thousands of hours of work over a lifetime to approach mastery of this subtle and challenging art.

Slips and readdiction can occur during the long process of growth and transformation that is recovery. Yet slips and episodes of addiction are not just momentary failures. They are also gifts. They provide an opportunity for growth and change—if only you persist in your recovery.

Readdiction occurs when you fall back into a sustained pattern of addicting, with the resulting destructive consequences. Most episodes of readdiction begin with a slip. Slips are the first one or two times you use an addictive substance or engage in an addictive behavior before compulsion and loss of control set in. The risk of readdicting is enhanced by limited recovery skills, the stress of the damage of addiction on your life, lack of support, physical discomfort, and post-acute withdrawal. These factors make the first year of recovery the time of highest risk for readdiction. Cognitive difficulties, commonly from the brain damage caused by alcohol, methamphetamine, or other toxic substances may also impair your ability to recover. Fortunately, the risk of readdiction reduces with time as you heal, fix your life, and develop recovery skills and supports.

Avoiding the Slip and Fall

One key recovery skill is learning to not let a slip turn into a recurrence of addicting. Those who expect perfection in their recovery will consider a slip a sign they have irreversibly failed. Then they give up and give over to the addiction. A slip then becomes a full-blown recurrence of addicting.

Develop a "slip management plan." Hope for the best and plan for the worst, as no one does recovery perfectly. Though slips and episodes of readdiction are not inevitable, they are common. This is why you need "slip insurance."

A slip management plan has three parts. The first part is to have in place emergency contacts that you can ask for help in the event of a slip. You can think of this as your "911-RECOVERY" list. Emergency contacts might include a therapist, a recovery mentor, other recovery supports, or trusted friends. Commit ahead of time to being honest and transparent with your recovery contacts. Planning ahead allows you to experience the care and acceptance you will receive when you slip. This makes it safe to reach out if you slip.

The second part of a slip management plan is to learn from the slip. Something has gone wrong in your recovery when you slip. You are likely lacking in your practice of one or more of the Touchstones. Explore, discover, and understand where and how you fell off your recovery path in the first place. Learning techniques include processing with an addiction professional or with someone experienced in recovery. Journaling can help you to explore the sequence of events, the circumstances, the thoughts and feelings that triggered the slip. Work to understand the anatomy of the slip. Then let this understanding teach you what to do differently next time.

Finally, make necessary changes. This might include increasing supports, going to more recovery meetings, reducing stress, removing triggers, or enhancing your self-care. This helps you get back into recovery. In this way, you prevent the failure of a slip from defining you and instead let it teach you. You harness slips for change and growth. Slips can be a blessing if managed properly.

Slips result from a process that started long before you actually slipped. Rather than one singular event, a slip results from a cascade of events. Negative emotions commonly trigger slips. If you do not know how to reduce your pain in healthy ways, the urge to addict to feel better arises.

When you look deeper, you see that negative emotions arise from non-acceptance, unrealistic expectations, or unskillful behavior. Unskillful behaviors include dishonesty, a failure to assert yourself, or some other failure to take care of yourself. Maybe you became complacent and lost your healthy respect for the illness within you. Perhaps you gave up recovery activities and supports because you thought you were cured. Whatever the case, you experienced a process of BUTA (building up to addict). By understanding a slip, you understand the warning signs—signs you were not well—before the slip. This teaches what you must practice going forward to maintain a sound mind, including acceptance, gratitude, humility, self-care, respect, accountability, and integrity.

Many slip because they got away from their personal recovery program.

They forget that addiction is always within them. Recovery loses its place as the number-one life priority upon which everything else depends. No one slips by attending too many meetings. Slips and readdiction happen when there are too many years of sobriety and not enough days of recovery. This is why you should persist in your personal recovery program until the day you die. Recovery is about changing and growing. Understanding your slips gives you the direction for your continued development. Just get back up when you fall and move forward.

Tips & Tasks

Tips: Slips are gifts in disguise. Understanding a slip teaches you how to do recovery.

Tasks: Develop a slip management plan.

Analyze the process that led up to and triggered the slip or readdiction. Make necessary changes to your recovery plan.

Never give up. Recommit to your recovery as soon as possible after a slip or episode of readdiction.

Have Faith

Faith is an attitude of openness to Reality and a trust in the Universe. Faith is not a rigid clinging to a particular belief. Instead, it is receptiveness to the truth as it reveals itself when you open your eyes. When you have faith, you do not blindly believe in some set idea, but instead give credence to the authenticity of your own experience. It is easier to persevere if you have faith in the bigger picture.

At its core, faith is about your goodness and the goodness of Life. Some, especially trauma survivors, grow up with a general sense that they are bad, that others are bad, and that life is bad. These people lack faith. Thus, they live in fear. And fear is a one-way ticket to readdicting.

Open your eyes to the Reality of grace, resilience, healing, beauty, goodness, and love. See that a life spirit flows through you and connects you to the world. See that each moment of life contains innumerable blessings and possibilities. Love is everywhere.

Seeing this allows you to have faith in yourself, in others, and in the world around you. Although things seem imperfect on the surface, see beyond that to the hidden perfection of things. While things may seem hopeless, they are not. While we make mistakes, we are not a "mistake." Life is good, and you are good. Go forth knowing that if you do your best with the best of intentions, that the best possible will result. With faith in yourself, in others, and in Life, you prevent your fears from plunging you into hopelessness.

While we have little control, we aren't helpless. Part of faith involves believing you can make your life and the lives of others better. That is often the core of persevering. Successful people believe their efforts will eventually yield success. While we can't change much, nothing will change without effort. This applies to recovery and improving your life. If you think you can recover, you can. Having positive expectations of your ability to be effective in the world is essential. Don't let fear and hopelessness overcome you. Tell yourself you aren't a victim of circumstance. Success comes not from the cards you are dealt, but how you play those cards.

Don't look outside yourself for strength and confidence. Look within. See you are already successful in many, many ways; you made it this far. Even the most troubled have innumerable successes. If you are reading these words, you are capable of recovery. Believe in yourself. Rather than saying, "I can't do this," say, "I will give it my all." Your life is your own to live through your efforts.

Faith conquers fear. Have faith that if you practice your recovery skills, you will succeed in your continued recovery. Many find their own faith and hope by hearing the success stories of others who were once hopelessly lost in their addiction. Being around inspiring people inspires faith. See that, although suffering is everywhere, so is the overcoming of it. This helps you to believe in something you cannot yet see yourself.

Faith fuels resolve. If you resolve to succeed, you will succeed. Your only limitation is your own mind. Deciding to do the work of recovery is the first step. It takes courage, but the courage is within you, strengthened by your faith. All you need is the courage to say, "I'll try."

Don't lose hope because the dream of recovery seems so far away. Everyone's recovery starts where they are, with their first sober hour. Even though it may be the darkest of hours, remind yourself that this will pass, as everything does. Darkness turns to light if you have faith in the possibility of recovery and commit to do the work. Even at your worst, the best still lies within you, waiting to be realized through the practice of recovery.

Hope and faith can be difficult to feel at first. You may have to borrow the hope of others. If you don't believe, you can make believe until the first successes kindle your faith. There is wisdom in the saying, "Fake it until you make it."

Given the choice of optimism vs. pessimism, optimism is far better. Negativity will only keep you trapped in a negative place where you cannot bring yourself to the practice of recovery. However, optimism fuels faith.

Look at the lives of others. Take in what they have to say. See that you can find happiness and serenity by disengaging from your addiction. Have faith in the solution by doing the following:

- Renounce a self-oriented way of life.
- Let go of your compulsion to control.
- Dedicate your life to a set of higher principles, such as love and service.
- Stop running from your pain.
- Deal with life on life's terms.
- Accept things just as they are so you can make the next moment better.

You lose faith and hope in your ability to recover when you look back on the mistakes of the past and take these to define who you are. The past only predicts the future if you let it. Bolster faith by living in the present, engaged and listening carefully to what the present has to say. Live each moment fresh, wisely and skillfully to create a better future.

Faith is boosted by the freedom that comes from seeing you are not your thoughts, feelings, and actions. You are not your past. You are free to see Reality and to do the "next right thing." Have faith that you are not doomed, no matter how low you are. Recovery is real. It is yours if you do the work asked of you.

Have faith in the power of recovery and the spirit of love that pervades the Universe. Your faith will fill you with a new hope that, no matter what the outcome, everything is OK. Hope that your actions may make a difference in your life and the lives of others. Hope you will live one more day without addicting. If you live a life of recovery, you can hope that your life and your relationships will eventually heal.

Faith also gives another kind of hope. That is the hope you can manage whatever comes your way. You can hope that although life may bring tremendous hardship, you can minimize your suffering by saying "Yes" to Reality.

Nurture faith by breaking down dreams into small, daily steps. Have faith you can take the next step. Your faith in the next step will take you to your dreams. Have faith that if you do good, then good will eventually come back to you. As you grow your faith, your perseverance will also grow. Like any other habit, perseverance is a trait that can be developed. As you truly believe and are willing to dedicate yourself to knowing you can handle life's obstacles and challenges, you will discover a certain confidence in your ability to protect your sobriety and not fall into the trap of readdicting.

Tips & Tasks

Tips: Faith helps us persevere in hard times.

Faith arises from perceiving Reality accurately.

Tasks: Foster your faith by observing the successful recovery of others. Open your eyes to the healing, love, and grace that surround you.

Enhance your faith by doing good so that you can know good.

Practice Patience

Recovery requires patience. Practice patience, especially with yourself. Nothing great, including your recovery, happens overnight. Recovery takes time. You benefit most from a "slow recovery." Make "Slow but sure" your motto. Success goes not to the swift or strong, but to those who keep practicing the skills of recovery. You can't rush recovery, as everything happens in its own time. Just as it takes nine months to have a baby, so it can take years to create a stable and fulfilling life free from addiction. While you cannot speed up the process, you can slow it down by becoming impatient and giving up. Don't let mistakes and failures hold you back. Patiently practice the skills in the Touchstones to transform missteps into steps toward success. Remember failure is not in messing up, but in giving up.

CHAPTER 11

TOUCHSTONE 10: DEVELOP HEALTHY RELATIONSHIPS

You are who you run with.
If you want to be a winner,
Run with the winners.

We need one another to get by. From birth until the day we die, we are interdependent with those around us, and are designed to love and be loved. Yet loving and being loved can be a messy affair. No one does it perfectly. We are all porcupines at a ball. We invariably poke one another as we dance. Our skill level varies. Some are expert dancers, while others cannot dance at all.

There is a paradox in human relationships; we are simultaneously both alone and connected. We are both autonomous and interdependent. Balance what you want and need for yourself with what others want and need from you. To be harmoniously both for others and yourself is one of the most difficult of all human achievements. It requires multiple self-care and interpersonal skills. This Touchstone discusses these skills.

Learning to Have Healthy Relationships

This Touchstone addresses key relationship skills you must possess for your recovery. Healthy relationships are both a practice and an experience. Through practicing the skills in this Touchstone, you will gradually experience an emotional transformation so you experience what it's like to safely love and be loved. Like riding a bike, this can seem awkward and unfamiliar at first. However, with practice these relational habits gradually become almost second nature. This is the transformation. Although you cannot change your character or erase the wounds of the past, you can change your relationship to your character so you don't destructively act out.

I start with the importance of recovery supports, followed by the practice of assertiveness. Guidance on how to develop a healthy social network follows. I then explore sharing your thoughts and feelings with others. A discussion follows on refraining from attempting to fix or change others. To complement the discussion of sharing feelings, I touch on not acting on the urge to isolate. As all healthy relationships require you to be both humble and respectful, I devote a section on this. I then discuss the importance of not socializing with people who are addicting. I conclude with a discussion of relationship repair through making amends.

Develop Recovery Supports

Recovery supports are those people who you surround yourself with to ensure you maintain your sobriety and prevent readdiction. These include the following:

1. Recovery mentors
2. People at recovery meetings

Let's unpack each one at greater length.

Recovery Mentors

Recovery mentors are people with recovery skills and experience living life according to the Touchstones. They commit to helping you with your recovery as part of their own spiritual growth and recovery work. In the 12-step fellowship, this person is a sponsor. You can find recovery mentors in other places, such as through your existing social networks or at other recovery-based meetings. Professional recovery coaches also serve as recovery mentors.

Recovery mentors are usually older. They serve as a father, mother, big sister, or older brother figure. They are tough, kind, and wise. They do not judge you, although they may judge the wisdom of your actions. They offer hope, encouragement, guidance, and support. They are there to help you get up when you fall. They reduce your self-alienation by giving you a forum in which to be vulnerable and share what you're doing, thinking, and feeling. They help you with shame by not shaming you. They help you with forgiveness by forgiving. They help you articulate your dreams and achieve your goals by providing a sounding board and wise advice based on their own recovery experience. This is an important relationship to your overall success in recovery. Work to develop this relationship in the early part of your journey.

Many people check in with their recovery mentors every day. They "get current," meaning they let their mentor know everything they felt, thought, or did since the last time they spoke. This requires honesty and transparency. You can't fully benefit from a recovery mentor if you are not completely truthful. A good mentor will not judge you no matter what you say, although they may gently call you out on your unskillful actions. When processing a mentor's advice, consider the merits of their suggestions, following what you intuitively know to be good for you and politely disregarding the rest.

It is very important to call your recovery mentor when craving, upset, or in trouble. This is when you need them most. Early recovery usually requires that you clean up the wreckage of your addiction. You need the encouragement and guidance of others. People's thinking in early recovery is usually diseased. Like a bad neighborhood, don't go into your mind alone. This is where a recovery mentor can step in to help keep you safe and sane.

Though a relationship with a recovery mentor is one of love, it's not a friendship. Friendships are mutual. You cannot easily fire a friend. Your recovery mentor should focus solely on your recovery, with the only "reward" being inherent in helping you. Only you can do your recovery, but you cannot do it alone. It takes strength to ask for help. It is a sign of weakness to feel you must do life on your own, with no one's help. This brittle independence is a sign of insecurity. A person who feels this way is afraid of feeling weak and vulnerable should they ask for help.

Meetings

In addition to recovery mentors, recovery meetings have rescued millions of people from addiction. Although meetings are not for everyone, they still serve as a dominant way that people recover. For some, a meeting a day keeps the detox away. People who think they don't need meetings to recover often do.

Every meeting consists of three meetings: the meeting before, the actual meeting, and the meeting afterward. Often, the meeting before and the meeting afterward are the most valuable. They let you have one-on-one conversations with people in recovery and make personal connections. Come early and stay late to take advantage of these opportunities to build recovery supports.

You find support from others in recovery at meetings. You connect at these meetings with others, and develop relationships that help you stay sober. Meetings reduce your sense of shame and isolation. You see you are not alone. Meetings give hope as you witness the successful recovery of people who started out devastated and destitute because of their addiction. Meetings also teach life lessons as you listen to the challenges people face and how they dealt with them. You experience belonging. You discover a new strength in union.

Each meeting has its own personality. Meetings vary by recovery approach, such as 12-step meetings vs. Refuge Recovery meetings vs. SMART Recovery meetings vs. the many other types of meetings discussed earlier. Meetings also vary by type of meeting, such as step meetings vs. speaker discussion meetings in the 12-step tradition. They can also vary by who attends, such as meetings just for women or men. In the 12-step tradition, there are both open and closed meetings. Open meetings are open to those who do not identify themselves as suffering from addiction. Closed meetings are only for those who identify themselves as suffering from addiction.

Meetings are a tool. They require skill to use effectively. People new to recovery can make the mistake of socializing with others who are also new to recovery. This usually leads to disaster. Another too frequent mistake is to seek romantic relationships at recovery meetings to cope with loneliness or sexual frustration. This often leads to a bad outcome as people with weak recovery and relationship skills often get together during a time of fragility. It is best to use meetings as recovery meetings, not as sources for romance. If you develop social relationships at meetings, make sure your new friends have several years of solid recovery.

Many find meetings difficult. They may feel embarrassment or shame. They may be too shy to meet others. Some compare themselves to others in meetings, concluding that they are "not as bad" as the people they meet. You will disagree with what some people say. When this happens, take what is useful and leave the rest. Identify with the similarities. Don't focus on the differences.

Meetings are often difficult at first, but become more comfortable with time. Just listen and learn at first until you get to know people and develop a sense of comfort. Go to many different meetings until you find a few you like. Then, go to those meetings regularly to develop recovery relationships with the other regulars. While you may not want to go to meetings, go anyway because it is good for you. Bring your body; your mind and heart will follow. You will eventually want to go to meetings because you feel so much better afterward.

Instead of talking to those who are also young in their recovery, associate with the "old timers" around the coffee pot at break time. Don't go out with the smokers, as those who smoke are not in total recovery—they are actively destroying themselves via their tobacco addiction. Instead, seek people with many years of total recovery from all addictive substances and behaviors. Talk with people you like and would like to be like.

Meetings require discipline. Schedule them, Make them a first priority. Don't let anything except emergencies get in the way. Go to meetings both when you want to and when you don't. As with exercise, forcing yourself to go to a meeting often ends with feeling much better afterward. Regular meetings support recovery. Those who skip often slip.

Everyone benefits from being supervised by and accountable to others. Without this, chaos would reign. Your recovery supports keep you accountable in your recovery. Invest time and effort into developing them.

Tips & Tasks

Tips: Mentors and meetings provide the support, guidance, supervision, and accountability needed to recover.

Tasks: Obtain a recovery mentor as soon as possible. Make sure they meet the criteria discussed in this section.

Keep current with your recovery mentor.

Go to meetings, even if you are uncomfortable.

Experiment with different recovery approaches. Go to different meetings until you find the ones that are right for you.

Give meetings time to experience the benefits. Use meetings skillfully as described in this section.

Be Assertive and Authentic

"Be who you are and say what you feel, because those who mind don't matter and those who matter don't mind."
—Dr. Seuss

Assertiveness

To be assertive is to take care of yourself by being strong, clear, firm, and confident with others. This is different from being aggressive, when you lash out in anger, hurting others because you hurt. Assertiveness is an important relationship builder. It allows you to create and maintain boundaries. When you are assertive, you negotiate with others for what you want or need with kindness, care, and respect. When assertive, how you say it (with kindness) is more important than what you say.

E.E. Cummings said, "To be nobody but yourself in a world which is doing its best, night and day, to make you everybody else means to fight the hardest battle any human being can fight, and never stop fighting." Assertiveness is necessary, as we all are vulnerable to mistreating each other out of our own needs and lack of awareness. If you act like a doormat, even the greatest of saints will wipe their feet on you. If you do not take charge of taking care of yourself, who will? Assertiveness comes from knowing it's up to you. When you stop treating yourself poorly, others will follow suit, while those who do not will fade from your life.

People fail to assert themselves out of fear or lack of self-regard. They are afraid of upsetting others by calling them on their behavior. You may fear others will dislike you or reject you. You may fear they will judge you, or they will abandon you. You may have learned that your needs are not important. Maybe you were taught to sacrifice yourself for others or that taking care of yourself is "selfish." To be assertive, let go of needing others to be happy with you. If someone asks you for something you do not want to give, be OK with their anger or disappointment when you say "No." Set yourself free from the need for others to like you. Pleasing everyone at all costs is violence against yourself. It is a formula for failure.

Let go of others' opinions of you, as that is none of your business. Accept and love yourself first to relieve others of the obligation to accept and love you. To experience yourself as autonomous and whole apart from what anyone thinks of you is freedom. Have faith that if you act with love and integrity, you are good, no matter what anyone else thinks. Few may agree with you, as when people first spoke out against slavery. Truth always starts out as a minority. Society would not advance without assertive truth tellers.

Assertiveness takes practice. The following techniques will help when you are dealing with hurtful or upsetting behaviors:

First, get calm. Being assertive when boiling with anger does not work. Practice the anger management techniques discussed earlier. Wait for the right time and setting to talk to someone, usually in a quiet, private place. When you do talk, be calm, be relaxed, make direct eye contact, and keep an open posture that reduces defensiveness. While you work to stay calm and respectful, you also allow yourself to be authentic, letting your facial expressions and tone of voice reflect how you are feeling.

Second, point out the behaviors that are upsetting you. State the problem clearly. You might say, "When you are late . . ." or, "When you ask me to work extra hours without pay . . ." or, "When you put me down . . ." Be careful to just state facts. Label specific behaviors. Don't make judgments. Saying, "When you forget about our dinner date . . ." is much better than saying, "When you are a thoughtless jerk . . ." You also want to avoid generalities such as "you always" or "you never."

Third, follow your description of the behavior with "I feel" statements. Stick to "I" statements that show how you feel in response to someone's behavior. You may say that you feel upset, frustrated, angry, hurt, or disappointed. When making "I feel" statements, be careful not to label, accuse, judge, or interpret the other person's behavior. "I feel hurt when you are late because you only care about yourself" is not as effective as "I feel hurt when you're late." When you make "I" statements, you take ownership for your feelings. You don't blame others for how you feel. "I am angry" is much better than "You make me angry."

Fourth, voice your requests for behavior change. After expressing your feelings and the behaviors that caused these feelings, say what you would like. Be clear, direct, and firm. For example, you may say to a partner, "When we work on a project together, I feel frustrated when you discount my preferences and opinions. In the future, I need us to come up with what we'll do based on an equal consideration of both our preferences and ideas." As you make requests, take care to make sure you are considering both your needs and the other person's needs. Try to come up with a resolution that is fair to everyone. This builds equality and trust. It also helps to invite brainstorming and problem solving so that the other person becomes a partner in finding a solution to the problem.

Fifth, you might add on what you will do if the disturbing behavior continues. In doing this, you lay out clear consequences for the other person should they persist in their behavior. To the person who is chronically late, you might say, "The next time we get together, I will wait for 10 minutes, but after that I will leave." Or, to someone who loses their temper and breaks things, you might say, "I get terrified when you lose your temper and break things. I need for you to not break things. If you continue to break things, I will call the police." Be careful to only state consequences you will follow through on. People may not change their behavior if they do not think you will follow through.

Sometimes you can pave the way for assertive communication by providing empathy and validation. If someone is yelling at you because you upset him or her, say, "I can see that you are very upset right now. Your being upset is understandable. But it scares me when you yell. I need for you to stop yelling at me now or I will need to end our conversation."

When dealing with people who are attacking or criticizing you, assertive communication means not arguing with them. Don't engage in a fight. Don't take what they say personally. Don't make it about your own worth or integrity. Let their words roll off your shoulders. Instead, listen for what is legitimate in their concerns and provide empathy and validation. This takes the wind out of the other person's sails; what are they going to say? It takes two to fight. If you don't fight, there will be no fight.

Respectful Authenticity

Be "respectfully authentic" when you are assertive. This helps to build healthier relationships. Work to be both spontaneous and appropriate. Be truthful, but speak the truth with compassion and care so as not to use truth as a weapon. Be authentic by being true to yourself. Say how you feel and what you need. Accept your feelings if you are upset or angry, but don't hurt others. Say what you think while protecting, as much as possible, the other person's feelings. Say what you mean, but don't say it mean.

Being true to yourself means being true to that which flows through you from beyond you. When you are true to yourself, you are true to your True Self, the self that exists within you to savor and nurture life. This Self is not something you create. It is not something you decide. You don't fabricate who you "should" be. The True Self is not a thought. Instead, it's something you experience when your mind settles down in silence and stillness. It is from silence and stillness that authentic love and compassion arise and flow through you. To live from your silent, still consciousness is to be authentic.

To be authentic, listen to the voice of your conscience that wordlessly speaks the truth. You cannot be authentic unless you look, see, and listen to the truth that stirs in your heart before thought. Honor your rational intuition.

Just as each one of us is unique, so our paths through life are also unique. When you are authentic, you blaze your own trail, rather than following a path that someone else says you should follow. It someone tells you that you cannot do something, do it anyway if it's the right thing to do.

As with any skill, assertiveness and authenticity become easier with time and practice. The rewards of being authentically true to yourself and assertive are great. When you are authentic and assertive, you escape victimhood. You secure your recovery by protecting yourself from harm.

Tips & Tasks

Tips: Being assertive and authentic protects you from harm and helps others to treat you better.

Tasks: Memorize the assertiveness steps in this section.

Make a list of people who are imposing on you or hurting you. Write down ahead of time what you want to say to them. Then make arrangements with them to assert yourself. Do so at the appropriate time, place, and in the appropriate manner.

Listen to your conscience. Honor the True Self that flows through you from beyond you. Practice being respectfully authentic in all your interactions.

Develop a Healthy Social Network

Andrena Sawyer said, "Life is hard. Find some really good people to walk through it with. It makes things a little easier." It is crucial to recognize that unhealthy relationships promote addiction. Developing healthy relationships requires healthy people. Recovery almost always involves changing your social network. In addiction, you may have socialized with others suffering from addiction. In recovery, you do not. Many fail to secure their recovery by continuing to socialize with friends and family who use. This almost always leads to readdiction.

People in the active addiction phase need each other to normalize, rationalize, justify, and support their addiction. Two addicting people are like two crawfish in a bucket; as soon as one crawfish tries to climb out, the other one pulls him or her back down into the bucket of addiction.

Shift from seeing your drug-using "friends" as "cool," to seeing your sober friends as the people who are really the "cool" ones. People lost in addiction are not capable of being true friends, as their agenda is their addiction, and not the love of friendship. This makes them dangerous to be around if you are not solid in your recovery.

Creating a Healthy Social Network

To ensure you do not readdict, you should work to create a strong and healthy social network to support you and your sobriety. Cultivate relationships with those committed to your recovery. Your recovery and your relationships go hand-in-hand. Only associate with those solid in their recovery if they suffer from an addiction.

Since no one recovers alone, choose friends who will help promote your recovery. Use them for inspiration, support, hope, and guidance. Be with people who will inspire and promote your consciousness to live according to the Touchstones of recovery outlined in this book.

Develop healthy relationships by first cleaning up your life and becoming whole. Get sober. Obtain the treatment needed to heal. Take care of yourself. Treat others with the kindness and consideration you would like. True friendships are between whole people forming friendships, not between broken people seeking others to become whole. Although everyone is worthy of love, achieving a sense of wholeness, integrity, and abundance in your life will attract the love of others. Become the right person to attract the right people. Surround yourself with as many supportive, healthy, loving people as you can who can love you while you learn to love yourself. Open your heart to the open-hearted. Let those relationships go that do not advance your growth.

Many who have lived in the street culture of addiction need to live by a new set of rules. Replace:

- Dishonesty with honesty
- Fear with love
- Intimidation and coercion with mutuality
- Violence with non-violence
- Exploitation with collaboration

If you do not make these changes, healthy people will see through your destructive behavior and put up boundaries to protect themselves. Once you're free of shame and are acting with love and integrity, make new connections. Pursue your passions in social settings. Get involved with volunteer work. Join clubs and interest groups. Join a religious or spiritual community. Help community service organizations. Consider joining a gym. Seek out healthy people in solid recovery at your recovery meetings. There are hundreds of ways to meet healthy people with similar interests and values.

Use love as your guide in cultivating a healthy social network. It is through your loving relationships that you find the strength and courage to face life. Love cures loneliness, emptiness, and hopelessness. Love takes the pain of life and makes it bearable. Conversely, it is love from which the joy of life flows. Love fosters belonging. Loving connection with others reduces the fear of being flawed and imperfect. Love gives peace in the midst of the storm of life.

If you have a history of neglect or trauma, you may find it difficult to allow others to love you. Trauma and neglect can damage trust. You may fear others will betray or hurt you. You may fear others will see your fundamental unworthiness. Your shame prevents loving connection. Rather than cultivating relationships with healthy people who value you, you pursue the unhealthy people who use you, abuse you, and reject you. Relationships can be heaven or hell. For too many with trauma and neglect, they are hell.

Healing happens when you substitute your attachment to addiction with attachments to others who are healthy.

Everyone wants to be happy. Nearly everyone wants to love and be loved. Everyone is afraid of being hurt and rejected. Remind yourself that we are all wounded and vulnerable. Knowing this, cultivate your friendships with the utmost care and respect.

Resolve Conflicts

Conflict is inevitable in any healthy relationship. The way you manage conflict determines the success of a relationship. When conflict arises, work it out. Walk away only as a last resort. This is how you preserve your marriage, family relationships, and friendships. When mistreated, assert yourself as discussed above.

If someone is upset with you, listen carefully. Try to understand. Reflect back your understanding of their experience. Apologize if appropriate and change your behavior if necessary.

Talk out disagreements. Come to a common understanding or agree to disagree and to live and let live. Adjust your expectations to what friends and family are willing and able to do. Ask for what you need, but don't make demands or coerce others. By adjusting your expectations to the Reality of the situation, you enable yourself to let go of poisonous resentments.

Tend to your relationships every day. As Ralph Waldo Emerson once said, "Go often to the house of thy friend, for weeds choke the unused path." Invest in your family and friendships, as the return on investment is joy, peace, and belonging. It is no longer "me" and "you," it's "we" and "us." In oneness, you need not readdict to manage life's difficulties. You cannot secure a healthy recovery without a healthy lifestyle of doing healthy things with healthy people. This is why developing a healthy social network needs to be a priority.

Tips & Tasks

Tips: Recovery requires a healthy social network.

Tasks: Remove destructive people, including those caught in active addiction, from your life.

Prepare yourself for healthy relationships by resolving shame and acting with love and integrity.

Seek out healthy people.

Invest in your healthy relationships. Tend to them.

Preserve positive relationships by resolving conflicts.

Share Your Thoughts and Feelings

Sharing is part of healthy relationships. We share our thoughts and feelings with others, just as they share their thoughts and feelings with us. It is in seeing and being seen, in knowing and being known, that you avoid isolation. By sharing, you let others help you.

They say a sorrow shared is a sorrow halved while a joy shared is a joy doubled. This is why it's so important to share your pain. When you do so, you are no longer alone. You have a choice; you can either talk and prosper, or addict and die. This is why some people in recovery meetings will say, "If you pass, it's your ass."

When the opportunity presents itself, share. You are better off picking up a phone than picking up a drink or drug. Help is often just 10 digits away. By talking about your feelings, you make them more real. Talking it out also separates you from your feelings. It helps you get unhooked. After talking about them, you are better able to address them.

Men have a particularly hard time with sharing, as society teaches men that sharing painful feelings makes one weak. This may be one reason why addiction is more prevalent in men than in women. Unfortunately, many men reject other men who show their vulnerability. Men must be selective in sharing their pain. An essential skill of recovery is the ability to be vulnerable and appropriately disclose to appropriate others. For many men, their therapist, their recovery mentor, close friends, family, and other recovery supports serve as safe sounding boards.

Authentic sharing entails vulnerability. Share with safe people where it is safe to be vulnerable. Remember that it is a sign of strength to be vulnerable with those who care for you. It requires courage. Be courageous when you share thoughts and feelings with others.

You are only as sick as your secrets. Recovery requires honesty and transparency with a select group of people who you can trust, who will not judge you, and who have your best interest at heart.

Tips & Tasks

Tips: We stay on track by transparently sharing our thoughts and feelings with safe, healthy people.

It is the strong person who has the courage to be vulnerable.

Tasks: Share yourself daily with those who care for you, who will not judge you, and who can help you sort things out.

Don't Try to "Fix" Anyone

Part of being a good friend or partner and building healthy relationships involves not trying to "fix" anyone. It doesn't work. You can't fix people. People must fix themselves (if they want to). You have no right to tell others how they should live their lives. No one likes when others tell them they're dysfunctional. Change must come from within. You can help and support others. You can even offer advice if requested. But give others permission to disregard your advice.

It is your job to clean up your own side of the street while letting others tend to their side as they wish. Since living your own life is a full-time job, you don't have time to live someone else's life for them. When it comes to feeling whole and fulfilled, a particular relationship isn't the problem, nor is it the solution.

If someone is causing you pain, you have three choices:

1. You can be assertive, share your distress, and ask for what you need.
2. You can accept behavior that someone cannot or will not change.
3. You can limit or let go of relationships if they're harmful or unfulfilling.

These are your three choices. Trying to manipulate, coerce, harass, or nag a person into submission will only generate resentment and resistance.

Some people try to fix a spouse or partner because they're not willing to end a harmful relationship. They may be terrified of being alone. They may feel un-whole and be using the other person in a futile attempt to make themselves whole. Whatever the case, sacrificing your well-being for the sake of maintaining a destructive relationship is not wise. That choice leads back to addiction. People set on trying to fix the problem behavior of another person are destined for disappointment.

Hold others and your relationships lightly in your heart. Love, live, and let live. Take care of yourself not by fixing others, but by setting limits, putting up boundaries, asking for what you need, negotiating, problem solving, and letting go of destructive relationships.

Tips & Tasks

Tips: Trying to fix other people does not work.

Tasks: Focus on cleaning up your own side of the street.

Take care of yourself by setting limits, putting up boundaries, asking for what you need, negotiating, problem solving, and letting go of destructive relationships.

Don't Isolate

The opposite of connection is isolation. The opposite of sharing your pain is keeping it to yourself. Isolating is a warning sign of impending readdiction.

Everyone needs some time for solitude. Solitude can revitalize you. Yet solitude differs from isolation. In solitude, you're alone in the context of connectedness to others. In isolation, there is no connection.

We need others to maintain our sanity, as anyone in solitary confinement or stranded away from others will attest.

A person in active addiction treats loneliness with isolation. Addiction isolates you by cutting you off from others. Be with and around others so you can make the connections that sustain your recovery. Recovery meetings are important because they treat addiction's isolation.

Balance solitude with healthy doses of human connection. Don't be alone too much. Some are "loners." Their fear of rejection makes it difficult to connect. They may suffer from social anxiety, fearing being the center of attention. They may fear acting foolishly or that people will judge them. If socializing is a problem, get treatment, as isolation will only fuel readdiction.

Apart from meetings, there are many other ways to decrease isolation. You might volunteer, join a local club or interest group, join a community service organization, or join a spiritual or religious organization. You can support a cause, such as a political group or a social cause. Online groups exist that offer an easy way to connect. Then there is always the telephone.

Remember that just as you need people, other people need you.

Tips & Tasks

Tips: Isolation fuels readdicting. Connection fuels recovery

Tasks: Balance solitude with healthy companionship.

Get treatment if you have difficulty socializing.

Practice Humility and Respect

Humility and respect go hand in hand. If one is humble, then one shows others the respect they deserve. Respect depends upon humility. If someone is respectful, you know they are also humble. You have an equal respect for both self and others. You value others because others are innately good, important, and valuable just because they are. This is respect. You don't respect people because they earn your respect. Instead, you respect others because, as a humble person, you are also respectful.

Humility

Ernest Hemingway said, "There is nothing noble in being superior to your fellow man; true nobility is being superior to your former self." To be humble is to be modest in one's view of oneself. Humble people lack self-importance, feeling so secure in their own goodness that goodness is no longer an issue. While they take their recovery seriously, they do not take themselves seriously.

When you are humble, you are not grandiose, nor do you cast yourself into inferiority. Instead, you are "right-sized"—neither too big nor too small. Though humility reduces us to our proper size, it does not degrade us. Humility elevates our status to a place of value and worth, but does not inflate.

When you're humble, you are realistic about yourself. You recognize not only your strengths and accomplishments, but also your weaknesses and failings. People suffering from active addiction have a hard time with humility because of their shame. To become humble, you must come to accept and value yourself, even with your addiction, other illnesses and disabilities, flaws, and weaknesses. Although recovery from addiction requires a certain healthy humiliation, to become humble is to become free from humiliation. When your self-worth is no longer an issue, you can let go of your egotistical self-preoccupation and achieve humility. As C.S. Lewis once said, "Humility is not thinking less of yourself, it's thinking of yourself less."

The opposite of humility is pride. While humble people may take pride in something well done, they are not proud. They don't consider themselves above others, or take pride in the gifts they did not earn, such as their talents. Proud people put their will above everyone else's. They consider themselves more important than others. The world serves them, rather than them serving the world. Recovery works for those who believe in God and those who don't believe in God alike, but not for those who believe they ARE God.

When you let go of pride, you feel equal to everyone else. Humble people consider everyone special, including themselves, but no one is more special than anyone else. They realize that they are unique, just like everyone else. Humility gives people permission to be ordinary. This is a great relief. Humility sets us free.

Humble people value others as much as they do themselves. When you value others, you are open to listen and learn from them, knowing you don't have all the answers. Humble people are comfortable being wrong. They are open-minded. They don't have to be right. It's not about who's right as what's right. Humble people are teachable. They are secure in being fallible. With this security, others can educate and influence them.

Humble people don't talk about their accomplishments. Recognizing their limitations and imperfections, humble people also recognize the potential to do better. Humble people are not self-satisfied or stagnant. They improve themselves and the world. They let their accomplishments speak for themselves. They don't draw attention to themselves. They neither need nor want to. Their agenda is the group, not self-aggrandizement. When praised, they point out with gratitude those who helped them along the way. Rather than elevating themselves, they recognize others.

Develop humility by combining self-inquiry and self-acceptance while seeing and accepting your place in the order of things. Acceptingly see yourself for exactly who you are, with all your character virtues and vulnerabilities.

Accept your imperfections and limitations, knowing you will be wrong and make mistakes every day of your life. Because you accept and value yourself, you need not pump yourself up into something greater than you are. Because you are OK, self-preoccupation recedes and you attend to what Life asks of you. While you take care of yourself, you also forget yourself because you see it's not just about you. You humbly step down from your throne and join in as an equal with the masses.

Respect

Respect involves practicing the Golden Rule, which says treat others as you would want them to treat you. Better yet, respectful people practice the Platinum Rule, which says treat others according to what is good for them. Respecting others is thus a practice of love. You show concern for others in your actions. If you can be of help, you help, going the extra mile if you can be of service to another person.

Being humble, you realize we are all equally deserving of being treated well, and thus with respect. Don't hurt or take advantage of others. Don't exploit others. Take care not to mistreat others. Take responsibility for policing yourself, setting rules for yourself for how you treat others. This allows for others to trust you, for they know you will not disregard their interests. Besides building trust, respect also generates goodwill, as it's human nature to want to do well for someone who does well for you. Respect nurtures love.

When you are respectful, you respect others' needs. Since everyone wants to be understood, try to understand. Since everyone wants affirmation of their inherent worth, affirm and validate others as innately good. Since everyone wants to be asked rather than ordered around, ask for what you want others to do. Since everyone wants to be given choices, give others choices. When you are respectful, you respect these universal human needs.

We show our respect in a thousand daily acts of kindness, consideration, and courtesy. Greet and acknowledge people. Be kind always, knowing that in their own way, everyone you meet is having a hard time. Don't lash out when angry. Be polite. Don't be rude. Being rude is disrespectful. Being disrespectful is not an option.

Showing respect involves listening. Listen carefully to others. Value their opinions, even if you disagree. Show consideration for people's preferences.

Part of being courteous is being reliable and trustworthy. Show respect by telling the truth, keeping your word, doing what you say you will do, and being on time. When you act with integrity in these ways, you also build trust and goodwill in others. Respectful people show gratitude and appreciation for the good that others do. They give specific praise when praise is due.

To practice being respectful, first practice humility, or your respect will not be authentic. Humility and respect are not destinations, but daily practices. Through the daily practice of balanced acceptance, appreciation, and care for self and others, you will develop a strong social network of respectful people. They will trust and value you in response to your valuing them and being trustworthy. It is karma. What you put out comes back to you multiplied.

Tips & Tasks

Tips: Humble people have a balanced appreciation and acceptance of themselves and others.

Healthy relationships require that you be respectful, which requires that you be humble.

Tasks: Develop humility by combining self-inquiry with self-acceptance.

Commit to being an unconditionally respectful person. Make this a daily life practice.

Heal Damaged Relationships

Joyce Rebeta-Burditt said, "Alcoholism isn't a spectator sport. Eventually the whole family gets to play." The victims of addiction include those around you. You have a significant impact upon others, for good or for ill. Like waves rippling out from a pebble thrown into a pond, addiction damages you first, then those closest to you, and then those closest to those people. Addiction's destruction thus spreads outward, with huge costs and burdens to society in the form of crime, unemployment, underemployment, disability, and disease.

Few victims of addiction leave others untouched. Addiction leaves a long trail of hurt, disappointment, sadness, grief, anger, broken relationships, and missed opportunities. Though even the best of us can harm others, addiction multiplies the harm you cause a thousand-fold, for addiction has no regard for anyone other than itself. Most people have deceived, cheated, manipulated, and exploited others during their active addiction phase. They have blamed others for their difficulties. They didn't meet their responsibilities to others. They have neglected their important relationships. They have abandoned others. They may even have been violent in an intoxicated state.

Part of developing healthy relationships in recovery includes healing the relationships you have damaged in your addiction if possible. Sometimes you cannot heal the harm you have caused. You may have lost contact with someone from the past. You may have so traumatized someone that to have further contact would cause further harm. Don't attempt to make amends if it will harm the other person.

Be clear about what you're doing and why when making amends. Don't try to repair relationships to relieve guilt or to restore a relationship for your benefit. This is common in early recovery. Your benefit is not the reason for making amends. Making amends is for the benefit of the other, not you. The purpose is to heal the harm you have caused others. You only benefit from the peace of mind of knowing you helped someone you harmed. Make amends with hope, not expectations. Hope the other person will benefit. Be clear about this intention. While you may hope to restore a relationship, don't make amends for this reason.

Making amends springs from your respect and care for others. Since you are not perfect and make mistakes daily, there are plenty of opportunities to hurt or disappoint people in the normal course of your life. This is why making amends is a lifelong practice. Maintaining healthy relationships means healing the ongoing harm we inflict upon others.

Consider whether to make amends in person or by letter. Email is somewhat less formal, so a letter is usually preferable to express the seriousness of your intent. If at all possible, make amends in person, as making amends is best when interactive. Making amends in writing is not as complete. If it is best to meet in person, consider the best place to meet. Sometimes it's best to meet in a neutral, public place, depending on the relationship. It should be a quiet and private setting.

Fixing the Broken

If you have caused pain or suffering in others, work to heal these damaged relationships. They will weigh on you and poison your serenity. Broken relationships may even threaten your sobriety. Repairing relationships through making amends is an 8-step process:

1. Ask permission. First, ask for permission to make amends. This is an act of respect, allowing the other person to decide if they wish for you to make amends to them or not. Respect that some may not wish to have contact with you. Depending on the relationship, you may ask for permission directly, in writing, or through a mediator. A possible statement might be: "I realize that I have harmed you. I want to offer you the opportunity for me to make amends. I wish to repair the harm I have caused you if possible." If someone does not wish to engage with you, respect this. Short of the full 8-step process, you may wish to write a letter to them that acknowledges the harm you have done and expresses remorse.
2. Acknowledge. Second, acknowledge the harm you have done to the degree you understand it. List the hurtful things you did. Follow with the commitments and obligations you didn't fulfill.
3. Develop and express empathy. Empathy means knowing another person's experience. This is perhaps the most important step. Ask the other person what impact you have had on them. This is a listening and understanding step. Seek to understand through listening and asking questions. Repeat what you have heard to insure you understand. This lets the other person know you understand their experience. Don't argue or disagree. You are not doing this to judge whether someone's experience was right or wrong. You are attempting only to understand the impact you had. Strive to understand every action you took that was upsetting or hurtful, and the full emotional impact you had.
4. Be accountable. Once you have acknowledged your behavior and demonstrated your understanding of the hurtful impact you have had on the other person, you then need to take accountability for your behavior. While you might offer explanations of your behavior, make no excuses. Don't say things like, "I was unaware," or, "I didn't realize," or, "I didn't mean to." Don't blame your behavior on others or play the victim. These evasive maneuvers will undo the amends-making process. What the other person needs from you is ownership

and accountability. Even if you were unaware, you still hurt someone. Own this with no excuses. There are no excuses. In recovery, live a "no-excuse" life.

5. Express remorse. It is only after you have shown empathy and taken accountability that you can then say you are sorry and that you regret what you have done. Apologies ring hollow if the other person does not know that you fully understand how you harmed them. Taking authentic accountability paves the way for the other person to accept your apology.
6. Invite forgiveness. After expressing remorse, you can invite forgiveness in order to relieve the other person from the pain of resentment. Invite forgiveness for the sake of the other person and the relationship, as forgiveness is healing for the other person. You might say, "I hope you can forgive me so that the pain I caused will ease." In asking for forgiveness, ask, don't demand. Do so with humility, as asking for forgiveness is not to assuage your guilt. Demanding forgiveness is not respectful. It is up to the other person to allow for forgiveness if they wish, not you.
7. Make a no-harm commitment. People need more than your remorse to heal. They need to know you will change your behavior. Don't make amends unless you can commit to not harming again. Don't make amends to people you may hurt again. This sets people up for further hurt and disappointment. Hurting others again destroys trust. Saying, "I'll try to," or, "I'll try not to," is not good enough. Say, "I will," and, "I won't," and mean it. Once you say it, do it. You must act with integrity for others to trust you. Walk your talk. When you say you will not harm again, follow through and change your behavior.
8. Make restitution. Sometimes you can make up for what you have done. If you manipulated someone into giving you money for your addiction, you can set up a payment plan to pay it back. If you stole something, you can replace it or provide compensation. If you damaged something, you may be able to fix it. Restitution is for both you and the person you harmed. It helps you to restore your dignity and integrity by cleaning up the messes you have made.

Only make amends after careful preparation. Be sure you are emotionally ready to hear and acknowledge what you may hear. Prepare in advance what you might say during the acknowledgment step. Go over your amends with a trusted friend, a family member, or a recovery mentor to make sure you have it right. You may want to role play what you will say. Keep in mind, however, that the most important part of making amends is listening and understanding. Prepare yourself to hear the pain you have caused. Once you make amends, show your love in your actions. Make ongoing, living amends, fixing what you can fix and attending to any pain you have caused.

You cannot protect your sobriety alone. It literally takes a village of healthy relationships filled with love and mutual care to sustain your recovery. Work hard each and every day to cherish the people in your life. As you grow, they grow. As they grow, you grow. Incorporate your loved ones into your life. If your addiction harmed someone, take the time to heal the relationship. Your loved ones are the people that help you plant the seeds and nourish the garden of Life.

Tips & Tasks

Tips: Restoring and maintaining healthy relationships require the making of amends when we hurt others.

Tasks: Make a list of all the people you have harmed.

Identify to whom you can make amends and the best way to make amends.

Execute the 8-step amends process in this section with each person you have harmed.

CHAPTER 12

TOUCHSTONE 11: TAKE ACCOUNTABILITY

"It is wrong and immoral to seek to escape the consequences of one's acts."
—Mahatma Gandhi

Addiction is a disease of blame. You blame people, places, and things for why you use. You blame your bosses, your partner, your jobs, the weather . . . even your addiction for your unhappy life. Addiction and personal accountability do not mix. In your addiction, you wear the victim costume and go onto the stage of Life to play the role of a victim.

Recovery requires abandoning the victim role. Instead, take accountability for your life. Wake up and realize that you make your own luck, blessings, and happiness. Everyone encounters difficult circumstances in life. Life is hard. Winners do their best with the cards they're dealt, turning misfortune into opportunity. While you are not accountable for everything that happens to you, you are accountable for your attitude and how you respond. That is the foundation for the eleventh Touchstone.

Without accountability, there is no responsibility. Recovery involves taking responsibility for your life and for the impact you have on others. This is your first order of business, as everything else depends on this. Put yourself in the driver's seat of your own recovery, while inviting as many helpful people as possible to ride with you.

Through taking accountability for your choices, you empower yourself to make the right choices that will free you from addiction and bring happiness. By empowering yourself, you take control of your life. Accountability helps you survive and prosper in the face of anything the world throws at you.

The first section of this chapter addresses taking accountability for caring for yourself, as this is your responsibility. I follow with a discussion of living with balance and savoring life. I then describe the practice of positivity and renouncing the destructive habit of blaming others. I then explore the need to take responsibility for managing your vulnerabilities. I follow this with a section on meaning and purpose. Following this, I focus on facing and overcoming fear to empower yourself. The final section lays out how to achieve your life goals.

Take Care of Yourself

The purpose of life is to nurture and savor life. You cannot do this if you are not vital. Take good care of yourself so you can care for others. Life has given you the precious gift of a fragile and fleeting life. It is your duty to Life to take care of your life. After all, there are no second chances.

Christian Nestell Bovee once said, "Your first and last love is self-love." This is as it should be. Self-love is only a problem when it stops there and does not extend to love for others. Self-care is not selfish as long as it's part of a larger love. In fact, part of self-love is to love others, as selflessness is the ultimate form of selfishness.

People fail to love themselves in many ways. Self-love is absent in addiction. People neglect themselves for the sake of the addiction.

Some also neglect themselves because others told them they are not worthy. Feeling unworthy and un-whole fuels love addiction. People with love addiction sacrifice themselves for the sake of the relationship. They cross from interdependency to dependency. Their excessive focus on others shows the need to focus on caring for themselves.

Some live passive lives, depending on others to care for them. They lack the drive to put themselves in charge of their own lives. In recovery, you commit to taking care of yourself first and foremost. This is your job, not someone else's. Don't let addiction, lack of self-worth, or fear prevent you from nurturing your own well-being. This becomes a conversation of personal accountability more than anything else.

Self-love saves relationships; when you love and accept yourself, you relieve others of the burden of having to love and accept you. This frees them to love you freely without obligation.

It's wrong—some would say a sin—to harm yourself. Though you have this choice, harming yourself is a choice to destroy Life. You weren't given the gift of life to destroy it. Care for yourself by choosing recovery.

Another way people harm themselves is by creating unnecessary stress. Life is stressful enough. Don't add to it. You choose how much stress to take on. Managing stress is a key to taking care of yourself.

Take care of yourself by balancing work, love, and play. Work benefits from time away from work. Balance nurturing and savoring life. Nurture yourself. Commit to caring for yourself as your second priority after the first priority of staying sober, so that in your vitality you can nurture and savor Life.

Remember that taking accountability for your life includes taking accountability for caring for yourself.

Tips & Tasks

Tips: We are accountable for taking good care of ourselves. Self-love is our job, no one else's.

We cannot fulfill our purpose to nurture and savor life if we do not take care of ourselves.

Tasks: Renounce self-hatred and self-neglect.

Commit to taking care of yourself every day as your highest priority after working your recovery. Take responsibility for your self-care the way you would take responsibility for caring for your own child.

Savor Life

You exist in part to savor life. Accountable people recognize that and work to enjoy the moments within their lives. You are Life's way of experiencing Itself. You are not here just to survive and reproduce. Nature has endowed you with the ability to experience beauty, wonder, awe, mystery, pleasure, joy, and laughter. Best of all, you can experience love. There is a loving life spirit that flows through you. This spirit calls on you to savor this brief life.

People who savor life are less prone to negativity. Less negativity means less risk of readdicting.

Were you to be in touch with the miracle of this moment, you would deeply savor:

- The simple experience of breathing
- Seeing a tree or a person
- Feeling the sunlight on your face
- Hearing water flowing or the wind in the trees
- Hearing the voices of loved ones
- The simple taste of water
- The smell of a flower or of the fresh air

Each moment is an opportunity to savor the profound gift of existence. People who complain of boredom need only wake up and open their senses to take away their boredom. When awake, nothing is boring.

Too many people live life in a trance. Our default mode of consciousness is to be lost in thought. People ignore their experience of Life. They habituate to the point of blindness. They lose the capacity to savor Life. We can all fall into this rut if we are not mindful.

Practice meeting each moment of life fresh. Be like a child seeing something for the first time. In Zen, this is called "beginner's mind." Be fully present to this moment, seeing each moment freshly, separated from the incessant thoughts that normally fill Awareness. With time and practice, thoughts die down. The mind stills for longer periods. In this stillness, you make direct, full contact with Reality. In this contact, you experience (initially very fleeting) a sense of oneness or unity with What Is. You can lose a sense of self-other when you are fully present to the Present. In that unity, you experience the Sacred and the mystery of existence. Each moment becomes both your first and last. This is the experience of savoring life.

The journey is the destination. This present moment is the destination. It is all there ever is. If you take the perspective of your lifetime, then the final destination is your death. Ask yourself, "Am I living to die, or am I living to live?" If you are living to live, then life is about the journey as it unfolds each moment of each day. Savoring life means to keep your focus on the present journey and not just on the future goals you hope to achieve. While goals are important, remember that the purpose of goals is to enhance the experience of this moment in the future. It is always and only about this moment.

Practice savoring each moment. This will enhance your experience of existence and thus help to keep readdiction at bay.

Tips & Tasks

Tips: Part or our purpose of life is to savor life.

Savoring life protects against readdiction.

Tasks: Practice encountering each moment fully, as if it were both your first and last. Practice presence.

Constantly note the miracle of your existence.

Practice Positivity

Winston Churchill said, "A pessimist sees the difficulty in every opportunity; an optimist sees the opportunity in every difficulty." Good looks, money, or status do not produce a happy life. Happiness and longevity come from living a positive life. Positive people live longer, suffer less medical illness, enjoy life more, have lower rates of depression and stress, feel better, and function better. Part of achieving the rewards of recovery includes practicing positivity. Positivity prevents the negativity that triggers readdiction. Accountable people focus on how to produce a positive life for themselves and those around them. It becomes a lifestyle choice in the end.

Positivity is an attitude that affects how you experience yourself, others, and your situation. It also affects how you behave. When you are positive, the glass is half full rather than half empty. Positive people are optimistic and hopeful, as opposed to negative and hopeless. Rather than seeing problems, positive people perceive opportunities. They appreciate the good amid the bad. Positive people focus on their blessings rather than on what's wrong. They focus on obtaining what they want instead of ruminating on what they don't have. Positive people make things better while negative people complain. Positive people attract positive people and take part in positive activities. Since they put out a positive attitude and do positive things, positivity comes back to them.

How do you cultivate positivity? By practicing positivity. You practice being positive both with yourself and others. Let's discuss that in greater detail.

Positivity Toward the Self

Positivity toward yourself means cultivating a positive appreciation of your experience of life and of yourself. Practicing positivity means practicing mindful appreciation of this present moment, moment by moment, appreciating the simple gift of conscious experience. Appreciating the moment also means practicing gratitude for what is good in your life. This might include showing gratitude for:

- Those who love and support you
- Enough food to keep you alive
- Shelter
- The many comforts and conveniences of modern life
- Human civilization and knowledge
- Freedom
- The arts
- Nature's beauty

Positive people smile, laugh, and enjoy simply living. They live each moment to the fullest. Positive people don't worry about the future. They know if they take care of this moment, the next moment will take care of itself. They know that, while you can't redo a beginning, you can make the best of today and create a new ending. This is positive recovery.

Positive people mindfully note negative self-talk and substitute negative thoughts with positive ones. Examples include changing:

- "I can't," to "I can if I practice and get help if I need it."
- "I'll never succeed," to "I'll keep trying until I succeed."
- "No one likes me," to "I'll work on being more likable."
- "I'm no good," to "I'm good enough."
- "I'm a negative person," to "I can learn to become more positive with practice."

Positive self-talk comes more naturally with conscious practice. Make it a life habit to notice and gently let go of negative self-talk, substituting negative thoughts with positive, self-appreciating and self-affirming thoughts. If you grew up neglected or abused, you may have a lifetime of hearing negative appraisals of you. These leave you feeling unworthy, making positive self-talk something that does not come naturally. This is why it takes intentional, repeated practice.

Positive people work on improving themselves and their lives. They are active, not passive. They don't hold back, giving it 100%, unafraid to do new things and take the necessary reasonable risks. While downtime and relaxation are important, positive people keep it in balance.

To stay positive, filter out negativity. Negativity is all around us, with almost all media reporting on negative events to the neglect of stories on human love, achievement, courage, triumph, and heroism. While it's good to be socially aware, don't let the media inundate you with negativity or set your life agenda. Instead, focus on positive events rather than negative events. This is more realistic. Though evil and tragedy make the news, goodness, grace, and love are far more prevalent.

Part of filtering out negativity includes filtering out negative people. These are the people who:

- Judge you
- Put you down
- Give you negative messages about yourself
- Abuse you

Negative people use negativity to control you or make themselves feel better at your expense. They are not accountable, and suck the joy out of life. Practicing positivity includes setting up boundaries to prevent negative people from causing you harm. Don't engage with negative people. Stay positive, and walk away. Practice not taking others' negativity personally.

Because positive people feel positive about themselves, they take care of themselves. Because they are committed to positive action, they end negative habits, including:

- Addicting
- Associating with negative people
- Overeating
- Isolating

- Failing to exercise
- Getting inadequate sleep
- Being passive

Positive people lead active, balanced, meaningful lives while taking care to nurture their own well-being.

Start a positivity practice by making a list of the positive habits of a positive life. This list will include:

- Working your recovery
- Balancing work, love, and play
- Exercising
- Taking time daily for silence and stillness
- Eating healthy
- Doing positive things with positive people
- Taking on a meaningful and challenging project
- Exercising your creativity
- Learning something new each day
- Giving to others

Remain accountable to this list. Work on each of these over the course of your days, week, months, and years. Once you have your list of positive life habits, build them into your life routine, one-by-one.

Positivity Toward Others

Practicing positivity also includes positivity toward others. Once positive about yourself, you can turn this attitude and practice outward toward others. Positive filtering with others involves focusing on the good qualities and positive actions of others. Positive people give specific praise freely to others to show their appreciation. A positive appreciation makes it easier to accept the negative traits and behaviors of others. A balanced perspective makes the negative more bearable.

Promote positive change in others by catching them doing something positive. Point out the positive to reinforce the positive. Don't participate in negativity with others. Don't complain or gossip. Be accountable for your actions toward others. Instead, discuss what can be done to make things better. Point out the good things people have done. By helping others to put things in a more balanced perspective, you cultivate positivity in others.

Being positive with others means being kind, supportive, and giving. Affirm others, especially in the face of their failures, mistakes, and difficulties. Avoid making negative assumptions of others or judging their actions before learning all the facts. Positivity with others requires dropping negative judgments of people. Positive people take the risk of trusting trustworthy people, connecting with them, enjoying them, and caring for them. Since love begets love, with time, the positive person finds him/herself immersed in a world of positive, loving people.

Practicing positivity is a key recovery skill. Positivity helps protect you from readdiction. Life truly is what you make of it. When you realize this, you can focus on the positive and promote the positive in all aspects of your life.

Tips & Tasks

Tips: Positivity prevents the negativity that triggers readdiction.

Tasks: Cultivate positivity by practicing positivity towards yourself and others as described in this section.

Live Blame-Free

Steve Maraboli said, "Take accountability . . . Blame is the water in which many dreams and relationships drown." Blaming is as destructive as it is pervasive. Everyone experiences the urge to blame. This is especially true for those raised in harsh and punitive families. Blaming others for your own actions and reactions not only damages relationships, it also keeps you from learning and growing. Part of taking accountability in recovery includes stopping blaming others for your actions and reactions.

When you blame others, you do one or both of two possible things:

1. You make others out to be bad and then use that as justification for your own bad behavior.
2. You take on the victim role.

Here are examples of blaming behaviors:

- A man beats up someone who is disrespectful.
- A woman says something hurtful to her girlfriend and then gets mad at her when her girlfriend gets upset with her.
- An alcoholic man blames his boss for being unfair to him when his boss fires him for missing work.
- A man with an opioid addiction cuts off ties with his parents when they call the police after he steals and pawns his mother's jewelry.
- A man beats his girlfriend because she slept with another man.
- A man doesn't speak to his wife for a week because she forgot to pick him up from work one evening.
- A man gives the finger to another driver when that driver cuts him off.
- A woman blames her depression and anger on her abusive husband, yet fails to do anything to improve her situation.
- A woman sues her doctor for getting a severe infection after surgery because of failing to take her antibiotics as prescribed.

In each of the above examples, the blamer holds somebody else responsible for his/her actions or feelings. Why do we do this? Because some find it intolerable to take accountability for their actions and feelings. Accountability makes them bad.

Blaming springs in part from fear—fear that you are not worthy and valuable despite your mistakes and imperfections. We are especially vulnerable to blaming others for bad behavior we also engage in. Thus the saying, "You spot it, you got it." Blamers hold the unrealistic belief that they cannot be imperfect and make mistakes. They link imperfection to defectiveness. Their actions equate to their self-worth, so they must make all their unskillful actions someone else's fault. To blame is to be unaccountable out of fear of accountability. If you were to take accountability, by the blamer's reasoning, you too would be unworthy and deserving of mistreatment.

Although others may engage in bad behavior, it never justifies making them out to be bad and then using that justification for treating them badly. Blamers lack humility and respect when they blame and then hurt others. Blamers blame to give themselves permission to mistreat others, rather than addressing injustices with care and respect. By devaluing others, blamers justify punishing them for their misdeeds.

Remember, there is a difference between blaming and holding others accountable. When you blame, you make someone else responsible both for an event and for your response to it. You don't take accountability for your role in the event or for your reaction. When you hold others accountable, on the other hand, you hold them responsible for their actions while also holding yourself accountable for your actions. Thus, you might hold someone accountable for paying back the $100 they stole from you rather than beating them up or slashing their tires.

A common form of blame is to blame others for your hurt and anger rather than taking responsibility for your emotional reactions to others. While fear, hurt, and anger are all common and normal emotional reactions, you are still accountable for how you process these emotions. As Eleanor Roosevelt once said, "No one can make you feel bad without your permission." While we don't choose our feelings, we can choose how to manage them so as not to cause harm.

Blaming destroys relationships, damages lives, and causes unnecessary pain, stress, and turmoil. The stress resulting from blaming can trigger readdiction. Blamers not only hurt others, but, true to the law of karma, they harm themselves. They suffer from failed jobs and relationships. They often invite harm, such as when they mistreat someone and that person retaliates. We hear of drivers who flipped off another driver, only to have that driver stop and beat or even kill the person who insulted them. There is no doubt that blaming is bad for everyone.

Renounce Blaming

There is a solution to blaming. It starts with awareness of when you are blaming. Other people, especially mature, healthy people, can help you with this if you only commit to listen to their feedback. When you notice you are blaming, stop and reflect, with humility and self-acceptance, upon what happened. Identify your role in what happened.

Second, take accountability for your own behavior. You are rarely a victim. You are responsible for what you bring upon yourself, for what you let others do to you, and for your responses. See that someone's bumping into you might not have happened if you had been paying attention. Accepting your bad behavior does not make you bad if you acknowledge that we are all imperfect. Without the life-and-death need to protect your imagined infallibility, you can give up the judge, jury, and punisher roles when bad things happen. Letting go of fault-finding allows you to focus on improving the situation.

After awareness and acceptance comes owning your emotional reactions and your actions. You, and only you, are accountable for your actions and reactions. Commit to unconditional respect for others. Part of respect is giving up any entitlement you might have to cause harm. Stop using and abusing others. Take a personal vow of no harm, which includes not blaming others. Do the psychological work necessary to work through your negative emotions so you can take care of yourself while respecting others.

As with all recovery skills, living a blame-free life requires practice, patience, and persistence. Stopping this destructive behavior greatly improves the quality of your life as well as the lives of those around you.

Tips & Tasks

Tips: Blaming arises out of a lack of self-acceptance and avoidance of accountability.

Blaming hurts everyone and fosters addiction.

Tasks: Stop blaming by accepting that you are imperfect and taking accountability for your emotions and actions.

Manage Vulnerabilities

So how do we manage our vulnerabilities? Once again, it starts with accountability. Knowing your vulnerabilities is to know the roots of your addiction. Vulnerabilities fall into two categories: disabilities and character vulnerabilities.

Disabilities can be physical or psychiatric. If paralyzed from the waist down, you must manage your disability with some aids such as a wheelchair and the help of others. With all disabilities, ask for what you need.

The same is true for psychiatric illnesses, including addiction, ADHD, mood disorders, anxiety disorders, and psychotic disorders, to name a few. Many people fail in life due to their inability to acknowledge their illnesses and ask for the resources and help they need to manage their disabilities. This is why the third step of the 12-step fellowship, in which you "humbly" reach out and ask for the help and guidance you need, is so important. Taking accountability for your life includes knowing what you need and asking for it.

Vulnerabilities include character vulnerabilities. You get to know both your virtues and your vulnerabilities by looking at yourself with honesty, radical self-acceptance, and curiosity. Self-knowledge comes from two simultaneous processes. First investigate your perceptions, thoughts, feelings, and behaviors. Second, open yourself to the feedback of others, asking yourself the value in what others say. What others say and do to you can be your greatest teachers.

As you look within, note common themes experienced by most victims of addiction: anxiety, trauma, shame, depression, hopelessness, and loneliness. There may be feelings of being unlovable, unworthy, defective, afraid, and inadequate. You may need to be loved at all costs. These, and other destructive emotions, make up the foundation for your habitual destructive ways of acting.

While we all have virtues, we also have what the famous Swiss psychoanalyst Carl Jung called a "Dark Side." No one is immune from destructive thoughts and feelings. There's a little larceny in all of us.

Fortunately, for most of us, love-based motivations regulate selfish motivations. Most of us limit our actions according to a personal set of morals and values; examples include honesty, fairness, patience, tolerance, and accountability. Yet, everyone is vulnerable to greed, desire, fear, and anger. Sometimes these forces get the best of us, leaving our Dark Side in charge. The mind is very subtle. You may think you're motivated by good intentions. Yet dark intentions can contaminate good intentions.

Don't Take Yourself Personally

How do you develop this sense of innate goodness? The first step is to not take your character personally. While you are responsible for your actions, you have no control over the automatic stream of perceptions, thoughts, and feelings your brain generates. You didn't choose the temperament you were given or the basic character you developed. These were visited upon you. Just as you cannot take credit for your gifts, so you also cannot take responsibility for your destructive thoughts and emotions. All you are responsible for is your actions. Despite your character vulnerabilities, you can do the next right thing. You can act with love and integrity despite your thoughts and feelings. The only time you lose free will over your actions is when you have:

- Brain damage
- A psychotic disorder

Even these don't take free will away completely. For example, if caught in addiction, you almost always have the choice to ask for help and to choose recovery.

Who You Are

In not taking your character personally, you stop basing your identity on your thoughts, feelings, and perceptions. See that you are not your thoughts, feelings, and perceptions. Sense the field of pure, spacious, empty Awareness in which perceptions, thoughts, and feelings arise. This is the one constant amid the whirlwind of perceptions, feelings, and thoughts. Awareness is ever-present and unchanging. This empty Awareness is who you are.

Who you are—your Awareness—is pure. It is beyond judgment. Don't judge yourself for being who you are. Your Awareness is whole and complete. It is your pure goodness, your loving life force. From Awareness comes knowing, without thought, what is true, right, beautiful, and good. It is the basis of your rational intuition. See there's nothing wrong with you. Your habitual actions cause the trouble when you act destructively, yet they are not you.

Once you experience who you truly are, see your character virtues and vulnerabilities. See that they do not detract from your essential wholeness and goodness.

Vulnerabilities and Recovery

Recovery involves the transmutation of vulnerabilities into virtues. Appendix A in the back of the book details the most common vulnerabilities that drive addiction and the opposite virtues for you to cultivate in your recovery. Start your character analysis by writing down your virtues and vulnerabilities. It is also useful to give the above inventories to someone who knows you well, someone you trust. Their input can help you to see traits you may not see in yourself.

Once you identify your main virtues and vulnerabilities, write about them. Go slow and deep. Explore each of your character traits, one at a time. Write about the things you have said and done that reflect each character trait. This requires time for contemplation and reflection. Don't rush the process. Take your time to get the most out of this exercise. This process will help you to be much more accountable to yourself and to those around you. You are pushing the envelope, evaluating, and analyzing your personality to ensure you are hitting the mark.

Close family or friends, a therapist, and a recovery mentor help guide and support your self-exploration. Share your character traits. Let them ask questions to help you deepen your self-knowledge. Let them give feedback, helping you to see yourself more clearly. Let them affirm your gifts. Others help you, through their acceptance and support of you, to overcome any shame or embarrassment that might arise. Besides not taking your character personally, the acceptance and forgiveness of others helps you to accept and forgive yourself. In the process of discussing your character traits with others, you see we are all fundamentally the same; we are all subject to fear, anger, hurt, and desire. We are all vulnerable to acting impulsively on destructive feelings. The only differences between us are matters of degree.

When exploring yourself, focus on the feelings that drive addiction. Note the events that trigger these feelings. Upsetting things happen to everyone every day. It is not your circumstances that define you or fuel addiction; it is your reaction to your circumstances. Part of your character includes the way you habitually react to things, either positively or negatively. It includes your general attitude and outlook on life. Negative attitudes drive negative behaviors, including addicting.

Explore your first important relationships, such as with your father and mother. Note how you have learned to relate to others; your early relationships set the template for how you relate to others now. If your early relationships were destructive, your current relationships may also be destructive. People recreate what is familiar to them because it's all they have known. This is part of what makes up your character. By looking at the way you relate to others, you see what is both healthy and unhealthy in your relationships. This will be very important self-knowledge as you go about developing healthier relationships.

See how your perceptions lead to your thoughts, how your thoughts lead to your feelings, and how your feelings lead to your actions. Observe how your repetitive responses create habits. These habitual ways of acting make up your character. Next, as you review the impact of your character on your life, see that your character creates your destiny.

With awareness of your weaknesses and vulnerabilities, your potential is virtually limitless. You are fortunate that the insight of self-knowledge enables you to transform. Gandhi once said, "As human beings, our greatness lies not so much in being able to remake the world . . . as in being able to remake ourselves." You are blessed to have this greatness within you. By facing and accepting the truth of who you are, you give yourself the opportunity to "remake yourself." This is a cornerstone of recovery.

Tips & Tasks

Tips: Everyone has virtues and vulnerabilities.

Knowing and accepting vulnerabilities is the beginning of managing them. Seeing is freeing.

Shame prevents growth. Change requires acceptance.

Tasks: Conduct a thorough character inventory. Name it, claim it, then tame it.

Don't shame it. Don't take yourself personally. Practice radical self-acceptance.

Armed with awareness and acceptance, manage your vulnerabilities so they don't hurt your ability to nurture and savor life.

Develop Meaning and Purpose

Meaning and purpose help to keep you sober. Without meaning and purpose, the temptation to give in to cravings to self-medicate exists without a counterbalancing force that sustains your motivation for recovery. As John Maxwell once said, "A difficult time can be more readily endured if you retain the conviction that your existence holds a purpose, a cause to pursue, a person to love, a goal to achieve." Meaning and purpose are unique to each of us. Consider the tale of three masons who were building a church. The first said he was working to earn money so he could eat. The second said he was working to provide for his family. The third said he was working to create a testament to the glory of creation. Though they were doing the same work, the meaning and purpose differed.

The meaning of Life speaks to the question of why you exist. Meaning and purpose are closely linked, as the meaning of Life springs from the purpose of Life. Your purpose is to nurture and savor Life. Yet we each nurture and savor life differently. Making meaning is a personal, creative process that continues throughout your life, changing as you grow through the chapters of your life. When you are young, you find meaning in finding satisfying work and developing relationships. Many then find meaning and purpose in raising a family. In later years, people find other ways to connect and contribute to their community.

Practically, people find meaning in many ways:

- In their connections with others
- In realizing their full potentials
- In giving to others
- In pursuing truth and understanding
- In appreciating the experience of existence, being mindful of themselves and the world around them

For many, a lack of meaning and purpose leads to lives, as Henry David Thoreau once said, of "quiet desperation." Many pursue meaning in acquiring things, their lives committed to the bumper sticker that says, "He who dies with the most toys wins." Yet meaning does not lie in your possessions. Others focus on their personal achievements to the neglect of their connections to the world that sustains them. Once they achieve their goals, they experience emptiness. They are left with the tragic sense of a precious life wasted.

Once you get into recovery, one of your important life tasks is to develop your own personal sense of meaning and purpose. What does nurturing and savoring Life mean for you? To begin this exploration process, you must first reflect on your current motivations. Why do you do what you do? Why are you striving? And what, really, are you striving for? What is your "life agenda?" Look closely and honestly. Is it to get rich, to be taken care of, to get revenge, to have as many pleasurable experiences as possible, or to escape a painful Reality? Why do you do what you do?

Do you work for your own needs alone, to support your family, to contribute, or all of the above? Do you seek friends for the benefits you receive, to give, or both? Do you strive for achievement and perfection out of a drive for self-realization, or because you are not worthy unless you have achieved greatness? Do you live out of fear, or out of love? Do you celebrate Life, or just exist? These questions require honest and careful reflection. With careful inquiry, you see the meaning and purpose of your life.

For nearly everyone, meaning and purpose involve connection. After looking within, look without. What does the world ask of you? Part of getting into recovery and developing a sense of personal meaning involves letting go of the self-absorption of addiction that causes such emptiness. Meaning and purpose include connecting to others. Many who suffer from addiction experience compulsive self-centeredness. Overcome this by practicing self-acceptance and then self-forgetfulness. Forgetting yourself, focus more on connecting with others. You will keep feeling as you do if you keep doing what you are doing. When you embrace service to others as part of your newfound meaning and purpose, you will feel better.

Once you see the truth of how you are living, ask yourself if this is what you truly want. Look within and ask, "What are my passions? What are my dreams? What is my life vision? What will bring me true fulfillment?" Ask these questions not once, but every day, as the answers change. Sometimes you ask and no answer comes. Ask again, and again, until the answers come. Often, the answers come when you allow yourself to become silent and still. Listen to what the stillness has to say. Through stillness, you know the True Self that animates your life. You see that your true meaning and purpose are to let go of fear and to love in the ways unique to you. This is true recovery.

Fulfilling your meaning and purpose requires that you have dreams. Dreams give you direction and give form to your meaning and purpose. Your dreams emerge from your passions and gifts. Pursuing your dreams requires harnessing your passions. You will fail without authentic passion for what you are doing. This is why you must first discover your passions to create your dreams.

Your dreams make up your life vision. Without dreams, you have no goals. Without goals, you drift through life, unfulfilled, unable to realize your meaning and purpose. This is why you must dare to dream. You will not create the life you want if you do not seek it out through dreaming.

Dreaming is a lifelong process. No matter your age, there are always dreams yet to be dreamed. Effective dreaming requires boldness combined with realism. As Haut Denim once said:

> It is not the job of dreams to be sensible or logical. It is the job of dreams to be nigh on fucking impossible. To scare the holy shit out of you. To push you to the very limit. To find what you are indeed capable of. To push you beyond what common sense says you can do. That's the job of dreams.

Dare to dream great dreams that "common sense" says you cannot achieve. Remember that what is realistic is greater than the dictates of common sense.

Dreaming springs from optimism, hope, and imagination. Imagination is more important than knowledge. Imagine a better tomorrow than today and then act today to fulfill your dreams for tomorrow. Dream of a better world that does not yet exist. Then make it a Reality. Leave no stone unturned. Set no limits to your dreaming. Explore all options that your passions and gifts will allow. Imagine a better world to set the stage for creating it.

Dreaming also springs from desire—desire to realize a better world and a better life. Without honoring your desire to become, you will become nothing. As Randolph S. Bourne once said, "Your real duty is always found running in the direction of your worthiest desires."

Pursuing your dreams requires courage. Take courage in knowing that something much more important than your fear of change awaits you. Have the courage to go forth into the unknown, doing what you have never done before, and persisting even when others say you can't. Have the courage to unshackle yourself from the chains of your self-imposed limitations. Have the courage to shoot for the moon, knowing you might miss. Take the risk. Don't allow yourself to suffer the defeat of failing to realize all you are. With courage, you will achieve your dreams and realize the pleasure of doing what others say you cannot do.

Pursuing your dreams requires commitment and perseverance. No great achievement comes easily in one day. Pursuing your dreams requires creativity and resilience, as you constantly improvise, adapt, and overcome inevitable setbacks. Push through obstacles, never giving up.

As you grow older, take care to never let regrets replace your dreams. Your dreams should die with you. As Langston Hughes once wrote, "Hold fast to dreams, for if dreams die, life is a broken-winged bird that cannot fly."

Pursuing your dreams requires action. Otherwise, dreams remain only dreams. You achieve greatness by acting on the dreams and the surrounding opportunities. Dreams will not become a Reality without your taking action. Don't wait for the "right time." The time to act is now. Start where you are, with what you have. Don't wait for things to happen. Instead, act now to make things happen. If you don't change now by taking effective action, your life will not change. If you want something you've never had, you have to do things you've never done.

Tips & Tasks

Tips: Meaning and purpose keep addiction at bay.

The purpose of life is to nurture and savor life.

The meaning of your life is a unique byproduct of your passions and gifts.

Making and executing on a plan to realize your life vision fulfills part of the meaning and purpose of your life.

Tasks: Look within to see what motives currently drive you. Then listen in stillness while asking what is the meaning and purpose of your life. Note how your current motives match up with your meaning and purpose.

Dare to dream.

Develop a life vision by dreaming of the life you want to live.

Make your vision a Reality by executing on a plan to realize your life vision.

Face Your Fears

Part of taking accountability for your life includes facing your fears. Being accountable means not letting unhealthy fear dictate your actions.

Nelson Mandela said, "The brave man is not he who does not feel afraid, but he who conquers that fear." At its core, recovery involves transitioning from fear to love. Part of taking accountability for your life includes taking accountability for facing and working through the fears that prevent you from creating the life you want. Unhealthy fear underlies all that is dysfunctional and destructive in your life.

Fear isn't always unhealthy. Fear is necessary for your survival. Healthy fear keeps you out of harm's way. Fear is unhealthy when you let it dominate your life in areas where it's not helpful. These include fears about your value and worth, of loss, of failure, of rejection, and of the inevitable distresses of life. Letting go of these fears brings you the freedom to focus on loving yourself and others.

Fear and anxiety are closely related. We say we are fearful of actions, such as meeting new people, confronting someone, or of flying on an airplane. We speak of being anxious about future events, such as losing a job or relationship, or getting sick. We will use the term "fear" to include both fear of actions and anxiety about future events.

Unhealthy fears fall into one of four categories:

1. Fear of failure
2. Fear of rejection
3. Fear of harm
4. Fear of loss

1. Fear of Failure

An unhealthy fear of failure stems from the unrealistic beliefs that failure is bad and that if you fail, *you* are bad. Some are tortured by perfectionism, which leads to procrastination, which leads to paralysis. It is not true that you must never fail. Failures are small successes in disguise if you learn and grow from them. All significant achievements result from a series of failures. Believing that you are "a failure" when you fail is a toxic manifestation of performance-based self-esteem. Don't link your self-worth to your achievements. Your self-worth rests not in what you do, but in who you are. The other side of a fear of failure is a fear of greatness as explained by Marianne Williamson:

> Your deepest fear is not that you are inadequate. Your deepest fear is that you are powerful beyond measure. It is your light, not your darkness that most frightens you. You ask yourself, "Who am I to be brilliant, gorgeous, talented, and fabulous?" Actually, who are you not to be? You are a child of the Universe. Your playing small does not serve the world. There is nothing enlightening about shrinking so that other people won't feel insecure around you. You are born to make manifest the glory of God, which is within you. It is not in just some of us, it is in all of us. And as you let your own light shine, you unconsciously give other people permission to do the same. As you are liberated from your own fears, your presence automatically liberates others.

Liberate yourself from your fear of failure by giving yourself permission to be great. Disregard the negative messages of others. Don't let them hold you back.

2. Fear of Rejection

All human beings need to belong and be loved. No one likes rejection. While unpleasant, you need not fear rejection. People who fear rejection feel rejection confirms their unworthiness. They lack compassion for themselves. Part of recovery is a commitment to your own unconditional value and to unconditional compassion for yourself. With these two commitments, you can overcome rejection by not taking rejection or negative judgments personally. Rejection is about the other person, not you. Your unskillful behavior may lead to rejection, criticism, or negative judgments of you. This says nothing about your inherent value and worth. Healthy people handle rejection triggered by their own unskillful behavior as an opportunity to learn and grow.

3. Fear of Harm

It is natural and good to fear harm. This helps to keep you alive. Your fear becomes unhealthy, however, when you let your fear of harm prevent you from doing what you need to do. Harm includes both physical pain and emotional distress. A person with aichmophobia (fear of needles), for example, has an unhealthy fear when they refuse an injection of an antibiotic needed to save their life. People who self-soothe by addicting bring on the tremendous suffering of addiction out of their fear of experiencing their authentic distress caused by trauma, disease, or unskillful living. Thus, one of the key steps in recovery is to face your fears of emotional and physical distress and bear the pain to heal.

4. Fear of Loss

Finally, people will fail to take effective action out of a fear of loss. They fear the unknown. Thus the saying, "The devil you know is better than the one you don't." Fear of loss fuels fear of change, for change involves both giving up and getting. People with this fear will stay in unhappy jobs and relationships out of a fear of losing what they have, although what they have causes unhappiness. The fear of loss is a big part of why people "settle" in their lives and don't act to fulfill their dreams.

Failure, rejection, loss, and harm can bring on great distress. All unhealthy fears arise from a fear of distress, which then blocks effective action. Unhealthy fear of distress occurs when you sacrifice your integrity out of a fear of the consequences. An example would be when you tolerate harassment, abuse, or unethical behavior at work out of a fear of retaliation or job loss should you "blow the whistle." The fear of the distress of rejection and loss can block you from doing the right thing.

Consequences of Unhealthy Fear

Fear has many good consequences. It can keep you honest and accountable for your behaviors. For example, we don't break the law because we fear going to jail. Healthy fear causes you to avoid risky situations, to make plans to minimize risk, and to get away when you do find yourself in danger. People with a lack of healthy fear get into trouble and even die prematurely. Their excessive and inappropriate risk-taking and failure to avoid harm causes them not to take needed precautions.

Unhealthy fear, however, strangles your vitality. It causes you to avoid doing what's necessary to improve your life. It prevents you from achieving your dreams, leaving you with disappointment and regret. Too many let opportunity pass by because they lack resolve to take action despite their fears. By rendering you powerless and inhibiting action, unhealthy fear leads to failure, depression, apathy, and hopelessness.

People who try, out of fear, to protect themselves by not taking action to improve their lives prevent themselves from experiencing joy and happiness. As John Greenleaf Whittier once wrote, "For of all sad words of tongue and pen, the saddest are these, 'it might have been.'"

Rewards of Conquering Fear

Facing and overcoming unhealthy fear vitalizes you and enables you to achieve your dreams. When you move from fear to love, you experience freedom. While fear still arises, your commitment to living a life of love enables you to do what is right for yourself and others. Learning to manage fear keeps you on track in the face of the risks of failure, rejection, loss, or distress. When you become free to act despite fear, your world changes. You will develop surprising new capabilities and encounter new opportunities. Learning to manage unhealthy fear will literally change your life. Take a look at Appendix A in the back of the book for self-assessment tools to help you inventory your fear.

Tips & Tasks

Tips: Recovery involves facing and working through fear. Unhealthy fear prevents growth and self-realization.

There are four main fears; fear of failure, of rejection, of harm, and of loss.

Tasks: Take an inventory of your fears.

Overcome fear by practicing the fear management techniques in the appendices:

- Processing it to understand it.
- Making peace with it.
- Quelling it.
- Making friends with risk and failure.
- Deepening your faith.
- Committing to a passionate vision.
- Taking action.

Achieve Your Goals

Henry David Thoreau said, "I know of no more encouraging fact than the unquestionable ability of man to elevate his life by conscious endeavor." At the end of it all, the purpose of accountability is to better position you to achieve your goals and cultivate happiness. As in all of life, success in recovery comes from having a passion-driven life vision. Then you need goals and a strategy to realize your goals. Other success ingredients include a commitment to yourself, positive success habits, and daily effort.

First and foremost, success requires a life vision. If you don't know where you're going, you won't get there. We have already discussed discovering the meaning and purpose of your life and then translating that into the dreams that make up your life vision. You will fail without a passion-driven life vision. Your vision gives you direction to your efforts. By now, you should have big, but realistic dreams. You can visualize yourself in your future life being your future self. As much as possible, see in your mind's eye what your new life vision looks like and feels like. Experience it in your imagination, with as much specificity, completeness, and clarity as possible. Part of visualizing your life vision includes visualizing yourself realizing that vision. When you visualize success, you see yourself overcoming the obstacles before you.

When discovering your life vision, focus on how you want to improve your life and the world around you. Life vision is about improvement and progress, not about proving and perfection. Your passion, derived from your meaning and purpose, gives you the motivation to commit, to stay disciplined, and to work hard for what you want. While vision gives you direction, passion gives you the energy needed to realize your vision.

To succeed, give yourself over completely to your life, as half-measures or partial efforts will not work. Half-hearted efforts yield half-hearted results. Greatness and success come from a total, lifelong devotion to what you do. Your passion-driven vision enables you to devote yourself completely to your life.

Yet achieving your goals requires more than just a clear vision, passion, and mastery of unhealthy fear. It also requires good strategy and good habits, as they help you to work smart, with maximum efficiency and effectiveness. I will now discuss strategies and habits for success in recovery and life. The two are the same.

Strategies for Success

As you can imagine, accountability is the first strategy for success. Don't keep your life vision a secret. Share your dreams with others. Talking about your life vision makes it more real. Others can help you develop greater clarity. Make a public commitment to your dreams. This creates a social network of people to whom you are now accountable.

There is a saying that, "He who fails to plan, plans to fail." You will fail without a detailed action plan. This is why the second strategy is to develop an action plan, or "life plan." Your plan empowers you to move from being reactive to being proactive. By being proactive, you switch to making life happen, instead of letting life happen to you. You are now in charge of your success.

Write down your vision-based life plan not only for clarity, but so you can go back and revise it. Your life vision should be a grand one of a life of purpose and meaning that also has a healthy balance of work, love, and play. You should have big goals in all these areas. Your goals should challenge you. You should shoot for the stars, aiming high, while also being realistic. Becoming an NBA superstar may be a noble goal, but is not realistic if you have never played basketball and are four feet tall.

To develop your life plan, first write down all the big goals you want to achieve. You will work backward from there down to the specific tasks you need to accomplish. As Steven Covey says, "start with the end in mind" and plan backward. Big goals might include:

- Getting a rewarding career
- Raising a family
- Getting in shape

The big goals should match your big dreams, but also be realistic. Make "SMART" goals:

- Specific
- Measurable
- Achievable
- Relevant
- Time-based

Examples include:

- "Out of my love for animals, I will obtain a job as a veterinary technician in the next three years."
- "I will get my body fat percentage to below 18% and run a 10k road race in the next 24 months."

We all have two big goals. These are your Core Goals. One is to secure and maintain a stable recovery. The other is to secure and maintain your health and vitality through proper self-care. Without attaining and maintaining these two goals, you cannot attain any others. Make these goals your first priorities.

Break down the big goals into medium goals. Achieving big goals entails achieving multiple medium goals. To become a Vet Tech, for example, medium goals might include:

- Graduating from a Vet Tech training program
- Becoming a volunteer at a local animal shelter to gain work experience
- Creating a resume
- Becoming knowledgeable about Vet Tech job opportunities

While big goals may take several years to achieve, medium goals take less time—ranging from months to a few years.

Once you have written down all your medium goals, break them into smaller goals. For our examples, small goals might include:

- Gain admission to a Vet Tech school
- Join an exercise group
- Join a dating service

Some people call these small goals "objectives."

Now put your small goals into their proper sequence. Then write down the tasks you must do to achieve each goal. Tasks should be clear and specific. For example, accomplish applying to Vet Tech schools by:

- Finding out what schools are available by researching on the Internet

- Getting applications and application requirements by calling, emailing, or downloading
- Completing and submitting applications with required fees
- Going to interviews
- Accepting an admission offer

When you have your list of tasks, schedule them. Put them on a timeline in their proper order. Scheduling tasks requires that you schedule your priorities. Priorities come first, and the schedule follows. Schedule "first things first." This allows you to go from being overwhelmed by the many tasks before you to just tackling the highest priority tasks before you one by one.

Since your first priority is recovery, schedule recovery activities first. Then schedule tasks to ensure your survival and vitality. Examples include:

- Eating
- Shopping
- Sleeping
- Cleaning the house
- Getting exercise
- Taking breaks
- Going to church
- Praying or meditating
- Hanging out, relaxing, having fun, and connecting with others

Schedule self-care, including solitude and stillness, or it will not occur.

Sometimes a task can seem overwhelming, such as completing admission or job applications. In this case, break a big task into several smaller tasks. You might break completing admission applications down into:

- Reading the admission application instructions
- Making a copy of the admission application
- Gathering information required to complete the application
- Finding a friend to help type up the application

- Proofreading the application for errors
- Signing the application
- Making a copy of the completed application
- Putting the application in an addressed, stamped envelope
- Mailing the application

Schedule these smaller steps as time allows. Remind yourself that if you complete a series of the right small tasks every day, you will eventually realize your dreams. Your life vision will become a Reality.

Schedule tasks according to the guidelines proposed by Stephen Covey in his book *The 7 Habits of Highly Effective People*. Covey categorizes tasks according to whether they are:

- Important or unimportant
- Urgent or non-urgent

Success comes from first doing the urgent and important tasks—the emergencies, such as sending out a check for the rent that is due tomorrow. Then focus on the non-urgent and important tasks. Keep emergency tasks to a minimum by living an orderly life that is as simple as possible. Simplicity goes a long way in reducing stress and allowing you to focus on what is most important.

Try to eliminate unimportant tasks. You may want to either delegate them or drop them. Discipline yourself to stay focused on the important tasks.

Once you have a written plan, revisit and revise it as necessary. Monitor and measure your progress. Success comes from overcoming the inevitable obstacles that arise. Work to overcome these obstacles. Adjust tasks and timelines as needed. Review the tasks for your small goals. Reprioritize and reschedule as circumstances change. Stay committed to your goals, but be flexible in how you achieve them. While big goals rarely change, medium and small goals may need to change as you encounter roadblocks and learn. Be focused and disciplined, yet flexible. Improvise, adapt, and overcome.

Put together meaning, purpose, dreams, vision, passion, strategy, and success habits, and you have the ingredients for a successful life. Success requires work. Life works for people who do the work. Commit to the work of living a successful life now, for now is not too soon. As you develop your accountability skills, you will find your new focus on responsibility for your actions and decisions actually helps you create a more organized and structured life. You will find that as your accountability increases, so does your success in life. All you have to do is do the work, starting today.

Tips & Tasks

Tips: Success in life requires a life vision, a life plan, and the intentional practice of success habits.

Tasks: Create a life plan as described in this section.

Practice the success habits until they become automatic.

CHAPTER 13

TOUCHSTONE 12: CULTIVATE YOUR SPIRITUALITY

We live in a more and more secular society that rejects blind dogma that does not abide by reason and rational intuition. If you have difficulties with religion, don't throw the baby of spirituality out with the bathwater of dogma. Our secular culture does not encourage a daily spiritual practice or give directions on how to cultivate spirituality.

Addiction is a disease in which spirituality has gone awry. At its essence, recovery entails spiritual healing that transforms your relationship to everything. This can seem overwhelming. In this Touchstone, I break down spirituality into specific, practical, manageable components to set forth a method for cultivating your spiritual health, and thus your recovery. No matter the case, spirituality is an absolute and necessary part of recovery and overcoming the grasp of addiction.

What Is Spirituality?

Definitions of spirituality have common themes. Spirituality entails an intuitive sense of "something more," beyond the five senses. There is a deep interconnectedness with Life that gives a sense of unity or oneness. With this sense of oneness, you shift from living solely for your own individual survival to living for the One Life of which you are a part.

Spirituality arises from the human cerebral cortex. As with biological, psychological, and social functions, spirituality is also a neuropsychiatric mind-brain phenomenon. The cerebral cortex of the brain has three major functions:

1. To **perceive** the world
2. To **understand** the world based on your perceptions
3. To **act** skillfully to enhance your survival and well-being, based on your perceptions and understandings

Spirituality mirrors these three cortical functions:

1. To **experience** (perceive beyond the five senses) unity, oneness, mystery, wonder, awe, beauty, goodness, grace, peace, serenity, meaning, purpose, gratitude, and healing.
2. To **know** (understand) the **Truth** beyond thought, utilizing your rational intuition, or direct knowledge without thought, that is consistent with your reason. Examples include:
   - That life is a miracle
   - That everyone is sacred
   - That Reality is perfect exactly as it is
   - That we are all interdependent parts of a greater whole
   - That love, healing, and grace operate in our lives
3. To act to nurture and savor all of Life, including yourself, based on your spiritual experience and resulting awareness of Truth beyond words. To love. To live your life with coherence and integrity. To be in harmony with Reality.

Summing this up, spiritualty is the capacity to act with love, compassion, and wisdom with peace both within and with others.

Spirituality exists as a uniquely human faculty. It enables you to savor life and to experience a much deeper meaning of life than just mere survival. Spirituality serves a higher organizing function, impacting your biological, psychological, and social functioning and well-being. It is your well-developed spirituality that brings you true happiness, meaning, purpose, fulfillment, and peace. Your spirituality allows you to look back on your life from your deathbed with satisfaction, knowing you loved well and left the world a better place.

The following are some components of a healthy spiritual practice:

- Engaging in an ongoing search for Truth

- Living for something greater than you—something that gives you purpose and meaning
- Living ethically, according to what is true, good, and right
- Reflecting, praying, meditating, or contemplating, in silence and stillness
- Cultivating wonder
- Cultivating gratitude
- Seeing the sacred in all things and people
- Practicing humility
- Practicing mindfulness
- Practicing acceptance and forgiveness
- Living out of love instead of fear

We explore all of these in greater depth in this Touchstone. Healing also involves spiritual healing and growth. Just as no one does recovery alone, no one heals and grows spiritually alone, or at least not as fully as they would with the help of others. Cultivate your spiritual growth by:

- Reading spiritual literature such as holy texts and books on spirituality
- Obtaining a spiritual teacher
- Joining a spiritual community
- Implementing a daily spiritual practice

At its core, recovery is a spiritual matter. Both spirituality and recovery refer to your way of being and living. We know that people who cultivate their spirituality reduce their risk of readdicting.[11,12] Through spiritual practice, you develop a positive identity, integrity, a rich inner life, meaning, purpose, and interdependence, all of which promote recovery.[13,14] Higher levels of spirituality correlate with greater optimism, social support, resilience to stress, and less anxiety. This indicates that spiritual practices promote recovery by enhancing well-being.[15] Your spirituality enables you to get high on life instead of by addicting. Without a healthy spirituality, negative states make you vulnerable to readdicting.

Describing Spirituality

Describing spirituality is like describing the taste of water. Words can point to the experience, but to understand spirituality you must experience it. Many people think or feel that spirituality is the same as religion. But that is not the case.

Spirituality involves a harmonious relationship with Reality. What you experience, understand, and do are all in harmony. It is a coherent way of living.

Spiritualty involves seeing "what is." When you look, you see. When you listen, you hear. You wake up to the Now.

With new insight and "outsight" inspired by your awakening, you commit to a way of doing. You engage in mutuality. You give. You serve. You love.

Spirituality and Religion

Spirituality is not religion. Religion is a defined set of beliefs, rules for how to live, and rituals. Spirituality transcends beliefs and rules. It is universal, such that even a devout atheist possesses the capacity for spirituality, as spirituality is not about a belief in God, but a direct experiencing of Truth. Conversely, many devoutly religious people have a poorly developed spirituality, their lives characterized by fear, conflict, judgment, hatred, inauthenticity, violence, or disconnection. While religion concerns itself with belief, rituals, and a moral code, spirituality concerns itself with experience, understanding, and loving action. It is far better to directly know Truth than to "believe in" some manufactured idea. Experience always trumps belief. This is why religions arise from spirituality.

Religion, however, can help cultivate spirituality. Religious disciplines and rituals help to discipline the mind, cultivate integrity and devotion, promote loving service, and deepen spiritual experience. Teaching spiritual fundamentals such as love, mutuality, compassion, acceptance, and forgiveness provides valuable guidance to millions. The support of a religious community can promote members' spiritual growth. The words of spiritual titans such as Jesus Christ, the Buddha, and Mohammed can inspire and help shape spiritual understanding when filtered through your rational intuition.

There is another paradox of religion vs. spirituality. It involves managing fear. Religion provides a sense of support and security in facing the fundamental insecurity of Life. Religion can bring people together as they face uncertainty, loss, and pain. Yet religion can be problematic when centered too much on security. Ideally, religious practices promote spiritual transcendence of fear.

Spirituality and Experience

Spirituality involves the connection to Reality beyond physical sense perceptions. You intuit something more. You sense the ground of being that permeates everything and of which you are a part. Some people call this experience "transcendence." This is an experience beyond thought. While not measurable or describable in words, it is nonetheless real.

In a state of deep meditation or contemplation, you experience your pure Awareness, your true nature, apart from your thoughts. This Awareness flows out and is one with everything. Feeling yourself part of something greater than yourself stirs you to live your life to serve the One Reality of which you are a part. From oneness springs love.

Spiritual experience also informs your authenticity. As you switch from operating based on thought to operating based on your authentic experience, you come into alignment with a greater loving life force that flows through you. You experience your authentic, true self, apart from manufactured ideas and beliefs about who you are or who you should be. Living from authentic, direct experience flips your relationship to your mind; rather than your mind being in charge and using you, your True Self is now in charge and uses the mind to serve Life. Thinking consciousness then submits itself to the service of what is true, good, and right beyond words. You have contacted and submitted to your "higher power" (Reality), based on direct, authentic spiritual experience.

Cultivate your spiritual experience of Oneness through the practices of silence, stillness, and mindfulness. In stillness, you experience connection. You experience unity with all that is. From this comes a wealth of positive emotions, including love, wonder, awe, compassion, humility, respect, forgiveness, gratitude, peace, serenity, and acceptance. Shame, guilt, resentment, and judgment dissolve in the light of your Awareness, for your clear seeing reveals these emotions to be harmful. Experience your proper place as just one tiny part of an immense web of being. Stillness allows you to sense the vibrant ground of being all around and within you. Sense a deeper truth beyond thought. In one Zen practice, the meditator asks, "What is this?" The answer is always, "Don't know," because the mystery of Reality forever remains out of reach of the cognitive, thinking mind. By moving beyond the thinking mind to a direct experience of Reality, you develop clarity—a direct seeing and knowing of "What Is" beyond words.

Based on your spiritual experience, you develop spiritually-informed understandings of the world—of others and yourself. These understandings arise from rational intuition, the merging of direct knowing and reason. You see that:

- Your purpose, as part of Life, is to nurture and savor Life.
- Life is good.
- Others are sacred.
- You too are both good and sacred.
- All is perfect in its imperfection.
- We are interdependent upon one another for our survival and prosperity.
- There are rules by which Reality works, such as the law of karma.
- As one, everything affects everything else.

Positive experiences lead to positive understandings, which lead to positive actions. The experience of oneness and goodness, combined with your understanding of life derived from these experiences, influences your life agenda. Out of oneness and goodness comes the motivation to nurture and savor Life. This empowers you to act in harmony with Reality. You become "right with Life."

Experience, understanding, and action merge into one symphonic whole. They create a rich inner life and a loving way of acting. You become open, receptive, present, and engaged with Reality. Your openness enhances the ability to be flexible and adaptive to ever-changing conditions. Your openness also enables you to grow and change. You can let go of life-killing opinions that prevent you from seeing things as they are. Based on your understanding, fueled by your experience, you act with love toward both yourself and others. As you put good out, the world generously gives good back. What was once hell on earth now becomes heaven.

Spirituality and Addiction

Impairments in experience and understanding lead to impairments in behavior, including addiction. People with crippled spirituality lack either the motivation or the capacity to act with love and integrity. As a result, they cause great suffering to both themselves and to others.

For many people, addiction is spirituality gone awry. In the quest to feel good, people who fall prey to addiction instead feel miserable. They choose numbness as a substitute for peace. They indulge themselves to experience abundance. They seek gratification instead of fulfillment, and intensity instead of intimacy.

As addiction takes over, people sever their connections in exchange for their all-consuming attachment to their addiction. With the loss of connection comes separation and alienation. This makes the original longing for connection and harmony only grow greater. Rather than boosting spiritual experience, addiction poisons it. Rather than freeing people to be who they are, addiction robs people of their authenticity and enslaves them into bondage to the addiction. You no longer live to nurture and savor Life, but to serve the demands of the addiction. You lose your freedom and capacity to live authentically on Life's terms.

In addiction, the capacity to experience joy, wonder, and awe wither away. The compulsive preoccupation to get the next fix and the pain of recovering from using crowd them out. Gone is any sense of the sacred, substituted instead by cravings to get high, seeking to get high, getting high, and recovering from getting high.

Rather than submitting their life to a set of higher principles, victims of addiction submit their lives to the addiction. In addiction, you sacrifice your integrity. Abandoning what is true, right, and good, you do what you must to feed the addiction, even if that means acting destructively. When you sacrifice your connections for the addiction, you also sacrifice harmony.

As you put bad out into the world, bad comes back tenfold, true to the law of karma. Disharmony leads to conflict, which leads to stress, pain, and suffering. In attempting to suppress hopelessness, you sacrifice hope. In attempting to suppress meaninglessness, you sacrifice meaning. In attempting to suppress disconnection and longing, you sacrifice connection and belonging. Instead of securing your safety, you attempt to control the uncontrollable.

Whereas spiritualty leads to continuous growth and transformation, addiction leads to regression and decay. While spirituality enhances life, addiction destroys it. The antidote for the diseased spirituality of addiction is recovery. In recovery, your spirituality provides what you were seeking in addiction.

Spirituality overlays and organizes all aspects of human functioning, from the biological to the psychological to the social. As the overarching organizing force of your life, spirituality informs every aspect of your recovery. Going from addiction to recovery requires a change in your awareness of yourself in relation to everything else. It is your spirituality that ignites this change of awareness.

The gift of addiction is your suffering. Your suffering—the gift of desperation—spurs your spiritual growth. Thus the saying, "Religion is for those who fear Hell; spirituality is for those who have been there." You grow spiritually because you must. Your choice is to either change or eventually die from your disease.

There is a saying that the way to love is through a broken heart. Likewise, the way to recovery is through the heartbreak of addiction. Start where you are, in your woundedness. Then cultivate an authentic spirituality that works, unlike the addiction that almost worked, but did not. Recovery includes a recovery of your spirituality. In addiction, you lost your way. In recovery, you find your way back. Recover your capacity to encounter each moment of life freshly, with authenticity and integrity . . . with love.

Recovery entails cultivating your spirituality through spiritual practices. Through your spiritual practice, you taste Oneness. Belonging replaces longing. Your newfound integrity allows for the privilege of interdependence. You develop a new sense of meaning and purpose based upon your connections and belonging to something greater than yourself.[16] Through recovery, you replace addiction with a way that truly works. This is the gift of recovery.

To that end, let's look at some of the components of a spiritual life . . .

Section 1: Make Time for Spiritual Practice

Rumi said, "The breeze at dawn has no secrets to tell you. Don't go back to sleep." Spiritual growth occurs through intentional spiritual practices. These practices enable a process greater than you to transform you. You do not necessarily grow because of your practice, but neither do you grow unless you practice. This can be difficult to grasp, for we live in a culture of doing rather than a culture of allowing. Through your growth, fear gradually fades as you experience being a channel of love. The benefits of a spiritual practice are several:

- Cultivating a vital experience of Reality through the practice of presence
- Cultivating awe and wonder
- Fostering hope and faith
- Transforming anger into compassion and forgiveness
- Promoting serenity
- Promoting connectedness/interconnectedness
- Disidentifying with the ego; retrieving awareness from its immersion in thought
- Cultivating rational intuition
- Promoting positivity and gratitude
- Developing virtue
- Reducing vulnerability to stress
- Enhancing overall well-being
- Reducing the risk of readdicting

Spiritual practices vary greatly. They include:

- The practice of stillness and presence through prayer, meditation, yoga, tai chi, and qigong
- Contemplation on topics such as the sacredness of Life and on your blessings
- Journaling
- Spiritual reading
- Rituals; examples include daily affirmations and commitments to a virtuous life
- Loving service
- Practicing mindfulness to awaken spiritual vision

Together, these practices transform motivation from fear to love. They cultivate emotional wisdom so you can respond lovingly and intelligently rather than react impulsively. They cultivate virtue, which enhances well-being. They foster presence, rescuing Awareness from thought. This enhances the freshness, wonder, and awe of existence, enhancing vitality. These practices also cultivate wisdom. Finally, they promote self-realization through loving service to others.

Many practices share the common theme of taking you out of your mind and putting you into oneness. There is one destination with many paths. As Symmachus once said, "Everyone has his custom, his religion. One cannot reach so great a secret by one way alone."

Spiritual awakening starts with a change in experience, or perception. The transformation involves a shift of awareness from the incessant flow of thoughts to an awareness of Reality before thought. You move from a self-absorbed relationship with your mind to a direct, open relationship with the Now.

Spiritual growth and vitality start with the practice of stillness. In stillness, the busy mind quiets. The thought clouds clear away, revealing the stars of Awareness. Practices that still the mind include meditation, yoga, tai chi, and contemplation, including contemplative prayer.

Meditation, while it may sound complex, is really a very simple practice, although it's as difficult as it's simple. When you meditate, you sit still and alert. You pay attention to what is going on right now. You consciously, gently, and persistently pull Awareness out of its immersion in thought so that Awareness can experience the Now. Take a look at the resource section for this chapter, which includes a detailed meditative technique.

Non-religious contemplation is very similar to contemplative prayer, with the difference being that you are not imagining an answer from a higher being. As in all contemplation, you focus your attention on an important concern, such as, "What would make my life more meaningful?" You ask, and then listen, in stillness and silence, for the answer to come.

In all contemplative prayer, you return your awareness over and over again back to the one thought that is your question. You are like the person before dawn, sitting in the darkness, waiting for the sun to rise. The answers may come gradually, a piece at a time, in many forms, over a lifetime. Often, the answers start out as general principles that become more detailed and specific over time. For many, the answers change over time with the accumulation of knowledge, experience, awareness, and wisdom.

This process is mysterious. Truth does not necessarily come by asking, yet does not come unless you ask. Similarly, the transformation of recovery may not come from your recovery work, yet only comes to those who do the work of recovery. Your intentional efforts combined with allowance create the conditions for insight and transformation to occur. This is the essence of spiritual practice.

Benefits from meditation, prayer, and contemplation come from regular, consistent practice over a lifetime. Start with 5-10 minutes twice a day, when you first get up and before you go to sleep. Some say that if you are too busy, up your meditation time. There is wisdom in this. Busyness is a sign you must slow down, as it is harmful to your well-being. If you are too busy to be still, you are too busy. While it's good to be active, maintain a balance between doing and being. Making time for a daily spiritual practice is essential, like eating, sleeping, and bathing. Your efforts need to be intentional, gentle, persistent, and disciplined to experience positive results. In this way, make silence and stillness a regular part of your daily routine.

When you still your mind, you contact Reality, part of which includes the Reality of the heart. You see both outside and inside. Looking inside, you awaken to the truth of the heart and experience the important essence of life—love. It is in the "silent chambers of the soul" that you resolve life's dilemmas. In stillness, as part of your recovery, you recover from a broken sense of self. In stillness, you recover wholeness, your true nature. You realize you already are what you were looking for all along by addicting.

Dedicating yourself to a spiritual practice is a profound act of self-love. Give yourself the gifts of clarity, wholeness, and freedom. Break free of your thinking mind. You can then reflect on the negative, self-defeating thoughts that arise, let them go, and create a space within yourself for more positive, realistic thoughts to arise. In stillness, positivity replaces negativity as you experience the abundance of the Present.

Each of us moves in and out of spiritual awareness. If the sacred suddenly seems far from you, notice who moved and return to the Present. It is in your continuous returning to the Now that you develop and maintain your spirituality.

Maintenance of your spiritual fitness through spiritual practice is a key to recovery, as your spirituality is your first defense against relapsing. For many, their abstinence is contingent upon their spiritual condition. A rich inner life means you need less from the outside, including the objects of addiction, to feel complete.

Implementing a Spiritual Practice

Implementing a spiritual act is an intentional act. It is putting your willingness to be transformed into daily action. To implement a spiritual practice:

- Select two to three practices from the list above.
- Make time for silence, solitude, and stillness; 5-10 minutes twice a day is a good start.
- Develop a routine. Schedule your spiritual practices.
- Make your practice a priority. Don't let life get in the way.

Make your spiritual practice a daily life discipline. Practice with patience and gentle persistence. Don't force the results. Allow the transformative process to happen. Let yourself become a channel of love.

Tips & Tasks

Tips: Spiritual growth requires a spiritual practice. Spiritual practices create the conditions for insight and transformation to occur.

One component of a spiritual practice is silence and stillness in order to cultivate the direct experience of Reality.

Tasks: Select and schedule two to three spiritual practices. Practice them daily with gentle, firm, disciplined effort. Be patient. Combine intention with allowance and surrender to the process of transformation.

Section 2: Cultivate a Deeper Connection, Beyond Words, to Others and to the World Itself

It is ironic that despite our material abundance and comfort so many experience emptiness and angst. Emptiness arises from disconnection and alienation from each other and from the Sacred. Your social-spiritual state of disconnection feeds addiction. Loneliness and meaninglessness both seem to be symptoms of contemporary human culture. Too many have renounced the depth of a rich inner life and of deep connections to others in exchange for the shallowness and busyness of modern life, with its addictive obsession with materialism, consumerism, achievement, and status. We see an exchange of the spiritual for the material and of fulfillment and meaning for gratification.

All human beings long for wholeness through connection, both outward and inward. The longing for oneness stems from the simple fact that we are born alone, are solely in charge of living our lives, and die alone. This is the human condition. We are separate yet dependent upon Life for survival.

We compensate for the existential dilemma of separation and aloneness by connecting with others. We also connect with the transcendent through our practice of stillness.

Socially, start with a primary attachment to a parent, a friend, a partner, a teacher, a mentor, or even a spiritual guide. In recovery, your primary attachment might be to a sponsor, other recovery mentor, or other recovery support. From this primary attachment, spread out to make other attachments required for your survival and well-being. Develop relationships with friends, neighbors, coworkers, family members, and members of your community. The richer your social network, the greater your prosperity.

Yet even those with a healthy social network still experience a metaphysical longing. We long to connect with the unseen, "something more" of Reality. Many intuit that their internal representation of Reality is not Reality itself. Looking closely, you see there are aspects of Reality you can never experience, know, or understand through our limited sense perceptions. Our small, finite brains cannot ever fully comprehend the mystery of Reality.

When people speak of a connection to a higher power, or to something greater than themselves, they are speaking of a merging of identity. You and the rest of Reality are but one Reality. It is this resolution of the problem of separateness that makes you whole and resolves your longing. Realize that, although we are separate, we are also part of the One.

Make your "connection" with the transcendent by going within. Enter into silence and stillness. This inner gateway opens you to the experience of oneness. Solitude, contemplation, meditation, prayer, and a rich inner experience—these practices bridge the inner and the outer. The inner and the outer become one. Awareness breaks away from its immersion in a false self that the brain manufactures out of sense perceptions, thoughts, and feelings. Transcendent connection activates the true, authentic, wordless self. This transforms identity. Awakening to the truth of who you are transforms your life. You now live for the One of which you are a part. You see the false self for what it is, and in the seeing, it loses its grip on you. You are free to nurture and savor Life.

As you practice attending to the Now, in silence and stillness, trust in yourself and your experience. Be your own guru while opening yourself to spiritual guidance from teachers and spiritual literature. Yet, while resources outside of yourself are essential, they are no substitute for your own experience. Trust and honor this above all.

Tips & Tasks

Tips: We compensate for our separateness through connection to others and to the transcendent.

Tasks: Develop a rich social network. Connect and contribute.

Make the practice of silence and stillness part of your daily spiritual practice to connect to the transcendent.

Section 3: Practice Mindfulness in All Your Daily Affairs

Jonathan Larson said, "There's only you, there's only this, forget regret, or life is yours to miss. No other road, no other way, no day but today." Practicing presence in stillness every day is necessary, but not sufficient for spiritual realization. The point of spiritual practice is to bring that practice into the daily moments of your life. To live the full richness of your life, be present for it. Do this through mindfulness.

Mindfulness is a fancy word for intentionally paying attention to what is going on in this present moment with an attitude of friendly acceptance. You make an intentional, gentle, conscious, persistent effort to be aware of the Now rather than be lost in thought. Be present to the only thing that exists—this moment. Live in the timeless moment. Unlike your default, half-awake, habitual awareness that lacks conscious intention, the intention of mindfulness heightens awareness.

Awaken to your experience. Live each moment fresh, as if it were your first and your last. Consciously note your experience, whether your experience be of a thought, a sight, a sound, a smell, a taste, or a feeling. Practice an unconditional openness to your experience. Mindfulness is a befriending of your inner life. In mindfulness, you welcome your experience without judgment, whether pleasurable or painful, admirable, or shameful. All experience receives the same loving awareness.

Practice mindfulness by asking, moment by moment, "What is this?" Then ask, "What does this moment call for?" Asking allows answers to arise from your inner well of intuition.

If you can note your experience, you can name it. Naming frees you from the emotional grip of your experience. Naming helps you to realize you are not your thoughts, feelings, or perceptions. This takes the sting out of painful experiences. It frees you to do the right thing. Mindfulness, then, is the practice of purposefully noting your experience. It is an intentional waking up. By silently naming your experience, you separate from it. Awareness breaks away from its immersion in thoughts and feelings. With this separation of Awareness from the contents of Awareness, you cultivate freedom. You have the freedom to note and let go of negative thoughts and feelings—they are not who you are and they are not Reality. They are just thoughts and feelings. Don't get caught up in your thoughts.

Mindfulness is also a practice of humble respect for what is. Accept what arises in your mind without judgment. This is true whether your experience be positive or negative. Welcome all thoughts and experiences as honored guests into the chambers of your mind, even when the experience is negative and distressing. Mindfulness is thus not just a practice of intentional attention. It is also a spiritual practice of loving acceptance of what is. This puts you in alignment with Reality. You are in harmony. With acceptance, you find yourself enabled to stop grasping for or pushing away experience. With acceptance, you allow yourself to be fully present with what is without judgment. By dissolving a judging mind, suffering recedes. Friendly acceptance without judgment of even the most distressing and painful of experiences brings peace. This practice of open acceptance of this moment promotes equanimity.

By promoting acceptance, mindfulness facilitates change. Ironically, the more you grasp for or push away experience, the more you stay stuck in the craving and aversion that arise from your lack of acceptance. In mindfulness, stop rejecting Reality. Stop creating dissatisfaction. Cease pushing away your experience and longing for a different experience. It is then that the change you long for occurs. Positivity, clarity, peace, and wellness come to you.

Mindfulness enhances clarity. By looking, you see. By listening, you hear. With clarity comes a deepening of understanding. From understanding comes wisdom and intelligent action.

There are many other documented benefits of mindfulness, including boosting your immunity,[17] reducing stress by boosting positive coping and emotional well-being,[18] reducing depression, and preventing a recurrence of depression.[19] Mindfulness practice also reduces anger[20] and enhances relationships.[21] The practice of mindfulness changes the brain. It increases gray matter in the areas of the brain involved in learning, memory, emotional regulation, self-referential processing, and perspective taking.[22] Overall, mindfulness enhances both well-being and functioning.

There is a special role of mindfulness for recovering from addiction. In addiction, you are vulnerable to cravings and compulsions. You may find your mind ruminating. The addictive compulsion hijacks your will, causing you to act on addictive urges. In mindfulness, you stop making the disease of addiction, or compulsions and cravings, your enemy. Accept and note them. With both acceptance and noting, strengthen the capacity to abstain from doing what you know to be harmful. The freedom that mindfulness brings strengthens your capacity to act freely in the face of addiction. You can do what is right regardless of cravings and compulsions. Mindfulness empowers self-love over impulsive self-gratification. Because of this, mindfulness not only promotes your recovery by enhancing your overall well-being and functioning, but frees you from addiction's cravings and compulsions.

Cultivating Mindfulness

So how do you cultivate mindfulness? Although mindfulness is a conscious practice, it is also a way of being. It is a way of experiencing life. As with any habit, cultivating mindfulness requires intentional, committed, persistent, disciplined effort. Patience and persistence are essential. As with any spiritual practice, the practice of mindfulness takes practice. Being mindful is both difficult and simple. The brain only changes into a mindful brain with sustained, consistent effort over a period of weeks to years. Although it is hard, gentle work, it's well worth it.

Mindfulness is meditation in motion. It is being still while still moving. Many practice mindfulness by repeatedly returning to the breath, just as in meditation. They use the breath as an anchor that grounds them in the Now. Then they notice the moment repeatedly throughout the day. One mindfulness technique is to create alarms on a phone or watch. They can either ring or vibrate multiple times a day, reminding you to wake up to the moment. When you wake up, tune into what is going on: sights, sounds, smells, tastes, feelings, thoughts, and sensations. Lovingly note them and name them. Do this over and over again throughout the day.

Simple, repetitive activities serve as excellent opportunities to practice mindfulness. We all have routine activities we do every day, such as eating, bathing, driving, walking, exercising, and cleaning. Be mindful when doing these routines. Engage in these practices as if it were both the first time and the last time you perform them. For example, while driving, turn off the radio. Sense your body in the car. Note the cars and sights around you. Note the thoughts that arise while you drive. When you walk, pay attention to the sensations of your movements. Feel your feet on the ground. Notice the sights and sounds around you. Note the thoughts and feelings that arise. In mindful eating, devote your attention to the smell, taste, and texture of each bite, chewing slowly, noting the sensation when you swallow.

Another daily opportunity for mindfulness is listening. When you listen, attempt to listen 100% to what someone is saying. Note not only their meaning, but also listen to the music of their speech and observe their facial expressions and body postures. Give others the gift of your full attention. This helps you understand them. It also gives you an intuitive knowing of the other person's experience. Mindful listening promotes empathy. When you listen mindfully, you experience the other person's essence.

Commit upon arising to miss as few moments of life as possible. Solidify this commitment with your morning spiritual practices, but then carry it forward into your day, returning your attention again and again to the present moment.

Your goal is not continuous presence. Look for progress, not perfection. Be kind and patient with yourself in this practice. Do the best you can. That's enough. Though you miss many moments, there is always this moment to return to.

The practice of friendliness with the Present puts you in a loving relationship with Reality. Though you may be in distress, you do not suffer.

Your distress becomes like ripples on the surface of a deep, still pool—the pool of your friendly, acceptant, loving Awareness. You no longer fight with What Is. You work in harmony with It. Because of this transformation of your being, positivity, harmony, and love now characterize your actions and interactions with others.

Some engage in spiritual practices such as the practice of mindfulness to cultivate a special state of consciousness, such as the experience of unity or bliss. Others practice hoping it will make them "better" people. These are both mistakes. The goal is to be aware so you can savor life and respond intelligently to each moment.

Mindfulness enables you to see and hear. You cannot see if you don't look. You cannot hear if you don't listen. Mindfulness enables you to see the obvious, right before your eyes. When you look and listen, understanding deepens. Clarity arises regarding your thoughts, feelings, behaviors, and motives. Clarity also arises regarding others' thoughts, feelings, behaviors, and motives. You also see your impact upon others. Your clarity helps you see the consequences of your actions.

Mindfulness and Recovery

We often hear the slogans "One day at a time," "Just for today," and "Easy does it." These sayings spring from the practice of mindfulness.

One day at a time corresponds to one moment at a time. You attend to this moment instead of the past or future. Someone once said, "It's not the experience of today that drives people mad, it's the remorse of yesterday and the dread of tomorrow." In mindfulness, we live one moment at a time, with loving awareness. When you are mindful, your focus is on staying sober now, not tomorrow. Tomorrow will become now soon enough.

Don't become too preoccupied with either the past or the future. We waste many precious moments fretting over the past. Only a fool trips on something behind them. Dwelling on the past, you miss out on the abundance of the Now. Your past can consume you with pain and regret, thus the saying, "Look back, but don't stare." While you can't change the past, you can learn from it and bring your knowledge to the present moment. Don't look back, learn back.

While you need a life vision, dwelling on the future also disables you from being in the Now. If you live "just for today," you avoid overwhelming yourself with the future. Living fully in the Now, one day at a time, secures a better "Now" tomorrow.

"Just for today" empowers you, for you only have control over your actions in this moment. Today is the only day you can change. You have no control over yesterday or tomorrow.

"Easy does it" reflects the friendly, non-judgmental attitude of mindfulness. Easy does it means being harmoniously in sync with the Now. Work with Realty, not against it. Don't act violently out of non-acceptant condemnation. Keep the attitude of "Easy does it" in both good and difficult times.

You are born again each moment. Life gives you the opportunity to start anew. Since your thoughts shape you, mindfully attending to your thoughts in this moment empowers you to let go of negative thoughts and allow positive thoughts to arise. Feel the resonance of truth when your thoughts reflect the Now. In this way, mindfulness shapes the thoughts that empower you to shape your life.

Tips & Tasks

Tips: Mindfulness is the practice of paying attention to this one moment with friendly acceptance (nonjudgment).

Mindfulness promotes clarity. It helps us savor life. It frees us from automatically reacting to our thoughts and feelings so that we can respond intelligently to Life.

Tasks: Make mindfulness one of your spiritual practices. Start each day with the intention to be mindful.

Set alarms to ring throughout the day to trigger you to "wake up."

Practice mindfulness during routine activities such as eating, dressing, bathing, driving, or doing chores.

Practice mindful listening.

When cravings arise, practice mindfully noting them with friendly acceptance. This will lessen their power over you.

Section 4: Don't Believe Everything You Think

Rene Descartes said, "If you would be a real seeker after truth, it is necessary that at least once in your life you doubt, as far as possible, all things." It is an endless wonder how our minds create such a comprehensive representation of Reality, weaving together sounds, sights, smells, tastes, and physical sensations into a coherent whole. It is so powerfully comprehensive and rich it's understandable that we take our experience to be Reality, rather than a representation of Reality. We take our experience to be truth, rather than an approximation of truth.

This is a mistake. Your conscious experience is not Reality. Your experience is at most a limited reflection of Reality, with many aspects of Reality remaining forever beyond your direct experience. Thus, you cannot see radio waves, subatomic particles, magnetic waves, or gravitational waves. You cannot see the bending of space-time by gravity. You cannot see the vibrations of air caused by sound. Without a microscope, you cannot see the teaming microscopic life all around you in the air or on your hands. Much of the world is invisible to us. The fact is that conscious experience is a limited representation of Reality.

Perception leads to thoughts. Thoughts about Reality arise from your perception of Reality. Thoughts, which are based on words, are symbolic representations of Reality one step further removed from your direct experience of Reality. Thoughts are very seductive. We mistakenly take them to be who we are, even though our thoughts arise and disappear from moment to moment at the rate of about 70,000 thoughts a day. Renee Descartes fell into this illusion when he said, "I think, therefore I am." The fact is that the opposite is true; you are, therefore you think. You are not your thoughts, but the Silent Observer of your thoughts. This spiritual truth turns out to be important for your recovery because when you experience this truth, you free yourself from the tyranny of thought. You free yourself to both take your thoughts seriously but not so seriously at the same time. This freedom helps you recover from addiction by enabling you to act on what you know to be true, right, and good apart from your thoughts. Being the Silent Observer in recovery allows you to act on knowing rather than on fallible thoughts.

Thoughts about Reality are called beliefs. Beliefs arise not only from direct experience, but also from what others tell us. These are socially derived beliefs. Thus, we believe that:

- There is a Santa Claus.
- There is a city under the sea called Atlantis.
- A huge serpent called the "Loch Ness monster" swims in a large lake in Scotland.
- A tooth fairy takes your lost teeth when you sleep at night.
- Bigfoot roams the wilderness.

Parents and others also fill us with beliefs. Examples include: there is a heaven and hell, Democrats or Republicans are wrong, those people are bad, we are the best, and so on. We enter adulthood filled with stereotypes and prejudices we absorbed like sponges.

We also develop a vast number of beliefs based on the experiences of others, such as scientists and explorers, who share the knowledge gleaned from their observations. Sometimes this knowledge endures over time, such as that light travels at the speed of 299,792,458 meters/second. With time, beliefs based on observation may turn out to be false as we gain more evidence. Thus, we learn that the world is round and not flat. Many of our convictions of what is true turn out to be not true as we gather more information and correct mistaken assumptions.

Leaders, teachers, clergy, politicians, and other prominent people fill us with beliefs. Examples include beliefs about:

- How the world works
- Who is good and who is bad
- Who is right and who is wrong
- How we and others should behave

Whether for good or for ill, beliefs have great power, for beliefs direct your actions. They direct your growth or prevent it. They influence the decisions we make, both as individuals and as a society. An organized set of beliefs makes up a philosophy of life, a worldview, or an ideology. We blend what we know from direct experience with what others tell us to create the way we see things. This leads to different religions, forms of government, political parties, and ways of living. Our worldviews are founded on our beliefs. Our worldview dictates what we should do and how we should be.

Beliefs are a powerful and essential psychic tool upon which our survival depends. They dictate the workings of human civilization and the workings of our individual lives. Beliefs shape both our individual and collective destiny.

The problem with beliefs, given they are an abstract approximation of Reality, is that they can be wrong. Beliefs are fallible, as explained by Thomas Kida in his book, *Don't Believe Everything You Think.*[23] First, he points out we are much more influenced by anecdotal stories than by facts and statistics. Thus, when you hear about someone's bad experience with a product, you believe the story over the facts about how a product compares to other products.

The second source of error comes from our need to know and to be right. There is a human drive to simplify the ambiguous, to turn the gray into black or white. We unconsciously look for evidence that confirms our preexisting beliefs. Thus, if we believe the Government is either good or bad, we will notice evidence either way that confirms our bias.

We also tell ourselves stories to rationalize away what we don't want to see. We distort Reality when Reality is too painful. This is especially true with addiction. Victims want to believe they don't suffer from addiction. They may say to themselves:

- "Other people have it worse than I do."
- "If I use just this once, the cravings will go away and I'll stop tomorrow."
- "All my friends use, so it's fine for me to use too."
- "I'll just have one drink/bite/hit."
- "It helps me."
- "I can stop anytime."

The rationalizations people use to perpetuate addiction and avoid the painful truth of their loss of control are almost endless.

Your beliefs lead to expectations. Expectations are beliefs about what should happen. Negative assumptions lead to negative expectations while positive assumptions generate positive expectations. Glass-half-empty people will expect the worst, while glass-half-full people expect the best. It turns out that expectations can be self-fulfilling. Many people caught in addiction don't make an effort at recovery because they expect to fail. Conversely, successful people have the belief they can succeed, even if the path to success passes through multiple failures. Because of their positive expectations, based on the assumption they can succeed, they persist until their expectation becomes a Reality. We create the conditions over time to confirm our expectations. Hafiz noted this when he said, "What you speak becomes the house you live in."

The "house you live in" also refers to the false sense of self made up of thoughts and feelings. Part of recovery involves letting go of unrealistic, negative beliefs about yourself and others that arose from limited, skewed experiences. Challenge negative, destructive, and self-limiting beliefs. Hold a positive expectancy about your recovery to recover. Believing you are hopeless or incurable will only hold you back.

Believe you can recover from addiction because if you look closely, you see it's true. Having positive expectancies and beliefs about your recovery is not only essential, they're Reality-based. If you believe you will heal, the chances are more likely you will. Every belief either stimulates action or prevents action. If you have positive, Reality-based beliefs, you will pursue positive actions. If you have negative, unrealistic beliefs, you will either act negatively or not act at all.

Unrealistic beliefs lead to inappropriate expectations. This happens when you cling to beliefs about how things should be instead of accepting things as they are. This is a major source of suffering and conflict. Someone may be filled with resentment throughout their life based on the belief that people shouldn't be selfish. The fact is all of us are selfish at times, some more than others. This is how it is. Dropping the unrealistic belief that people should be unselfish all the time dissolves the resentment.

Realistic beliefs spring from spiritual experience combined with rational intuition. Examples include:

- The Universe is perfect as it is.
- Nothing "bad" happens (except from our limited, egocentric perspective).
- Order and chaos, good and evil make up the coherent Whole.
- You are part of the Universe.
- God (Reality) and the Universe are one.
- All people are deserving of respect.

These beliefs make up the spiritual understandings that inform your worldview. How then do you develop a healthy set of beliefs that are grounded in Reality? Base your beliefs, as much as possible, on direct experience combined with rational intuition. Ask, "What is this?" and, "Is this true?" This is the practice of mindfulness combined with critical thinking. Let go of old stories. Open to your experience. This is the source of your healing. Open yourself to what your experience has to teach you, even if it is painful. Listen more. Talk less. Make continuous, gentle efforts to see things as they truly are. Watch and note your thoughts. Don't try to control them, but also don't let them control you. Continuously stay open to changing circumstances and to new information. In doing so, you distinguish myth from truth, and fact from fiction.

Byron Katie, in her book *Loving What Is*, describes herself as a "lover of Reality." She constantly questions her assumptions and expectations by asking first, "Is this true?" If the answer is "Yes," she then asks, "How do I know 100% that it's true?" She has a healthy skepticism toward her thoughts, especially "negative" and "should" thoughts. She then asks how it feels to believe something you can't know for certain is true. Then she asks how it feels to drop beliefs not supported by Reality. Peace comes from dropping unrealistic beliefs. Thus, not believing everything you think is especially important when you judge others based on unrealistic expectations. This practice is respectful of others, for you accept others for who they are vs. resenting them for not being how you want them to be. By "loving what is," you honor others' rights and need to live life according to their nature and wishes. Move from demanding to desiring and from judging to acceptant tolerance.

The second practice is to get comfortable with not knowing. Get comfortable with mystery, paradox, and uncertainty. You can't simplify the complex. Not everything is explainable. Sometimes there are no answers. There's more "gray" than black and white. There are things we will never know, such as where we are. (Where is the Universe?) The human mind is limited in its capacity to know.

Part of not knowing is realizing there may be many valid perspectives. There is the story of the wise man who spoke to a fighting couple. When he heard the first person's account of events, he said, "You're right." When he heard the second person's story, he again said, "You're right." When someone confronted him on his waffling, noting that he had agreed with both parties, he again said, "You're right." This wise man was comfortable with the complexity of the gray that makes up human existence.

The third practice is to be comfortable being wrong. There is a saying that, "The world is divided into those who think they're right . . ." The fact is, there's something wrong if you're never wrong. To stay open to the truth, drop the need to be right. Hold your beliefs lightly. Question your beliefs. Seek feedback from others, taking in what the world has to teach you with an open willingness to discard old beliefs, which upon further evidence appear to be incorrect. Consider first impressions. Everyone forms impressions of others. Sometimes your impressions are right, but sometimes, as you get to know someone better, you realize your first impression was wrong. Again, humility is key. If you disagree with someone and later learn they were correct, be able to say, "I was wrong, and you were right." Maintain a healthy skepticism about the workings of your mind, realizing that it was your best thinking that got you into many difficult situations in the past. Thus the insightful saying, "My mind is out to get me." Knowing we all have a disease of perception, look for feedback from others to put things into a truer perspective.

Note and preserve the beliefs that can "bear the light of day." Mindful of the power of beliefs to shape your Reality, honor the positive beliefs that spring from your spiritual experience and reason. Embrace the beliefs consistent with your positive life vision. Discard negative opinions and misinformation. In this way, you develop the right thinking needed for your healing and recovery.

Tips & Tasks

Tips: Beliefs are not Reality.

Beliefs shape our destiny.

Tasks: Question your beliefs. Don't confuse them with Realty. Be open to new understandings.

Base your beliefs on direct experience combined with rational intuition.

Drop unrealistic beliefs.

Get comfortable with not knowing.

Get comfortable with being wrong.

Section 5: Live Both for Yourself and for Something Greater Than Yourself

Rabbi Hillel said, "If I am not for myself, who will be for me? If I am not for others, what am I? And if not now, when?" Resilient people live both for themselves and for something greater than themselves, including family, friends, community, their country, the world, Nature, and for a higher power that courses through them. The higher your level of living, the greater the cause, then the greater your resilience. The greater the cause, the greater your sense of meaning. Living solely for yourself leads to a small, empty, meaningless, petty life.

Humans need to belong. We have an inborn drive to be part of and contribute to the human family. You want to leave a legacy. What's most important in the end is how well you lived, how well you loved, and how you bettered the world.

If you live with a self-preoccupied desire to be happy and successful, you risk missing both. A focus on your contentment exclusive of others is a recipe for depression, for it leads to disconnection and isolation. When you focus only on your own personal happiness, you neglect the happiness of those around you, resulting in unhappiness coming back upon you.

If you focus just on your own personal success, you neglect the success of others. Instead of asking, "How can I be happy and successful?" ask, "What do I need to do to maintain my well-being while doing what Life asks of me?" Listening for and then answering the call to service brings the happiness and success you seek. When you put out good, the good of the world improves, resulting in good coming back to you. You simply cannot escape your interdependence. It truly is "one for all and all for one." By living this way, happiness and success come of their own accord without your grasping for them. They are a natural consequence of your self-forgetful devotion to Life.

In living for something greater than yourself, stop grasping for pleasure, happiness, self-fulfillment, success, or self-actualization. These are all like roses that wilt and die when you try to pick them, leaving you with thorns. By living to nurture and savor Life, pleasure, happiness, self-fulfillment, success, and self-actualization come as a natural consequence of your way of living. This truth is extremely important as you consider the "why" of your life—your life vision. Ask yourself, "Why do I eat?" If the answer does not include some form of self-transcendence, of living for the One Life, then well-being will not be yours. Your self-absorption will lead you back to addiction.

In addiction, you live in self-preoccupation, consumed by both suffering and concern for your survival. In recovery, you simultaneously go inward spiritually and outward to connect with Life. Ask yourself, "What is the 'why' of living?" When the answer comes to you, you experience a transformation of purpose as you devote yourself to living for the One Life of which you are a part. Serving Life well becomes your definition of success. Work to realize your hopes for your family and community. Work every day for a higher good. Extend yourself to others in love and service. Lose yourself in your devotion to your work and to others. Shift from a singular focus on self-interest to an interest in the problems and suffering of the world. Cultivate compassion and concern. It is this daily practice of devotion to something greater than yourself that brings true fulfillment as a byproduct of your actions, for giving is a gift.

There is another secret, besides service, to living for the One. That secret is surrender. In recovery, when you live simultaneously for yourself and others, you surrender to the loving, intelligent force that flows through you from beyond you. You let it transform you. You allow. Your True Self emerges.

Humbly surrender as well to the help, guidance, support, wisdom, and feedback of others. Open yourself up. Make yourself "intelligently vulnerable" to trustworthy people in the ways you can trust them. Shed the arrogance of unaccountable autonomy that characterizes addiction, and instead humbly embrace others, realizing that to live for others, you must let them in.

Some say you must sacrifice your life for some greater cause. This is what terrorist leaders say to suicide bombers. It is what Adolph Hitler said to his people. Even some of our politicians extol this "virtue." Self-sacrifice is unnecessary except in extreme life-and-death situations. Look for "both-and" solutions that meet your needs and the needs of others. Avoid "either-or" solutions that harm you. You must be good to be good for others. Self-sacrifice harms others when it puts you "out of commission."

In your dedication to leading a "no-harm life," look for "win-win" scenarios. This does not mean you don't compromise; you may defer exercise to complete an important project. You may take the kids fishing now and schedule time to read later. Be flexible, creative, and adaptive. Look for solutions that yield the greatest good for everyone, including yourself. It starts with your attitude. With the right attitude, things work out.

Whatever your life vision, your meaning and purpose must include service to others, to the world, and to Life if you wish for a fulfilling life that supports recovery. Greatness arises from the 10,000 tiny, daily, ordinary acts of love and service that make up your life. Though your light be tiny, it's still of great value. As Gandhi once suggested, practice being the change you wish for in the world. Tap into your authentic concern for the world. This concern arises spontaneously out of your experience of Oneness. See that living for something greater than yourself is a Reality mandate. It can be no other way. When you come into harmony with Realty, Life flourishes.

Tips & Tasks

Tips: Fulfillment comes from nurturing and savoring all of Life, both your own and the rest of Life.

Tasks: Make a daily commitment to live for a higher purpose. Dedicate your daily actions to something greater than yourself.

Section 6: Live According to a Higher Set of Principles

To flourish in your recovery, play the game of Life according to the universal principles that govern Life. Some disregard these principles. They have no moral compass. They do not submit their lives to a higher set of principles. They make up their own rules, accountable to no one but themselves. They do not live according to a higher set of principles because they put nothing higher than themselves. They pay a heavy price by disregarding Reality and putting themselves in charge of how the game of Life should be played. Arrogance comes at a heavy cost. At the extreme, people who don't live by a higher set of principles end up dead or in prison.

In addiction, you serve the addiction, so you follow the addiction's rules. These include doing anything, at all costs, to perpetuate the addiction. Morals, values, and other life principles become irrelevant.

You don't decide the principles for living. Life does. It is your job to figure them out using your reason, intuition, and your powers of observation. It is also your job to live by them. Look both without and within. Note how things work. See what is skillful and what is not, what is "right action," and what is not.

When faced with a dilemma, reflect on your life principles. Then ask, "Who is the person I need to be?" rather than, "What should I do?" If you live your principles, right action follows.

To flourish in recovery, you need a set of universal principles to live by. The 12 Touchstones in this book speak of many of these principles, such as making recovery your first priority, living with integrity, and so on.

But there are others. Refer to the resource section in the back of the book to validate these principles through what you know to be true, right, and good. Reflect upon the life principles outlined in the back.

In practicing these principles, keep in mind they are not rigid rules, but guidelines. Stay true to the guidelines, keeping in mind that what is right and good varies according to circumstance.

Make your own list of principles by which to live, in your own words. If you make it your own, you are more likely to live by it.

No one adheres to these principles perfectly all the time. Life is difficult and messy. We're all imperfect and limited. This is summed up in the core principle from which all other life principles arise:

Be good . . .
Accept when you aren't
Do good . . .
Accept when you don't.

Tips & Tasks

Tips: Successful living requires living according to a set of universal Life principles.

Tasks: Review the principles in the appendices. Then make up your own set of the most important principles for you. Commit yourself to living by these principles every day. Make this part of your daily morning intentions.

Section 7: Keep Perspective

One challenge of recovery is to stay sober in the face of stress. Life is difficult.

The road of recovery is full of bumps and potholes. You will face many difficulties, big and small, on a daily basis. Everyone finds it challenging to maintain inner peace and serenity when "bad" things happen.

Keeping a proper perspective on things helps you maintain both your serenity and your sobriety. By perspective, I mean seeing the whole truth about the way things are. Right perspective is the larger perspective in which you see your troubles in correct proportion. From this perspective, you see "bad" things exist only from a limited personal perspective. Even the most profound of tragedies, and the tremendous pain you feel in the midst of such tragedy, are part of the sacred Whole. Everything is exactly as it should and must be.

While we have little control over the world, we do have control over our attitude. You have the capacity, with conscious effort, to maintain a clear and balanced perspective on Life. You have a choice how you view your life situation. If you run out of gas and miss an important appointment, you have the choice to stand back and see this from a spiritual perspective: "bad" things happen. This comes with the gift we call Life. You add nothing to the situation by getting angry or anxious. Nothing comes from negativity and complaining.

Instead, improve the situation while savoring your existence. With every step you take to the gas station, remember you are blessed to be alive and able to walk to the gas station. Let go of needing Reality to be what you want. Humbly accept even the most painful of situations. Make friends with What Is. Realize any other attitude only brings suffering. Maintain your gratitude and appreciation for what you have instead of losing perspective by focusing only on what you do not have.

It's easy to forget how good things are. Our culture of entitlement does not help. It's human nature to focus on what is wrong instead of what is right. Looking at the news, we see an unbalanced focus on the dark while ignoring the light. We hear of murders and wars, but hear very little of the countless acts of love and heroism, and the many incredible human achievements that occur daily. As people look at the "news" of their lives, it's "what bleeds that leads" in the headlines of their consciousness. Keeping the larger picture in mind lets in the light, helping you to stay positive. The positivity of a spiritual perspective helps to keep you sober by keeping pain, and thus cravings, at bay. You see that most of the time, the glass is 98 ½% full.

Positivity leads to positive action. When you make friends with Reality, you empower yourself to improvise, to be creative, to adapt, and positively respond. Rather than kicking the car and pouting, you start walking. You call to explain your situation and reschedule your appointment. You improvise, adapt, and cope instead of giving up and addicting. Maybe you wave to someone with a friendly smile and end up getting a ride to the gas station.

Negativity, on the other hand, only hurts you. In losing perspective, you lose track of your goals. You lose sight of your purpose. You are distracted from your life vision. Your equilibrium is off. You lose your productivity.

We all can make mountains out of molehills. Yet artificially inflating your problems by losing sight of the whole only hurts you. It reduces your ability to solve problems. Remind yourself that if it doesn't matter, it doesn't matter. See the relative importance of a situation and put things in context. Is running out of gas a matter of survival, or an inconvenience? Will it matter 30 years from now that you had to reschedule an appointment for a later date? Most likely not.

Proper perspective includes seeing most problems as opportunities in disguise. Creatively overcoming obstacles creates a pathway to success. With the proper perspective, you see that most problems are not problems at all.

Many get knocked off track by their interactions with others. Someone may judge, criticize, or reject you. They may abuse you or exploit you. They may betray you or abandon you. It's challenging to keep perspective at these times. Remind yourself that it's never about your worth or value. That is a given. Usually, when it seems about you, it is really about the other person. Someone may criticize you because they envy you. Another person may snap at you because they're having a bad day. Rather than shrinking into a small, self-preoccupied perspective, commit to not taking others' actions and thoughts personally. Instead, strive to understand.

Since, in your spiritual perspective, you are perfect in your imperfection, open yourself to learn about your mistakes. Ask others, "Help me understand." Humbly recognize that your grasp on Reality is always incomplete. Drop defensiveness. There's nothing to defend. Move from hurt to care and concern. Transition from fear to curiosity. Become inquisitive. What can you learn? Move from reaction to investigation. Renounce prejudgment. Since you have made it a practice to not believe everything you think, investigate your assumptions. Your love for yourself and others allows you to learn.

Don't blow a criticism out of proportion. Don't turn it into a global condemnation of who you are. Remember the whole of who you are—you are a combination of strengths, talents, gifts, weaknesses, and vulnerabilities. Nothing is black and white, including you.

When you stay with an abiding care and concern for others, you are keeping the proper perspective. Love yourself and others as best you can. This is the proper spiritual perspective on relationships.

While we often let petty problems get to us, we also inevitably face bigger problems. These include serious illness, disability, our own impending deaths, divorce, and the deaths of loved ones. Our house may burn down. Someone may rob and beat us. Someone may rape us. We may lose our jobs or our fortunes. It is our job in these situations to be in pain, as these are all painful situations. Yet even in dire situations, empower yourself to bear the pain and stay positive by keeping perspective.

Life necessarily includes chaos and destruction. Life is not always fair. With humility, accept that Life is not always about you. Remind yourself, for example, that many, many people become sick, disabled, and die every day. Note that bad things happen daily. This is part of Life. See that death comes to us all—that you ultimately lose everything. If someone leaves you or betrays you, remember that no relationship is permanent or guaranteed. Remember that we hurt each other in large and small ways every day out of our pain, ignorance, and unskillful behavior. It is your job to maintain a perspective of hope and gratitude for the gift of Life in these painful times, even when facing death. Someday death will be upon you. At that time, your spiritual perspective will help you grieve and experience acceptance and gratitude for the life you had.

Keeping things in perspective enhances your resilience and keeps you in recovery. The resource section in the back outlines specific practices for maintaining perspective.

Tips & Tasks

Tips: Keeping a proper and positive perspective helps you stay sober in the face of life's difficulties.

Tasks: Practice perspective taking during difficult times as described in this section.

Section 8: See the Sacred in All Things and People

What does sacred mean? People have used this term to refer to God, or a divinity. I don't use that definition, as it does not include everyone's worldviews. A better definition of sacred is something deserving of our reverence because of its infinite beauty, value, or goodness. This definition allows everyone, even atheists, to contemplate the sacredness of Life without religious overtones.

Ask yourself if people, and even Life itself, are of great value and thus deserving of your reverence. In thinking about reverence for Life, you might ask yourself if Life (including you) is worthy of awe, respect, wonder, and admiration.

Are human beings worthy of awe, respect, wonder, and admiration? Why don't we always feel this? Should we?

To begin, notice that human beings have an incredible capacity to take the miraculous for granted. We become *habituated*, or get used to things. As we get caught up in our day-to-day routines, we lose our sense of the wonder of Life.

Take note of the mystery of self-aware consciousness. How is it that, through us, the Universe is aware of Itself? How is it that the neural symphony of our brains creates the music of human awareness? If this is not worthy of awe and wonder, what is?

Reflect on the mystery of beauty. Why does beauty even exist? Why can human beings experience the ecstasy of beauty?

The human brain is by far the most complicated structure in the known Universe, with roughly 80 billion cortical neurons. The brain has trillions of connections, and more possible connections than atoms in the Universe. It is baffling to think our brains, along with the rest of our bodies, developed according to instructions contained in only 46 submicroscopic molecules—our chromosomes.

The complexity of Life, with its almost infinite interdependencies, dwarfs the complexity of the human mind and body. Life happens in an intricate, harmonious balance.

It is amazing that the thousands of intricate, interwoven processes that sustain our life go on automatically, beyond our conscious control. Such is the astounding intelligence of Nature. Seeing this, we realize our lives are a miraculous, moment-to moment gift.

Everyone has but one brief moment of existence before death. Like flowers, we each bloom into the fullness of our lives and then wilt and die.

The fleeting, momentary nature of our existence gives a further sense of the preciousness of Life.

Reflecting on these facts of our existence stimulates wonder, awe, appreciation, and deep respect for Life, for others, and for the gift of our own lives. It is this profound reverence that makes people sacred.

How do you treat something you cherish? Think of how a mother cherishes her child. It is with the greatest of love, care, and respect. Once you come to your own reverence for the lives of others and for yourself, you treat yourself and others as a mother treats her child. You treat all of Life with love, care, and respect. This is what it means to treat yourself and others as sacred.

The following poems by the great Sufi poet Hafiz speak to our sacredness and the attitude we need toward others. For those uncomfortable with the word "God," substitute the terms "Spirit" or "Life-Force":

If God invited you to a party

If God
Invited you to a party
And said,

"Everyone
In the ballroom tonight
Will be my special
Guest,"

How would you then treat them
When you
Arrived?

Indeed, indeed!

And Hafiz knows
There is no one in this world

Who
Is not upon
His Jeweled Dance Floor.

In this poem, Hafiz conveys the idea that everyone is an honored guest on the "Jeweled Dance Floor" of life. Life is the party to which we have been invited.

The following two poems address the reverent attitude in which we attend to others.

How do I listen?

How
Do I
Listen to others?
As if everyone were my Master
Speaking to me
His
Cherished
Last Words.

Why not be polite

Everyone
Is God speaking.
Why not be polite and
Listen to
Him?

In these poems, Hafiz beautifully expresses the deep reverence he gives his fellow men. He sees others as "God speaking" to him, knowing that "God," or the sacred Life Spirit, is in everyone and everything, including us.

As both a miracle and a mystery, Life, including your existence, is precious beyond measure. You and others deserve to be treated with the utmost reverence and respect. Imagine if everyone on this small planet were to only see their own and others' sacred natures? What would that do to hatred, conflict, war, discrimination, injustice, and intolerance?

The Sufis emphasize that God is in everything. Physicists and other scientists understand that God, or the intelligent life force that arises from matter, is in all of matter, arising from the fundamental properties of matter. With this understanding, you realize that everything, including the chair you sit in, is sacred. Life arises from Reality and is one with Reality.

Seeing the sacred is yet another spiritual practice grounded in mindfulness.

When you become one with the Now, you experience the fresh, vibrant essence of Reality. You experience the sacred.

Practice returning your awareness to this present moment with reverence, humility, gratitude, and respect. Look. See Life's mystery, wonder, and beauty. Marvel at your awareness.

Seeing the sacred, treat yourself, others, and your environment with great care. Take a vow of no harm except in extreme life-threatening situations where no other option exists.

When your eyes are open to the sacred, several positive spiritual qualities arise within you and govern your behavior. You can summon these qualities by reminding yourself of the sacredness of yourself and others:

- Kindness. Treat both yourself and others with kindness.
- Appreciation. Appreciate the wonder and beauty of life, of yourself, and of others.
- Care. Care for yourself and others out of your reverence for Life.
- Respect. Guard your own self-respect and treat others with the respect their sacredness calls for. Refrain from gossiping or otherwise belittling others.
- Generosity. Given that your fellow beings are of infinite value, humbly give yourself over to the benefit of others.
- Tolerance. Since sacredness is unconditional, maintain your sense of others' sacredness even in the face of their destructive, hurtful, and otherwise unskillful behavior. Seeing the sacred mutes reactions of hurt and anger. It neutralizes judgment and condemnation of others. Do not retaliate. Treat others with unconditional care and respect, regardless of how hurt and angry you may feel. Do not retaliate. Instead, say to yourself and your actions, "God bless you." Accept people for who they are, even with their imperfection, ignorance, and negative emotions and behavior, while protecting yourself and others from harm.

Practicing these qualities out of your awareness of the sacred has a powerful impact. From your own self-love, you experience a waning of harsh self-judgment and criticism. The world is like a mirror. Being your best with others brings out the best in others. If you treat yourself with care and respect, others will do the same. Seeing the sacred in all things inspires love. As you love the world, the world loves you back.

The practice of seeing the sacred has a powerful effect on recovery. Seeing your own sacredness, you would do nothing to harm yourself, including addicting. Your profound appreciation dissolves the negativity that so often leads to readdiction. Hurt, anger, anxiety, grief, sadness, and other distressing emotions become like small waves upon the ocean of your reverence.

Continuously return your awareness to the truth that this moment is sacred, regardless of your conditions or circumstances.

Tips & Tasks

Tips: Everything is sacred.

Tasks: Seeing the sacred in yourself and others, treat yourself and others with kindness, appreciation, respect, generosity, and tolerance. Make a daily commitment to this spiritual practice.

Section 9: Count Your Blessings

Victor Frankl said, "The last of the human freedoms is to choose one's attitude in any given set of circumstances." Humans have a tremendous capacity to remember their troubles and forget their blessings. We quickly get used to and take for granted the many positive things in our lives. Thus, some might travel to an island paradise and after a few days complain of boredom, the heat, or the insects. They forget the incredible beauty that so impressed them upon their arrival.

We also take each other for granted. The antidote to this human tendency to take everything for granted is to count your blessings every day.

Nurture your positivity through the practice of gratitude. Make this a daily practice, especially in hard times when you are in distress. Remind yourself of all that you have. Reflect on the following:

- Life. Each day of existence is a gift. A day above ground is a good day.

- Consciousness. We are blessed by our capacity for self-awareness.
- Food. Most are blessed to have enough food to survive.
- Family and friends. Appreciate the loving connections that support and sustain you.
- Material goods. Never before have humans experienced the comforts, conveniences, and pleasures that our current civilization provides.
- Civilization. We have developed an intricate web of interdependence that enhances both our safety and the quality of our lives.
- Freedom. Not all people can say what they think (with limits such as hateful speech and threats). Not everyone can choose who will govern them.
- Human knowledge. Never have we known and understood as much as we do now about our world.
- Art. Visual arts, music, dance, theater, and other art forms deeply enrich our lives.
- Beauty. The natural beauty of others and of Nature is a gift for our enjoyment.
- Healing and grace. We are indebted to the remarkable tenacity and resilience of Life that supports and heals us.

These are just a few of our many blessings. No doubt you can think of more.

In recovery, gratitude helps to protect you from negativity. A loss of gratitude can trigger readdiction. The fact is that grateful people don't addict, and those in active addiction aren't grateful. You simply can't serve both positivity and negativity at the same time. A heart full of gratitude has no room for resentments. Practicing gratitude can cause a change of heart that changes everything. You succeed in life and in your recovery when your gratitude helps you to "be for" instead of to "be against" Life. The practice of gratitude also extends to gratitude for your "trials and tribulations," for these are usually blessings in disguise. Every negative has a positive. Be grateful for your pain, for pain is both a great teacher and motivator for growth. Thanks to healing and grace, your mistakes and your misfortunes become your greatest gifts, if you will only choose a positive attitude and learn from them. If anything, they teach acceptance.

Since change starts from within, an inner attitude of gratitude triggers positive changes in your outer life. As Lewis L. Dunnington has said:

> What life means to you is determined not so much by what life brings to you as by the attitude you bring to life; not so much by what happens to you as by your reaction to what happens.

It's not your situation as much as your reaction to your situation that determines what happens next. If you remain grateful in the face of adversity, this will inspire a positive and productive response to Life. Be grateful that there is more good than evil, that in the long run good trumps evil. As Jodi Picoult once said, "You can stick a candle into the dark, but you can't stick the dark into the light."

It is the wise person who, through the practice of gratitude, allows him or herself to enjoy the fruits of his or her strivings. Those without gratitude are condemned to work for what they want but never enjoy it. Happiness, like a butterfly, will only alight upon your shoulder if you become still enough to appreciate all that you have.

The practice of gratitude counters the ego's tendency to want more and more. There is never enough. In your wanting, you suffer. True success in life comes from knowing what you don't need. Don't disregard what you have in your wish for what you do not have. Cultivate the practice of "enough." The disease of "more" will fade as you practice gratitude for what you have. See that happiness comes from appreciating what you have vs. getting what you want. Notice that sometimes the worst happens because of getting what you wanted.

Melody Beattie once said:

> Gratitude unlocks the fullness of life. It turns what you have into enough, and more. It can turn a meal into a feast, a house into a home, a stranger into a friend. It turns denial into acceptance, chaos to order, confusion to clarity. It turns problems into gifts, failures into success, the unexpected into perfect timing, and mistakes into

important events. Gratitude makes sense of your past, brings peace for today and creates a vision for tomorrow.

The practice of gratitude, like so many spiritual practices, is rooted in recognizing the gifts of the Now. You cannot appreciate what you do not see. Live with gratitude now to transform a "bad time" into a good time.

To cultivate gratitude, write a gratitude list and count your blessings every day. Start each day with gratitude for another miraculous day of existence. Set out with intentions to savor and appreciate each moment. Practice keeping an attitude of gratitude throughout the day. This intention fills your life with grace. Taste the happiness that comes from gratitude for all that you have. This helps to keep you on track in your recovery.

Tips & Tasks

Tips: We all have much to be grateful for.

Living with gratitude generates positivity, which leads to positive actions, which leads to positive outcomes, which reduces the risk of readdicting.

Tasks: Make a gratitude list. Reflect on it every day. Commit each day to appreciating your many blessings.

Section 10: Live Life out of Love

The culmination of your spiritual practice and of recovery is to live life out of love instead of fear. As Winston Churchill reminds us, "You make a living by what you get, but you make a life by what you give!" It is to live out of abundance instead of deficit. Become like a candle that loses nothing by lighting a thousand other candles. Develop the capacity to love for love's sake alone, and not for anything in return apart from the gift of giving.

Achieve this capacity by first becoming whole and loving yourself, and second, by healing your relationships. First heal yourself and your life through the practice of these Touchstones. You can't give away what you don't have. You can only help others to the degree you have helped yourself. It is only in health that you can experience the happiness of helping others. This is why Step 12 of Alcoholics Anonymous—to help other alcoholics—is the last step of the transformation achieved by working the Steps. Whatever your method or path, be it through the 12-step fellowship or otherwise, the ultimate result is the realization of love.

Through your recovery and your spiritual practice, keep returning to gratitude, reverence, and wonder. This generates the compulsion to serve—to nurture Life. You want to give back for all that you have been given. You do not love because you should. You love because you must.

Just as you need others, so others need you. Life is waiting for you to recover so you can serve the Life that serves you. Loving is both a privilege and a responsibility. There is a place in Life that only you can fill. Each day is an opportunity to serve in countless ways. Pay it forward by giving your time, your talent, and your treasure. Share your knowledge and whatever wisdom you have gleaned from your experience.

Nurture others to realize their own potentials just as you are realizing yours. Through your faith in them and your encouragement, help others to see their own strengths and talents. Connect with others to learn of their burdens so you might share them. Yet do not foster dependency. Instead, empower. Broadcast your own wholeness and vitality to be a beacon to others. Share your faith and positivity. In being, show others how to be. In doing, show others how to do. As you have received so much without cost, give freely without charge.

One blessing and privilege of recovery is the ability to help others with their recovery. Through your own healing, you pass on the message of strength, faith, and hope. Through the living of your life, through the practice of your being, you show others how to live and be in recovery.

We also grow in helping others to grow. When you teach, you learn again. When you give wise advice, you give that advice to yourself. When you serve others, you serve yourself. As Ralph Waldo Emerson once said, "It is one of the most beautiful compensations of life that no man can sincerely try to help another without helping himself." Immersed in service, you forget yourself and become one with Life. This is the most rewarding of feelings.

True to the law of karma, the more you give, the more you receive. As you continuously give, so you continuously receive. Once you have secured your own health and vitality, you realize that the ultimate act of selfishness is to be selfless, for giving is its own reward. You discover that only in giving do you receive in full measure.

Spirituality is a thread that runs deep through recovery, and is often an antidote to addiction. Don't let the fact that it is the last Touchstone fool you. It is perhaps the most important in terms of realizing the joy of recovery. Many who have lost their spirituality find that they tend to replace it with addicting. But once you begin to cultivate your spirituality as outlined in this Touchstone, you'll find a more prosperous and fulfilling life is within reach.

Tips & Tasks

Tips: The culmination of recovery is to live out of love instead of fear.

Loving others is the greatest gift you can give yourself. Giving is a gift. The most selfish thing you can do is to be selfless.

Tasks: Prepare yourself to love others by first loving yourself.

Dedicate yourself each day to serving the One Life of which you are a part.

CHAPTER 14

ADDICTION: HOW FAMILY AND FRIENDS CAN HELP

Addiction affects not only the victim of addiction, but also everyone touched by him or her. Victims of addiction and their families, friends, and coworkers all suffer together. Addiction negatively impacts everyone in contact with the sufferer of that addiction. In the end, it is a group sport—everyone gets to play. So how can you detect addiction in a friend or family member? Start by asking yourself if your friend or loved one meets the following diagnostic criteria for addiction:

1. Do they take the drugs (including alcohol) in larger amounts or for longer than intended? For prescription medications, this might include not using the medication as prescribed.
2. Do they want to reduce or stop using the drug but just can't? They may try to set limits on their use, but end up using more than they planned, or more often than they intended.
3. Do they spend a lot of time getting, using, or recovering from the drug? Do they go to multiple doctors for prescriptions, try to get other people's medications, or buy medications or drugs off the street? Do they think about how bad they felt after their last use?
4. Do they have cravings and urges to use the drug?
5. Are they unable to manage responsibilities at work, home, or school because of drug use?
6. Do they continue to use a drug, even when it causes problems in relationships with family or friends, with the law, or at work? Do they have trouble getting along with co-workers, teachers, friends, or family members? Do others complain about how they act, or comment on

how they have changed? Do they have money problems due to loss of income or increased spending on drugs?

7. Do they give up important social, recreational, or work-related activities because of drug use? Are they isolating socially because of time spent addicting or to hide their drug use from family and friends? Have they lost interest in family, friends or activities they used to enjoy?
8. Do they use drugs again and again, even when it puts them in danger? This can include driving or operating heavy machinery while intoxicated, or purchasing illegal drugs from a drug dealer.
9. Do they continue to use, even though their drug use causes physical or mental problems? Do they have mood swings or bouts of anger and irritability? Are they fearful, anxious, or paranoid for no clear reason? Do they appear lethargic or "spaced out?" Does their energy level fluctuate from exhausted to energetic? Have they lost their motivation?
10. Have they developed tolerance, where they need more of the drug to get the wanted effect?
11. Have they developed withdrawal symptoms, which taking more of the drug relieves? Do they feel shaky, depressed, nauseous, sweaty, tired, or confused? Have they been feverish or had seizures? Have they been irritable or nervous?

If your friend or loved one has two or more of the above symptoms, they meet the criteria for a substance use disorder.

Other signs or manifestations of addiction include physical signs such as:

- Bloodshot eyes
- Dilated or constricted pupils
- Slurred speech
- Impaired coordination
- Bad breath
- Unusual odors on the body or clothing
- Shakes
- Frequent bloody noses
- Persistent coughs or sniffles

- Weight loss or gain
- Poor grooming or hygiene.

Behaviors that indicate possible addiction include:

- Stealing money, possessions, or prescriptions
- Other illegal behavior
- Borrowing money
- Erratic sleep
- Fighting
- Erratic behavior
- Lying
- Increased accidents
- Isolating from friends and family
- Hanging out with other victims of addiction
- Lying about one's activities or whereabouts, or having repeated unexplained outings, often with a sense of urgency.

Addiction corrupts character. Victims become self-centered, secretive, manipulative, and dishonest. They abandon their moral compass. They are no longer themselves. If you see a negative change in personality, suspect addiction.

The Impact of Addiction on Families and Others

Addiction hurts everyone. Households afflicted with addiction experience increased stress, tension, miscommunication, and other negative consequences like violence and poverty. Addiction turns a positive atmosphere into a negative one. Victims of addiction can be unpredictable. Since family members often cannot count on the victim, they lose trust in the victim. Families suffer from the loss of the victim's capacity to contribute, and from the victim's abandonment of their family for the sake of the addiction.

Then, families experience a variety of negative and painful emotions, including blame, resentment, hatred, anger, and fear. The trauma caused by addiction poisons family dynamics, creating an atmosphere of pain.

The damage caused by addiction depends on the family, the severity of the addiction, the personal characteristics of the victim, and the addiction. No two families are the same. Common consequences include:

1. Financial strain. Victims may lose their jobs or spend their money on the addiction. Bills go unpaid. Families go without necessities such as food and clothes. Some families even become homeless.
2. Isolation. Victims often do shameful things. Out of embarrassment, families withdraw from outside family and friends.
3. Enabling. Loved ones often shield the victim from the negative consequences of their behavior to "help" the victim.
4. Codependency. Partners may depend too much on the victim. Or, they may stay in the relationship even though it harms them. Partners often fail to take care of themselves. They may even get their sense of purpose and meaning from caring for the victim.
5. Enmeshment. The addiction may preoccupy family members. This can prevent them from living independent and fulfilling lives.

Addiction's damage can extend for many generations. Victims make poor role models. They destroy trust. Addiction damages ideas about what's normal in a family. These distorted ideas get passed on from generation to generation.[24] Growing up with the chaos and trauma of addiction hurts adult children's ability to parent. Adult children may be to be too protective and controlling of their own children. They may fear for the safety of their children. While well intentioned, hovering over children hurts their independence and autonomy.

Addiction also hurts others outside the immediate family. Extended family members can experience abandonment, anxiety, anger, embarrassment, or guilt. Extended family members may cut ties with the victim. They may even seek legal protection. Victims or their partners may ask for financial help from friends. Coworkers may have to take on an unfair share of the work, leading to resentment.

The addicted person abandons their loved ones for their addiction. Victims spend their time with other addicted individuals who will support and reinforce their addiction rather than with those who love them. Because of stigma and shame, families often hide the addiction from the world around them, keeping it a secret. This prevents them from getting help.

Impact of Addiction on Children

One in five people lived with a relative with alcoholism growing up. Others grew up with parents who had different addictions. Addiction devastates many children. Addicted parents often neglect their children. They abuse them. They are unpredictable, causing insecurity and anxiety. Sometimes the unaddicted parent may try to make up for the deficiencies of their addicted spouse.[25] The trauma to children is even worse if both parents suffer from addiction. Parents can't tune in to their children's emotional needs, so children suffer alone, without support.

Neglect, instability and conflict can harm children. Parents may leave children to fend for themselves. Parental unemployment may cause children to go without heat, food, or electricity—all essentials of life. Some children don't have a home. Children suffer as they see their parents suffer. It hurts them to see their parents struggle with mental illness, unemployment, legal problems, and divorce.

Without parenting, children may take on the role of caregiver for their addicted parent. They can become "parentified." This robs children of their childhood. They may develop denial to protect themselves from the pain of their parent's addiction.

Addiction poisons families. Healthy families become unhealthy families that harm children:

Healthy Family System	Addicted Family System
Self-worth is high	Self-worth is low
Communication is direct, clear, specific, and honest	Communication is shut down, unclear, and indirect. No one says what he or she really thinks.
Members express their feelings	No one says what he or she really feels
Rules are reasonable, firm, consistent, but flexible to change	Rules are rigid, unreasonable, and inconsistent.
The family is linked and open to their community	The family is isolated from the community. The addiction is shrouded in secrecy. No one discusses family problems outside of the family
The family supports each person in achieving their personal life goals.	Support of each family member's growth and individuation is lacking

Addiction damages the way addicted parents interact with their children:[26]

- *Rather than being positive, addicted parents can be negative.* They may complain, criticize, and condemn. Children may then believe they are not worthy and will fail in life. Addicted parents don't reinforce good behavior. Neglected children may learn that the only way to get attention is to misbehave. They may feel negative attention is better than no attention.
- *Some addicted parents put overly high expectations on their children.* They do this because of their own lack of self-worth. This can overwhelm children. Children then pull away from the demands of their parents. They give up on themselves. They become hopeless about their lives. Other children may become overachievers to please their parents. Unfortunately, no matter how well they do, they can't please their parents. This leaves them feeling depleted and defeated. In either case, the addicted parent deprives the child of the sense of their innate goodness apart from their behavior.
- *Addicted parents confuse their children by being inconsistent about the rules.* They may also be inconsistent about discipline. This leaves children feeling unsafe. They may misbehave to test their parents. Without consistent limits, children cannot predict how their parents will respond to their behavior. They can't behave according to how they know their parents will respond.
- *Addicted parents have impaired Reality testing.* They deny their addiction and any family problems. They don't see the harm they are causing to their children. They deny signs of abuse or addiction in their children, even in the face of plain evidence.
- *Addicted parents often retaliate against their children if their children show anger over their toxic family situation.* Children learn that it's not safe to express their anger, fear, or hurt. As a result, they suppress these feelings. Children may then act out their anger at school. Or they may turn to alcohol and drugs to numb their pain. People call this self-medication. Tragically, many children become addicted attempting to cope with their parent's addiction.

Addiction changes family roles. Some addicted family roles include:[27]

- The *Scapegoat*—the child who misbehaves and gets into trouble. They draw attention away from the real problem in the family—the addiction. They are often defiant. They may get in trouble with the law. Their behavior reflects the poisonous and chaotic atmosphere in the house. The scapegoat feels shame, guilt, and emptiness.
- The *Enabler* (caretaker)—takes care of the things that the victim needs or left undone. They compensate for the victim's impairment. They make all the other roles possible. They try to keep everyone happy. They make excuses and do not seek help. They present a problem-free image to the public. Feelings that drive their behavior include inadequacy, fear, and helplessness.
- The *Mascot*—uses humor to try to create balance and comfort in the home. They are the family jester. Their humor may be harmful. Their underlying feelings are embarrassment, shame, or anger.
- The *Victim* of addiction—often alternates between shame and rage, remorse and entitlement. They are usually exploitative, deceitful, and manipulative.
- The *Lost Child*—isolates from other family members. They are silent. They stay out of the way. They are quiet and reserved to avoid making any problems. They have trouble developing relationships. They are avoidant and shut down. They've given up on getting any of their needs met. Underlying feelings include guilt, loneliness, neglect, hurt, and anger.
- The *Hero*—generally an older child who overachieves. They appear confident and serious. They often take on a parental role. They may be obsessed with perfection. They need the family to look good. Their underlying feelings are fear, guilt, and shame.

There can be profound psychological damage of children of addicted parents. Children often feel guilty or responsible for their parent's addiction.[28] The parent may force their children to engage in illegal activities to support the parent's habit. This can leave children feeling guilty, ashamed, angry, fearful, confused, anxious, and conflicted. Because of the addicted parent's impairment, neglect, abuse, and inconsistency, children can't develop the capacity for trust they need for their future relationships.[29]

Addiction exposes children to violence. The consequences are serious. They include addiction, mental health problems, physical health problems, and reduced functioning. 30-40% of children who experience violence enter a violent relationship as an adult.[30]

Children of addicted parents are more likely to be emotionally, physically, or sexually abused. As much as 80% of child abuse involves alcohol or drug use.[31] This further increases the trauma experienced by the children. It makes them more vulnerable to developing an addiction themselves. Roughly two thirds of people in addiction treatment were physically, sexually, or emotionally abused as a child.[32]

When addiction impairs parents, the grandparents may pick up the slack.[33] This may be a saving grace for the parents' children.

Children suffer greatly when a parent is afflicted with addiction.[34] Lifelong consequences include poor self-image, loneliness, guilt, anxiety, helplessness, fear of abandonment, embarrassment, confusion, anger, and depression. They often try to keep their parent's illness a secret. They may develop poor school performance, truancy, physical symptoms, depression and suicidality, addiction, delinquent behavior, or risk taking behaviors. They can suffer from impaired learning ability, increased rates of divorce, violence, the need to control others, and increased rates of mental illness.[35,36,37]

Children of parents with alcohol use disorder are four times more likely to develop alcohol use disorder than children raised by sober parents. Because of weak attachments to their impaired parents, children may shift their attachments to drug-using peers. This is especially true in blended families where an adolescent is living with a divorced parent and stepparent. This increases the risk of cannabis use in adolescence.[38] These adolescents are at greater risk of long-term behavioral and emotional problems. They have more difficulty dealing with stress. They are more likely to marry someone who suffers from addiction or someone who is abusive.

Some children enter adulthood without much damage. They are resilient.[39] Some respond to the stress and trauma of addiction by developing mature judgment, autonomy, responsibility, strong moral values and a capacity to tolerate ambiguity.[40]

Impact of Addiction on Spouses and Partners

Addiction ruins relationships.[41] It can tear families apart. Partners often have to take on an unfair share of household responsibilities. Extended family members and close friends may have to financially help to compensate for the victim's failure to fulfill their responsibilities. Addiction leads to higher divorce rates. When both partners are addicted, the household atmosphere becomes even more toxic.[42]

Some partners will set limits, requiring that the victim get help and enter recovery for the relationship to continue as it is. Ideally, they will maintain some sort of caring connection while making a full relationship contingent upon recovery.

However, other partners may become overly involved with the victim's addiction to the point of dysfunction. They may attempt to sustain, save, or control the victim. They may feel trapped by financial or other social circumstances, such as having children together or have limited outside social supports.

Vulnerable partners often have low self-esteem and a tendency to deny their own needs and feelings. Out of their own lack of a sense of wholeness and their need for a relationship at all costs, they forego the need for a mutually accountable and loving relationship. They maintain a loyalty to their addicted partner, who does nothing to earn their loyalty. They may develop a "co-addicted" relationship where they:

- Adapt to and try to maintain the relationship at all costs, including the cost of their own well-being. They place the needs of the victim over their own needs. They have what some call a relationship addiction or love addiction.
- Attempt to control the uncontrollable, as only the victim of addiction can make the decision to ask for help to get into recovery.
- Enable the victim by defending them, providing for them, covering up their addiction, or making excuses for them.[43]
- Become excessively accommodating of the victim's behavior, compromising his or her own values and integrity to avoid anger or rejection.
- Overreact to disruptions, problems, and disappointments due to traumatic hypervigilance.
- Suffer from guilt, perfectionism, a need to please others, a

> compulsion to "fix" others, a fear of rejection, and a blurring of boundaries, where they take on the responsibilities of the victim.

Partners often experience chronic anger or resentment, stress, anxiety, or hopelessness. They may engage in inappropriate sexual behavior, such as having an affair, to get sexual and intimacy needs met. They may neglect their health and self-care. They often find themselves living increasingly isolated lives clouded by shame and stigma, while they put up a false front to the world.

Addiction increases the risk of violence in the home. More than half the defendants accused of murdering their spouses were intoxicated at the time of the incident.[44]

Addicted Children and Adolescents

It is traumatic to have a child suffering from addiction. Children with addiction bring conflict and crisis into the home.[45] Due to increased attention devoted by parents to the addicted child, siblings are often neglected. They may be left to fend for themselves, and may act out negatively to get attention. Addicted adolescents often have a parent who also suffers from addiction.[46] Adolescents are at greater risk of drug abuse when stressed. Common stressors are changing schools, moving, or divorce.

Warning signs of teen substance abuse include:

- Bloodshot eyes, dilated or pinpoint pupils, and using eye drops
- Missing money, valuables, or prescriptions
- Negative emotions, including anger, irritability, or depression
- Associating with lower-functioning, drug-using peers
- Loss of interest in activities or hobbies
- Secretiveness; demanding privacy, locking doors
- Avoidance; avoiding eye contact, spending less time with family members, sneaking around
- Dishonesty; lying about actions and activities
- Increased requests for money
- Acting irresponsibly; failing to do chores, homework, or follow through on commitments

Addicted adolescents are at increased risk for homicide, suicide, traffic accidents, and other injuries.[47] They can be violent and impulsive. They often break the rules, get into trouble with the law, and engage in risky sexual behavior. Adolescents with addiction also have an increased risk of psychiatric disorders, neurological impairment (especially with use of inhalants and solvents), and developmental impairment.[48,49] They associate with unhealthy, drug and alcohol-using peers. Consequences of addiction can include loss of educational opportunity, impaired social maturation, and a criminal record.

Parents often question or blame themselves for their child's addiction. When a child lives at home, parents can impose consequences and limits to get the child to accept treatment. This is more difficult for parents of young adults with addiction, especially when the young adult child lives separately from their parents.

Addicted adolescents in blended families face special challenges. Stepparents are generally less tolerant of the negative behaviors driven by the adolescent's addiction. Often both households reject the addicted adolescent who is acting out.[50]

Sometimes parents try to keep their addicted adult child afloat. They may fear what will happen to their child without their support. They may even fear for their child's life. Adult children may manipulate their parents with suicide threats to get financial or other supports.

Enabling addicted children shields them from the natural negative consequences of their addiction. This takes away ½ of the pain-hope equation needed for recovery. Sheltering the adult child also prevents them from going through the necessary "launching phase" of early adulthood.

When the Parent of an Adult Child Suffers from Addiction

Older adults can become addicted to alcohol or prescription medications, including opiates and benzodiazepines.[51] The statistics show that older adults consume three times as many prescriptions as younger adults.[52] They may abuse their medications to cope with health problems and loss. They then often hide their addiction. Sometimes their addiction presents as other medical problems. This can lead to children and providers not recognizing the addiction.

The addicted person may overwhelm their spouse, who doesn't know what to do or how to cope. Spouses may abuse or neglect the victim out of anger or fear. Other family members often need to help to manage the crises created by addiction. Grown children may have to take on a caretaking role for their parent. This role reversal can be difficult. It can cause stress for grown children, who may respond in unhelpful ways. For example, children may cut ties with their parents or not give any financial support.[53,54]

Addiction and Trauma

Addiction causes trauma. The trauma in families with addiction can have lifelong damaging consequences. Victims of trauma are more likely to suffer from Post-Traumatic Stress Disorder (PTSD) and depression. Both these conditions increase the risk of addiction as a coping mechanism.

Trauma survivors need help to heal. Therapy helps trauma survivors stabilize their lives, develop ways to recognize and voice their pain, and learn how to live with and bear their pain. Ultimately survivors can resolve their pain, transforming it through understanding, compassion, and forgiveness.

Treatment and Recovery

Since addiction damages the family as a whole, the whole family should seek treatment. This means repairing damaged relationships between everyone. Siblings can especially help addicted adolescents.[55] They can give healthy connection and nurturing. Healthy relationships and lack of conflict can protect the addicted adolescent. If other family members are addicting, therapists also need to attend to their addicting. The goal is to create a non-addicting family characterized by love, support, mutuality, honest and open communication, and accountability.

Families may need the help of multiple therapists to resolve their problems. These problems can include criminality, unemployment, domestic violence, abuse, and neglect. Healing a family often takes time and a team. Family members may need individual treatment, family therapy, or multifamily group therapy. Multifamily group therapy creates a positive, accountable recovery community where families can support and role model for each other. Providers need to communicate, coordinate, and collaborate with each other to provide effective treatment. Sometimes case conferences involving several providers can help to address conflicts, clarify treatment goals, and enhance the overall treatment.

When a partner suffers from addiction, the damage to both partners requires that both partners receive treatment to heal. Addiction is traumatic for everyone involved, so everyone needs care and attention.

Adolescents suffering from addiction often deny their illness. They will refuse treatment unless adults require it. It is essential to treat the family, especially any parental addiction, neglect, abuse, or other problems. The affected adolescent needs to return to a safe, stable, supportive, sober family environment. They should have supervision and therapeutic consequences for both sobriety and for recurrences of addicting. Addicted adolescents benefit from individual and group therapy. Mutual help groups such as Alateen, AA, NA, SMART Recovery, and others can also help adolescents recover.

Family or couples therapy is often necessary to heal the family. If family comes from a distance, intensive or extended family sessions may be necessary.

Affected family members may benefit from seeing a therapist themselves. They may find it helpful to attend mutual help groups. Options include Al-Anon, Alateen, Co-dependents Anonymous (CoDA), Adult Children of Alcoholics, Adult Children Anonymous, Families Anonymous, or Co-Anon.

Co-addicted partners with poor self-esteem or self-worth need help to find a sense of wholeness and worth apart from their addicted partner. They need outside support. They need help to stop enabling their addicted partner. Therapists should target any behaviors that reinforce the victim's addiction and the victim's unskillful or hurtful behaviors.

Treating addiction in blended families requires special considerations:

- There may be a need for more extensive education about the needs of the victim, the impact of addiction on the family, and what a family can realistically expect.
- It can be helpful for family members to exchange memories that they have not previously shared.
- A genogram can clarify each person's place and role in the family, and identify where addiction is and has existed in other family members.
- Therapists should help family members develop mutually acceptable language for referring to family relationships in blended families.
- Unhealthy family interactions need repair. A therapist first needs to develop trust with each family member by meeting and validating

each family member. Treatment begins with an alliance with each family member, where the therapist shows empathy to everyone.

Helping Someone Suffering from Addiction

The first step in helping a loved one with an addiction is acknowledging and accepting the Reality of things. See the truth of your loved one's addiction.

Next, educate yourself about addiction and recovery. Realize addiction is a neurobiological illness and not a moral failing. While the victim may have made unskillful choices then led to addiction, they are not responsible for having the illness itself.

With the above in mind, cast off any shame or embarrassment you feel about your loved one's addiction. Tell yourself that it is another illness, just like diabetes, that happens to affect the brain and not the pancreas or other body organ.

Several principles guide effective communication with people suffering from addiction. Take a positive approach that avoids confrontation:

1. Treat your loved one with the compassion you would give them if they had any other severe, life-threatening, chronic illness.
2. Remember that having an addiction makes one a sick person, not a weak or a bad person. Realize that addiction drives victims to do bad things.
3. Try to metabolize your hurt and anger into compassion and forgiveness. Make sure you approach your loved one with a supportive and loving heart. If you don't attack, accuse, vent, blame, or criticize, then they won't have to defend themselves. This will leave them more open to hearing your loving concern for them.
4. While you may hold them accountable for getting the help they need and for their actions in general, do not judge them for having the illness of addiction.
5. Avoid accusing your loved one, calling them names, or otherwise putting them down out of your own hurt and anger. Avoid negativity. Stay positive and hopeful.
6. Remember that their behavior results from neurobiological impairment. They are not themselves. Don't take what they may say or do to you personally.

7. Talk to them only when they are sober.
8. Try not to argue. Don't try to coerce your loved one by punishing them, threatening them, bribing them, or preaching to them. Simply state your observations, feelings, and love for them. Say what you hope for them, your wish for them to get treatment, and how you will modify the relationship if they don't seek help.
9. Talk to your loved one in a substance-free, supportive environment.
10. An addictions intervention specialist can support your attempt to help your loved one. They can help to orchestrate an intervention. An interventionist will help you prepare to maximize the possibility of a good outcome.
11. If possible, talk to your loved one with a group of family and friends that all care for them. Try to create the sense of loving community accountability. This will help them hear what you and others have to say.
12. Be concise and positive in your communications. Speak in short, simple, clear sentences.
13. Express how much you care about them. Tell them how much they mean to you. Remind them of all the good times and special moments you shared with them. Positive memories remind them how good life was before their addiction and of how good it could be again.
14. After establishing your love for them, gently raise your concerns for them. List specific behaviors you have observed, along with how these behaviors concern you or affected you. Tell them how their addiction is hurting you or others, but be careful not to blame or pass judgment on them. Use "I" statements, such as, "When you spend the night drinking, I feel abandoned, lonely and afraid of what you will do." In talking this way, you label your feelings.
15. If appropriate, you can reduce defensiveness by taking partial responsibility for your role in your relationship with your loved one. You might take responsibility for reacting out of anger, for judging, blaming, enabling, or for distancing yourself. Don't take responsibility, however, for things you didn't do.
16. Tell them you don't want to lose them or see further harm come to them. Offer to help them in any way you can. Ask them to get help, and offer specific treatment resources they can turn to for help. Tell them what the consequences will be if they don't get help. You may not

give certain material supports. You may separate to protect yourself from further harm. NEVER threaten to abandon them emotionally.

This approach reduces defensiveness. It lets the victim know you love and accept them. It also helps them to move out of the egocentricity of addiction and see the impact they have on people who love them. This is often the most powerful motivator for change.

When dealing with a child or teen with addiction, parents should:

1. Lay down rules and the consequences of breaking the rules. One rule is that you do not allow drugs and alcohol use. Make sure both parents agree with the rules and consequences. Make sure you can and will follow through on consequences, as hollow threats don't work. Mix positive consequences for not using with negative consequences of using. Try to keep the emphasis on positive rewards for not addicting.
2. Monitor your child's activity. Know where they are at all times. Know who they're with, and what they're doing.
3. Check for drugs: in backpacks, between books, in DVD or make up cases, in compartments in drawers, etc.
4. Create a positive family environment characterized by closeness, connection, support, and love. Catch your child doing something good and give well-earned praise freely. Make sure you connect with your child before you correct them. They need to feel loved and safe to hear what you have to say.
5. Know what your child is struggling with in life. What is stressing them? Are there problems at school? Are they being bullied or otherwise having peer problems? Make yourself available to talk to them. Try just to listen and show you understand. Then ask them what they need to help them through their difficulties. Explore with them what they can do. Be careful to avoid giving advice ("You should do this…") and instead make suggestions ("Have you thought about saying…"). Then ask how you can help.
6. Get help. Going to others diminishes the secrecy of your child's drug use. It creates more public accountability for your child. Rebellious children will often hear things better from a more neutral, outside authority figure. Options include a therapist, a mentor figure from

church, another beloved family member such as a grandparent, a close family friend, or a coach.

7. Be willing to engage in family therapy to create the best possible family environment for your child's recovery.
8. If all else fails, you may need to insist that your child go to a treatment program.

You can enhance your loved one's motivation for recovery in several ways:

1. Give them information on addiction with no pressure on them.
2. Ask them what they want to do. Help them develop ways to deal with their dilemma and reasons for changing that make sense to them, not you.
3. Give positive feedback for positive actions.
4. Help them build up a sense of hope they can change.
5. Acknowledge and accept them as they are in the midst of their disease. While setting limits and creating boundaries to protect yourself and not enable, make sure they know you love them just as they are, even when they are addicting. You may not love their behavior, but you love them. They should know they don't have to do anything to receive your love. Ironically, your acceptance of them with their addiction enhances the chances they will eventually choose recovery.

Remember that families can have a great influence on a loved one's addiction. Many people enter recovery because of family encouragement. As you continue to relate to your loved one:

1. Work to understand your loved one's triggers to addict. Then help them avoid these triggers.
2. Always communicate positively. Avoid negative behaviors such as yelling, screaming, pleading, manipulating, attacking, blaming, judging, or criticizing. Talk to them only when they are sober. Own your unhelpful behavior when appropriate, but hold them accountable for theirs.
3. Give consistent and reliable rewards for positive recovery behavior.
4. Support problem solving—both in your relationship and with their other difficulties.

5. Continue to practice good self-care. You are no good to your loved one or anyone else if you are no good. Relax, have fun, rest, get plenty of sleep, exercise, engage in a spiritual practice, and spend time with healthy people who love you.
6. Continue to set whatever limits and boundaries are needed to keep yourself safe. Protect yourself from abuse or violence.
7. Continue to encourage your loved one to accept help and work a recovery program.

Don't lose hope if your loved one can't see their addiction and the negative impact it has on them and those around them. Don't give up on them. Don't emotionally abandon them. Let them know you are there for them when they want help. Make yourself available to give emotional support. Keep the door open. If you must ask them to leave for your own well-being, for example, you might offer to visit them or to talk on the phone. Make sure they know you are there for them when they humble themselves, surrender to the need for help, and enter recovery.

Follow through on your consequences for your loved one if they continue to addict, but make it clear the many positive things that will occur should your loved one choose recovery. Follow through on these as well.

Don't cover up or make excuses for your loved one's behavior. Since pain is a stern but invaluable teacher, don't shield your loved one from the natural negative consequences of their behavior. Don't take over their responsibilities or otherwise do for them what they should do for themselves. This fosters an unhealthy dependence that takes away their sense of independence, autonomy, and dignity. While the victim may ask you for this type of help—or even try to coerce you into giving it—they will at the same time resent their dependence upon you. This can cause them to lash out at you.

Prepare for your loved one to try to manipulate you into supporting them again. Don't give into their manipulations. They may deny or rationalize their use, threaten you, or try to induce guilt in you. Don't buy into their attempts to get you to go along with their not getting treatment. Ignore their manipulations and stay firm with the need for them to enter treatment to avoid the negative consequences of addicting and to get the positive consequences of recovery.

Remember the "Three C's" of your loved one's addiction: you didn't Cause the addiction, you can't Control it, and you can't Cure it. You can't make anyone enter recovery. You can't "fix" anyone, including someone with an addiction. You also can't do their recovery work for them. Don't hide or throw out their drugs, alcohol, or drug paraphernalia in an attempt to control their addiction. Don't blame yourself for their illness. Never feel guilty or responsible for their behavior. Allow your loved ones to accept responsibility for their choices and actions.

NEVER use drugs, alcohol, or otherwise engage in the addicting behavior of your loved one with them.

If you decide it's safe to have an in-person relationship with a loved one who is addicting, see the victim only in substance-free environments. If they live at home, make sure the home is substance-free.

Get help for yourself. Seek out counseling or a support group. Some people benefit from Al-Anon or Narc-Anon. Read Dr. Meyer's book on the CRAFT approach to helping a loved one (in resources below). Talk about what you are going through with trusted family and friends. Focus on living a happy and fulfilling life while putting up boundaries and limits to protect yourself from being harmed by your loved one's addiction. Take good care of yourself.

Remind yourself that self-care is not selfish. If you are enabling your loved one out of your own shame, inadequacy, or feelings of unlovability, then own this. Renounce using the relationship to distract you from feelings of emptiness, loneliness, or fear. Instead, get help to achieve a sense of wholeness and fulfillment in your life apart from your relationship. Rebuild our own life. Create your own meaning and purpose apart from your relationship with your addicted partner. This will be better for your partner. If they enter recovery and go through their own life repair and integration, you will have two whole people enhancing each other rather than two broken people using the relationship in a futile attempt to create wholeness.

Let go of trying to control your loved one's behavior. Respect their autonomy and their need to make their own decision to change if they want to. Don't blame yourself for their illness or their behavior. Guard against their attempts to manipulate you by blaming you. Likewise, don't blame them for your own misery. Instead, take accountability for your own life. See your part in perpetuating the diseased relationship you have with your addicted loved one. Honestly look at yourself. Own your own unhelpful behaviors.

Getting help may show the victim that their actions are negatively impacting your life. It may also set an example for them that may inspire them to get help.

Set up boundaries and limit your relationship so as not to perpetuate the victim's addiction. Do not punish the victim. Don't give material support that in any way perpetuates the victim's addiction. If you feel you must give limited life-sustaining support, do not give money that the victim can use to buy alcohol or drugs. Instead, buy them the food they need or other life-sustaining goods and services. Try to not give material support unless your loved one has a medical or psychiatric disability. Giving material support can be harmful. It can foster an unhealthy dependency that robs a person of the opportunity to learn to take care of themselves and take accountability for their life.

Once your loved one surrenders to the need for treatment and enters recovery, give as much support—coupled with accountability—as you can. Do what you can to give or arrange for a sober environment to help minimize triggers for readdicting. Support their effort to get treatment and build recovery supports at mutual help meetings. Commit to a substance-free lifestyle with your loved one. Change any harmful patterns of behavior that promote addicting. Help your loved one minimize stress and maximize support. Encourage them to develop meaning and fulfilment in their life. Develop ways to play and have fun to reward their commitment to a life of recovery. Make sure they understand they need to work on their recovery consistently as they see fit to maintain the health of their relationship with you. Continue to hold your loved one accountable for abstaining from addicting and for getting back into recovery should they have a recurrence of addicting.

Be patient with your loved one. Recovery takes time. Addiction is a disease with remissions and recurrences. Be supportive when they readdict. Don't criticize, blame, or give up. Help them to let go of their shame for readdicting. Try to help them harness readdicting as a learning experience. But insist that they do what they need to do to get back into recovery.

Resources for family and friends of those who suffer from addiction include:

- Al-Anon.org—for family members of people with alcohol use disorder.
- Nar-anon—for family members of people with other drug use disorders.

- Gam-anon—for family members of people with gambling disorder
- Coda.org—for partners who identify themselves as having relationship dependency issues (co-dependency).
- Adultchildren.org—for adult children of parents who suffer from addiction.
- https://en.wikipedia.org/wiki/Community_reinforcement_approach_and_family_training.
- Get your loved one sober: Alternatives to Nagging, Pleading, and Threatening. Meyers, R. Wolfe, B. Hazelden. 2004.

CHAPTER 15

THE PROMISE OF RECOVERY

"The most beautiful people you have known are those who have known defeat, known suffering, known struggle, known loss, and have found their way out of the depths. These persons have an appreciation, a sensitivity, and an understanding of life that fills them with compassion, gentleness, and a deep loving concern. Beautiful people do not just happen."
—Elizabeth Kubler Ross

The joy of recovery emerges from a transformation of your experience, your worldview, and your actions. This transformation comes from following the Touchstones of recovery outlined in this book. It is not enough to simply read about them. True recovery calls for you to implement these Touchstones as foundational pillars in your life. The thing that changes in recovery is *everything*. While you may become abstinent, it's only the transformation that recovery work triggers that gives you the solution you were looking for. Keep the following Touchstones at the forefront of your mind and as an integral part of your life. These include:

Touchstone 1: Work on recovery

Touchstone 2: Create a positive recovery environment

Touchstone 3: Renounce addicting

Touchstone 4: Act with integrity

Touchstone 5: Heal

Touchstone 6: Love

Touchstone 7: Respect Reality

Touchstone 8: Grow

Touchstone 9: Persevere

Touchstone 10: Develop healthy relationships

Touchstone 11: Take accountability

Touchstone 12: Cultivate your spirituality

Recovery is challenging. It takes hard work over the course of a lifetime. It can be difficult. But it's doable. It's not easy, but you can recover if you only decide to do the work and persevere, humbly asking for the help you need with an open mind and an open heart. With recovery, you will become grateful for the pain of addiction. Each of the Touchstones in this book provides a part of the puzzle of the joy of recovery. No one Touchstone or area of focus will get the job done. Just like a car needs many different components, you need each of the Touchstones to keep moving in the right direction and shield yourself from addicting.

One key to a successful life is effective pain management, for life comes with both joy and pain. If you suffered from addiction, you likely managed your pain through reliance on addictive substances or behaviors. But in recovery, you practice a new way of managing pain by first minimizing unnecessary pain and then learning to metabolize your pain when it does occur in order to reduce your suffering. The truth is that recovery is the practice of optimal pain management.

While the disease of addiction is devastating, the promise of recovery is great, transforming a curse into a tremendous blessing. In recovery, you turn lead into gold, transforming your wounds into sources of wisdom, love, and compassion. These are gifts you can then share with the world around you, including your family, friends, and cherished loved ones.

Addiction gives you the gift of a prod to wake up and harmoniously engage Reality. In this engagement, practice *being* present with what is, *seeing* what is to be seen, and *doing* the next best thing.

You can only realize the blessings of recovery through gentle, persistent effort over a lifetime. Recovery is a dynamic way of being, seeing, and doing that, once achieved, you must maintain. It is a verb, not a noun. It is work. It requires an enduring commitment to a way of life as described in the Touchstones. Too many people wish for change without the willingness to do the work. The good news is that recovery works if you work it. This is eloquently captured in a classic passage from The Promises of Alcoholics Anonymous:

> If you are painstaking about this phase of your development, you will be amazed before you are half way through. You are going to know a new freedom and a new happiness. You will not regret the past nor wish to shut the door on it. You will comprehend the word serenity and you will know peace. No matter how far down the scale you have gone, you will see how your experience can benefit others. That feeling of uselessness and self-pity will disappear. You will lose interest in selfish things and gain interest in your fellows. Self-seeking will slip away. Your whole attitude and outlook upon life will change. Fear of people and of economic insecurity will leave people. You will intuitively know how to handle situations which used to baffle people. You will suddenly realize that God [Life] is doing for you what you could not do for yourself.

Be "painstaking" in your recovery. Fuel your commitment with the vision of recovery this book offers. But don't stop there. You'll also need the assistance, support, inspiration, and guidance of others. No one does recovery—or life for that matter—alone. Gather both courage and humility to reach out and ask for help, especially when you are lost in the clutches of addiction. Make recovery your first priority in life. Keep yourself in a positive state of mind, in a positive environment, surrounded by positive people. Take good care of yourself and give of yourself. Most importantly, never give up. Even when the light seems dim, continue to try your best to reengage and find the support and help you need. Always maintain your humble, surrendered willingness to be helped.

Recovery takes time. Be patient with the process. Enjoy each small step forward, grateful that the process never ends. Look forward to the next new achievement, the next new insight, the next transformation of your way of being, seeing, and doing.

Recovery does not happen by accident, but as a byproduct of intentional living. The Touchstones in this book are the fundamental building blocks for a life intentionally lived. A life of recovery is a life lived on purpose. Be mindful of your moment-to-moment intentions. Recovery occurs by making a conscious commitment to living for a higher purpose, in harmony with Reality. It will not happen by accident or without premeditation.

An intentional life of recovery is one in which you consciously work to meet both your basic needs and your spiritual needs. Do this by intentionally choosing to do what is true, right, and good, moment-by-moment. Put self-love before self-gratification. Consciously choose and commit to the practice of the several lifelong and recovery-enhancing habits described in the Touchstones. These habits make up your way of being, seeing, and doing in recovery. When you talk about "working" your recovery program, you are talking about the intentional cultivation of the Touchstones in your life.

Intentional recovery entails the patient and persistent practice of the positive recovery habits outlined in this book. Through these practices, you cultivate the possibility for the miracle of transformation to occur. Once you do, you'll never want to turn back. The joy of recovery is a wonderful thing. It is too good to give up. It uplifts, motivates, inspires, and directs you to a life filled with an abundance of happiness.

Several qualities of character benefit the practice of the art of recovery. I have discussed them in the Touchstones. Mindfully and intentionally cultivate these qualities as habitual ways of being and acting:

- Disciplined
- Committed
- Focused
- Clear
- Positive
- Acceptant
- Renunciation
- Submitted to a higher purpose
- Surrendered
- Interdependent
- Creative
- Flexible
- Persevering
- Courageous
- Generative

- Self-confident
- Intuitive
- Authentic
- Self-reverent
- Balanced
- Passionate
- Humble
- Honest
- Reliable
- Trustworthy
- Self-empowered
- Self-reliant

Cultivating these positive character traits is akin to replacing the bad habits of addiction with the good habits of skillful living. Take a daily inventory. Did you express these character traits in your life today? What did you do well? What can you do better tomorrow? With time, your efforts polish your character the way water polishes a stone. Through developing these positive character traits, you realize the Touchstones in your life and experience the joy of recovery.

Recovery, like life, is an adventure with both challenging and wonderful moments along the way. May you take this journey, and then enjoy it. Use this book along the way. It is your resource, friend, and reminder of the steps you should take each and every day to ensure you are on a path to joy. Addiction is a terrible monster to face, and no one should face it alone and without the support of many resources.

May this book be one of those resources. May it provide guidance and inspiration for your recovery journey.

APPENDIX A:
RECOVERY TOUCHSTONE ASSESSMENT

Scoring: 0 = Not at all. 1 = Very little. 2 = Somewhat 3 = Often. 4 = All the time.

To what degree do I:

Daily Recovery Practices	Score
Make recovery my first priority?	
Commit to lifelong recovery work?	
Develop my recovery skills?	
Stay wary of complacency?	
Recovery Environment	
Attend to my recovery environment?	
Minimize external triggers?	
Renouncing Addicting	
Pursue freedom from all addictive substances and behaviors?	
Avoid moving from one addictive substance or behavior to another?	
Manage distress and desire without addicting?	
Let go of what is beyond my control?	
Integrity	
Do the next right thing?	
Practice honesty?	
Put principle before pleasure?	
Healing	
Seek professional help?	
Manage stress?	
Address trauma?	
Manage emptiness?	
Loving	
Refrain from destructive behavior?	
Think before acting?	
Refrain from obsessing over others' faults?	

Let go of resentments?	
Refrain from judging?	
Cultivate compassion and forgiveness?	
Let go of shame?	
Manage anger constructively?	
Respecting Reality	
Not expect the world or others to be other than who they are?	
Not expect perfection from others or myself?	
Change what I can and accept the rest?	
Growing	
Learn from the past?	
Practice, practice, practice?	
Use slips and mistakes as opportunities for learning and growth?	
Pay attention to the feedback of others?	
Learn from pain?	
Persevering	
If I slip, immediately recommit to my recovery?	
Have faith in myself and the process of recovery?	
Practice patience?	
Healthy Relationships	
Develop recovery supports from those who have recovery experience and skills?	
Practice being assertive and authentic?	
Associate with those I wish to be like?	
Sit with my thoughts and feelings and share them with trusted confidants?	
Not try to "fix" anyone?	
Avoid isolating?	
Practice humility and respect?	
Have a healthy social network?	
Avoid socializing with anyone who is addicting?	
When possible, heal damaged relationships by making restitution and amends?	

Accountability	
Take care of myself so that I can care for others?	
Live with balance and savor life?	
Practice positivity?	
Live blame-free?	
Manage your vulnerabilities?	
Have a sense of meaning and purpose?	
Face my fears?	
Achieve my goals?	
Spirituality	
Take time for spiritual practice?	
Cultivate a deeper connection, beyond words, to others and to Reality?	
Practice mindfulness in all my daily affairs?	
Don't believe everything I think?	
Live both for myself and for something greater than myself?	
Live according to a higher set of principles?	
Keep perspective?	
See the Sacred in all things and people?	
Count my blessings?	
Live life out of love?	
Total	

APPENDIX B: RESOURCES

Chapter 2

A list of helpful organizations for promoting your recovery:

- Alcoholics Anonymous (www.aa.org)
- Cocaine Anonymous (www.ca.org)
- Co-Dependents Anonymous (www.coda.org)
- Computer Gaming Addicts Anonymous (http://cgaa.info/)
- Crystal Meth Anonymous (www.crystalmeth.org)
- Debtors Anonymous (www.debtorsanonymous.org)
- Dual Recovery Anonymous (www.draonline.org), for people with both addiction and psychiatric illness
- Food Addicts Anonymous (www.foodaddicts.org)
- Gamblers Anonymous (www.gamblersanonymous.org)
- Marijuana Anonymous (www.marijuana-anonymous.org)
- Narcotics Anonymous (www.na.org)
- Native American Indian General Service Office of Alcoholics Anonymous (NAIGSO-AA), (www.naigso-aa.org), a 12-step fellowship designed for Native American Indians
- Nicotine Anonymous (www.nicotine-anonymous.org)
- Overeaters Anonymous (www.oa.org)
- Sexaholics Anonymous (www.SA.org)
- Sex and Love Addicts Anonymous (www.slaafws.org)
- Shopaholics Anonymous (www.shopaholicsanonymous.org)

A list of Mutual Help Groups:

- Alcoholics Anonymous (AA) (aa.org)
- Adult Children of Alcoholics (ACA) (adultchildren.org)
- Al-Anon.org (al-anon.org) For family members of people suffering

with addiction.

- Cocaine Anonymous (CA) (ca.org)
- Food Addicts in Recovery Anonymous (FA) (foodaddicts.org)
- Food Compulsions Anonymous (foodcompulsions.wordpress.com)
- Gamblers Anonymous (GA) (gamblersanonymous.org)
- LifeRing Secular Recovery (lifering.org)
- Marijuana Anonymous (marijuana-anonymous.org)
- Narcotics Anonymous (NA) (na.org)
- Nar-Anon (nar-anon.org) For family members of addicts.
- Nicotine Anonymous (nicotine-anonymous.org)
- Refuge Recovery (www.refugerecovery.org) A Buddhist-oriented recovery approach emphasizing mindfulness, meditation, group support, and teaching on skillful living.
- S-Anon (sanon.org)
- Sexaholics Anonymous (sa.org)
- Sex and Love Addicts Anonymous (SLAA) (slaafws.org)
- SMART Recovery (smartrecovery.org). A self-empowerment program focused on monitoring and correcting addiction-promoting thoughts and behaviors.
- Women for Sobriety (WFS) (womenforsobriety.org)
- XA Speakers (xa-speakers.org) A collection of recordings from speaker meetings, conventions and workshops of 12-step groups.
- 12 Steps (12step.org) Resources for all 12 step programs. It contains an in-depth discussion and forum on the 12 steps.
- Celebrate Recovery (www.celebraterecovery.com). A Christian-based recovery movement.

A list of other online Self-Help Forums:

- AA Intergroup (aa-intergroup.org)
- Addiction Recovery Guide (addictionrecoveryguide.org)

- Addiction Survivors (addictionsurvivors.org)
- NA Chat (na-chat.com)
- Soberistas (soberistas.com)
- Support Groups (supportgroups.com) Covering a wide range of issues including: addiction, depression, anxiety and suicide
- 12 Step Forums (12stepforums.net)

Craving Management Techniques

There are many other ways to manage your cravings when they arise. Here are just a few:

1. Don't crave alone. Call someone and get together with them. Talk out your craving with them.
2. Don't make your cravings an enemy. They are just cravings. What makes them good or bad is how you respond to them. Remember that attitude is everything. Smile at them, knowing that enduring the distress of cravings is the pathway to healing. Smile, and say to yourself, "This is the feeling of healing."
3. When you get cravings, stop, pause, breathe, and think through the consequences of using. What will happen? How will you feel? Then think through the consequences of not using. What will happen? How will you feel?
4. Make a gratitude list. Carry it in your wallet or purse. When you get a craving, pull out your gratitude list and reflect on what you will lose if you act on your cravings.
5. Go to in-person recovery meetings, such as Smart Recovery, 12-step recovery meetings, LifeRing, Secular Organization for Sobriety, Women for Sobriety, Refuge Recovery, or church-based recovery programs such as Celebrate Recovery.
6. Go online to meetings and forums, such as those at www.smartrecovery.org or www.intherooms.com.
7. See a therapist once or twice a week. Attend a substance abuse treatment group.
8. Exercise.
9. Pray or meditate twice a day or more.

10. Journal. When you get a craving, write about how you will feel after you use, how it will impact others, and how you will feel if you don't use. Write about triggers or underlying feelings that are causing your cravings to arise.
11. Attend religious/spiritual/inspirational meetings.
12. Practice yoga, Tai Chi, or Qigong.
13. Go for long walks.
14. Read spiritual/inspirational/recovery literature, watch recovery videos, or listen to podcasts on recovery.
15. Engage in productive activities to distract yourself. Ask yourself, "What is the next best thing for me to do right now?" It may be getting the house cleaned, finishing a project for work, or catching up with friends. Substitute craving with a feeling of accomplishment.
16. Volunteer.
17. Give to someone.
18. Make a "Consequences Card." On one side list the benefits of abstaining. On the other side list the consequences of addicting. Laminate it. Carry it with you and review it whenever you get a craving. Also note the consequences of your addiction on those you love and who love you.
19. Sit with your cravings. This requires practicing meditation and mindfulness. If you have developed these abilities, you can engage in "Urge surfing"—watch your cravings like clouds in the sky of your awareness and wait for the cravings to pass. Center yourself in the still awareness that is your true self. From this place of mindful awareness, watch your thoughts and feelings as objects in your awareness. Don't allow yourself to get caught up in them. Let your Awareness unhook you from urges to use. Remind yourself not to believe everything you think, especially negative thoughts.
20. Envision the life you want to live. Imagine how acting on your cravings will/will not help you achieve your life vision.
21. Label cravings as just cravings and do not give yourself a choice. Remind yourself that every time you do not act on a craving, you strengthen your recovery. Label the craving as the "feeling of healing." Imagine how good you will feel when the craving has passed without addicting.
22. Distance yourself from any triggers. Get out of any high-risk or dangerous situations. Keep away from high-risk people.

23. Relax. Use deep breathing and muscle relaxation techniques.
24. If you rationalize or justify using, go over your thinking with your recovery mentor, therapist, or a recovery contact. Work to get clarity on your "mis-thinking."
25. When a craving comes, remind yourself that "this too shall pass." Comfort yourself with the thought that the craving won't last forever. Then practice the "4 R's" of craving management.
26. Practice thought-stopping techniques. Say "stop" out loud, visualize a stop sign, or snap a rubber band on the wrist. Note the thought, and direct your attention back to the Present. Identify the next right thing to do. Then do it without hesitation. Substitute craving thoughts with positive thoughts and images, such as images of healing, your ideal self, a future goal, or images of love ones. Pull out photographs of loved ones. You can also substitute craving thoughts with reflections on your consequences card. Reflect on the positive consequences of not using.
27. When cravings arise, don't "entertain the thought." Don't romance the addiction, thinking about the pleasure of addicting. This only seduces you into obsessing over "temporary gain" without seeing the much greater "long-term pain."
28. Some people benefit from medications to reduce cravings. For some, cravings are too powerful and craving management skills are too weak to manage cravings without medications. There is nothing wrong with using medication to help manage cravings as long as you do not use the medication as a substitute for recovery work.
29. Investigate the roots of the craving. What is threatening your well-being? What message might the craving be giving? Write in your journal to attain clarity, or explore it with a therapist or recovery support. Then address the pain with problem solving, perspective taking, or acceptance. If the problem, for example, is that you are lonely, pick up the phone or go to a meeting rather than numb it by addicting.
30. Soothe yourself. Treat yourself to something pleasurable that will not harm you or others. It might be a snack, entertainment, reading a good book, exercising, taking a bath, or playing a game.
31. Distract yourself. Busy yourself with reading, doing puzzles, knitting, playing a musical instrument, making models, learning to do something new, taking a course, playing video games (assuming you do not have a

tech addiction), going for a walk, listening to music, going to a movie, going dancing, going bowling, going to a sport event, making love, or doing research for a future project or event such as a vacation.

Chapter 4
The Pitfalls of Nicotine

Many in recovery continue to destroy themselves by using tobacco. 480,000 victims of nicotine addiction die every year from consequences of their addiction. Nicotine is one of the most addictive of all substances, on a par with opioids. Although roughly half of the 94 million tobacco users eventually quit, 45 million people continue to use tobacco, unable to stop.

Part of what makes nicotine addiction so insidious is that the lethal consequences of tobacco use are delayed. People do not experience immediate painful consequences to such a degree that they feel compelled to quit. Everyone knows that smoking, chewing, and dipping are harmful. But knowing this is not the same as having your life fall apart because of addiction, or nearly dying from an overdose. Immediate painful consequences bring about change more forcefully than delayed consequences. This encourages people to say, "I'll quit someday." Yet "someday" never comes until it is too late.

Several benefits of quitting other than health and economic benefits exist. Studies show that nicotine increases cravings for opiates, recurrence of addicting during detoxification from opiates, and possibly long-term opiate use.[56] Conversely, smokers who quit have more successful recovery from opioid use disorder. Tobacco use disorder is associated not only with higher rates of opioid use, but also of alcohol, cocaine, and cannabis.[57] Nicotine use is associated with higher rates of depression and anxiety. Fourteen studies have concluded that quitting smoking results in reduced rates of depression, anxiety, and stress.[58]

To quit nicotine, make a recovery plan. Prepare for quitting using the techniques in the section on preparing for recovery. The following nicotine cessation protocol gives other techniques to maximize the chances of quitting:

Nicotine Cessation Protocol

1. Make a 3x5 "Consequences Card." List reasons not to smoke/chew/dip. For example:

- Save money
- Enhance health
- Feel better
- Reduce risk of anxiety and depression
- Resolve guilt
- Have more energy
- Live longer
- Make those who love you happy
- Enhance integrity
- Enhance ability to meet friends and mates who do not smoke
- Be a role model to children/reduce their risk of smoking
- Enhance self-esteem
- Strengthen the ability to do what is right despite cravings
- Reduce the risk of using other addictive substances or engaging in addictive behaviors

Update your list as you think of new reasons. Carry your list with you at all times. Pull it out to review it every time you get an urge to smoke.

2. On the back of the card, list the bad things that will happen if you continue to smoke/chew/dip. Review these when the urge to addict hits.
3. Write a paragraph describing yourself at age 60 if you continue to smoke/chew/dip. Make it as detailed as possible. What will you look like? How will you feel? What diseases might you have because of your addiction? Then write a paragraph describing yourself at age 60 if you stop addicting with nicotine. Carry this in your purse or wallet. Review it when cravings arise.
4. Get two to four nicotine "supports." Make a promise to them to call them when cravings occur to review your list of reasons to not use nicotine and the benefits of quitting. Give them your lists.
5. Ask your co-workers, friends, and loved ones to be sensitive to the fact

that you are trying to quit smoking/chewing/dipping. Ask them not to use around you.

6. Set a "stop smoking/chewing/dipping" date.
7. Get rid of all nicotine products. Vow not to buy any more.
8. Don't put yourself in situations where you will be exposed to nicotine. Walk away from others who are addicting with nicotine.
9. If necessary, use bupropion, a nicotine replacement product, or varenicline.
10. If you slip, don't give up. Don't beat yourself up. Put out the cigarette or spit out the chew or dip as soon as possible. Throw away the nicotine product. Failure is not in picking up, but in giving up. Keep quitting until you succeed. Recommit over and over again.
11. If you smoke, practice a meditation: as you breathe in, say, "I'm killing myself." As you breathe out, say, "This is wrong."
12. Set rewards for not addicting. They can be small, medium, and big rewards. For example, going out to dinner every week could be a small reward. Going to a game or a spa once a month could be a medium reward. Going on a vacation once a year could be a big reward.

Most people who quit tobacco tried to quit an average of nine times. Success comes from perseverance. If at first you don't succeed, try and try again. With practice, you strengthen your commitment and develop the recovery skills and supports needed to succeed.

Chapter 6

An extensive list of addictive substances and potential medication treatments:

ALCOHOL

Disulfiram. Disulfiram is a chemical that interferes with the metabolism of alcohol. It blocks an enzyme that breaks down a toxic product of alcohol metabolism called acetaldehyde. When you drink on disulfiram, acetaldehyde accumulates in your blood stream, causing you to become hot, flushed, nauseous, drowsy, weak, and fatigued. You can experience a severe headache. You may vomit, have heart palpitations, or feel dizzy. Knowing this is in store if you drink, you abstain from alcohol. The typical dose of disulfiram is 120–500 mg daily. Someone taking disulfiram must avoid all alcohol, including in food. Disulfiram can be very dangerous for patients with psychotic disorders and some medical conditions. You must be highly motivated for recovery and have circumstances that mandate medication adherence. Otherwise, you will stop taking disulfiram when the desire to drink overcomes the commitment to recovery. Noncompliance is common. Since medications don't work unless you take them, the efficacy of disulfiram is limited. If medication adherence is mandated, such as when someone must take disulfiram to maintain their residence, then disulfiram can be effective. For people who take the medication, disulfiram promotes abstinence.[59]

Naltrexone. The FDA has approved naltrexone to treat alcohol use disorder. Naltrexone blocks opioid receptors in the brain. The stimulation of opioid receptors induces euphoria and reduces the discomfort of pain. Since alcohol induces some of its pleasurable effects by indirectly stimulating opioid receptors, naltrexone can reduce alcohol-induced euphoria by blocking endorphins from stimulating opioid receptors. For many people, naltrexone makes drinking less pleasurable. It breaks the positive feedback loop of addiction where the pleasure of the high causes people to want to drink more. The reduced reward of drinking can then result in less of a desire to drink. Naltrexone is good for people who lose control when they have one drink.

Naltrexone reduces heavy drinking, but does not always increase abstinence rates. As with other medications, naltrexone is most effective when combined with addiction therapy. Naltrexone comes as either a daily pill or as an every-four-weeks injection. Since many people do not take the pill regularly, the injection can improve adherence and thus recovery outcomes.[60] A typical oral dose is 50 mg a day. The intramuscular injection dose is usually 380 mg every four weeks. Naltrexone can cause liver inflammation, so clinicians check liver function tests, especially when just starting this medication. People usually tolerate naltrexone well. Side effects include nausea, headache, constipation, dizziness, anxiety, and insomnia. Since naltrexone blocks opioid receptors, narcotics will be less effective or ineffective for treating acute, severe pain at standard doses. People with acute pain syndromes requiring narcotic treatment need much higher narcotic doses and should stop taking naltrexone while receiving narcotics.

Acamprosate. The FDA has approved acamprosate to treat alcohol use disorder. Acamprosate interacts with an n-methyl d-aspartate (NMDA) receptor in the brain. It may help to restore a neurochemical balance between a calming neurotransmitter called gamma-aminobutyric acid (GABA) and an excitatory transmitter called glutamate. When you stop taking a substance you have developed a biological dependence upon, such as alcohol, you go into withdrawal. Acamprosate may reduce post-acute withdrawal symptoms (PAWS). Acamprosate may reduce cravings and compulsions to drink by making people feel better. Feeling better reduces slips and addicting by 14%.[61] It may work better in those with less severe alcohol use disorder who have just quit drinking. Acamprosate doesn't work in active drinkers; it seems to have effect only in people who are sober and engaged in a recovery program. The standard dose is 666 mg three times a day. Since the kidneys eliminate acamprosate, clinicians must reduce the dose in those with reduced kidney function.

Topiramate. Topiramate is an anticonvulsant medication developed to treat seizure disorders. Although not approved by the FDA to treat alcohol use disorder, some research shows that topiramate can reduce the number of heavy drinking days. It may do this by reducing levels of dopamine—a neurotransmitter associated with cravings and reward. People taking topiramate experience reduced cravings and compulsions to drink.[62] Topiramate can induce feelings of well-being. People taking topiramate often experience improvements in their overall quality of life. Just as suffering fuels addiction, reduced suffering promotes recovery. Topiramate can cause sedation, confusion, numbness and tingling in the hands and feet, mood swings, anxiety, and decreased appetite. Side effects increase at higher doses or when clinicians increase the dose too rapidly. The best success with topiramate comes when a prescriber starts a low dose and then slowly increases the dose over several weeks.

Ondansetron. Another non-FDA approved medication that reduces problem drinking in people whose addiction began before they were 25 (early onset alcohol use disorder) is ondansetron. Clinicians prescribe ondansetron to relieve nausea. Researchers believe ondansetron acts on serotonin receptors, causing a secondary decrease in alcohol-induced dopamine release. This then reduces the pleasurable sensations of drinking and compulsions to drink. Ondansetron at a dose of 4 mcg/kg twice a day increases the number of days abstinent in patients with a biological predisposition to alcohol use disorder.[63] Ondansetron is extremely well-tolerated. People can occasionally experience diarrhea, headaches, constipation, weakness, dizziness, and fatigue.

Baclofen. Baclofen is a muscle relaxant. It increases the secretion of gamma-aminobutyric acid (GABA), the major calming neurotransmitter of the brain. It thus has a relaxing effect. Like acamprosate, baclofen may reduce cravings and withdrawal symptoms.[64] It has been shown to induce abstinence from alcohol. The FDA has not approved baclofen to treat alcohol use disorder. We need more research to verify the efficacy of baclofen for alcohol use disorder.

Varenicline. Varenicline interacts with brain nicotine receptors. The FDA has approved varenicline to treat nicotine use disorder. Researchers later discovered that varenicline also reduces both cravings for and consumption of alcohol in males suffering from alcoholism.[65] The studied dosage was 1 mg twice a day. People generally tolerate varenicline well. It can cause nausea at higher doses, so it's best to take it with food. It can also cause vivid dreams and, rarely, nightmares. Early research suggested varenicline may induce depression or anger, but these findings have not born out.

Gabapentin. Like topiramate, researchers developed gabapentin to treat seizure disorders. Gabapentin also reduces neuropathic pain (nerve pain experienced as pins and needles). Gabapentin has a mild antianxiety effect. Gabapentin may work by promoting GABA activity in the fear center of the brain, the amygdala. This seems to result in reduced cravings for alcohol. In one study, gabapentin at doses of either 900 mg or 1200 mg a day increased abstinence rates from 4.1% with placebo to 17%. Gabapentin also cut the heavy drinking rate from roughly 80% to 56%.[66] Gabapentin reduces the symptoms of PAWS, including insomnia, anxiety, and depression. It also reduces cravings. Although gabapentin can cause drowsiness, dizziness, headaches, anxiety, and constipation, the large majority of people taking this medication experience no side effects.

Pregabalin. Pregabalin is a close analogue of gabapentin, with some studies showing it has an even greater anti-anxiety effect than gabapentin. It appears to reduce the release of the excitatory neurotransmitters, including glutamate and some excitatory monoamine neurotransmitters. Initial research reveals pregabalin to be very effective in treating alcohol withdrawal syndrome and in promoting abstinence after quitting drinking.[67,68] Like gabapentin, pregabalin also reduces the severity of PAWS, thus reducing cravings and rates of recurrence of addicting. Doses from 150–450 mg a day can be effective. Like gabapentin, pregabalin can cause drowsiness and confusion at higher doses. It is generally well-tolerated.

OPIOIDS

Methadone. Approved by the FDA to treat opioid use disorder, methadone is an opioid. It binds to and stimulates opioid receptors. Methadone is the most effective of all treatments for opioid use disorder. Patients most appropriate for methadone maintenance treatment are those with severe opioid dependence combined with impaired functioning. They benefit from the daily structure and supervision of a methadone maintenance treatment program (MMTP). Candidates for methadone treatment usually cannot achieve sobriety with other treatments.

Methadone acts as a replacement therapy. Patients take a controlled dose of methadone instead of heroin or narcotic pain relievers. Since methadone is an opiate, it eliminates cravings and withdrawal symptoms. At high enough doses, it blocks the effects of other opioids, helping to promote abstinence from street opioids. Methadone reduces crime and mortality due to the various consequences of illicit opioid use. It reduces opioid abuse by 34% and at least triples retention in treatment. Methadone usually restores patients' baseline functioning. Methadone maintenance patients enjoy more stable relationships, a return to productive work, and an improved ability to parent.

The three main drawbacks of methadone maintenance are inconvenience, side effects, and risk of overdose. Patients attending a methadone maintenance treatment program (MMTP) have to initially attend daily. Access to care is an issue due to the need to attend a clinic. With abstinence, treatment, compliance, and time, patients can earn up to a week or two of "take home" doses. With take homes, patients need only attend the clinic two to four times a month. Patients and staff need to plan for vacations by arranging for guest dosing at other clinics.

Methadone can cause fatigue and decreased motivation. Although many patients function just fine on methadone, some may feel dulled or apathetic. Finally, methadone can kill when combined with benzodiazepines, other sedatives, alcohol, and/or other opiates. Every year several methadone maintenance patients die of drug-related overdoses. An effective maintenance dose is usually 80–120 mg a day. Common side effects include sedation, reduced libido, and constipation.

Buprenorphine. The FDA has also approved buprenorphine to treat opioid use disorder. Buprenorphine is a partial μ-opioid receptor (MOR) agonist (receptor stimulator).[69] This means it only partially stimulates the main opioid receptor involved in opiate addiction. Buprenorphine is also a partial agonist at opioid receptor-like (ORL-1) receptors. It has mixed but primarily antagonistic (blocking) actions on μ-opioid (KOR) and δ-opioid (DOR) receptors.

Because buprenorphine only partially stimulates MORs, it does not cause as much respiratory depression as other opiates. This gives it a "ceiling effect," meaning that beyond a certain dose "ceiling" it does not have further effects such as respiratory depression and euphoria. This makes buprenorphine safe if taken without sedatives such as benzodiazepines or alcohol. It is an ideal drug for treating opioid use disorder because it eliminates cravings and withdrawal symptoms without causing significant euphoria, dulling, apathy, or sedation. It thus has little abuse liability.

Since buprenorphine binds to the MORs very tightly and stays bound to them for a long time, it blocks the actions of other opioids. Patients who slip on heroin or other narcotics often experience little or no effect, thus protecting them from a full-blown addicting. Unlike methadone, outpatient prescribers can give prescriptions for up to 28 days of medication for safe and stable patients, making buprenorphine treatment much more convenient than methadone treatment.

Patients who take buprenorphine responsibly and work a recovery program do well. They do as well if not better than patients receiving methadone maintenance treatment. Since outpatient buprenorphine treatment is less structured and supervised than methadone maintenance treatment, buprenorphine has greater risks of diversion and treatment non-adherence. This makes buprenorphine treatment less effective than methadone maintenance for people who have impaired functioning or who lack a sustained commitment to recovery. These patients need the extra structure and supervision that a methadone maintenance program provides.

Naltrexone. The FDA has also approved naltrexone to treat opioid use disorder. Naltrexone is a medication that blocks MOR receptors. If someone taking naltrexone uses opioids, the opioids cannot stimulate the opioid receptors. This prevents the user from getting high. With enough naltrexone in their bloodstream, patients will not return to addicting if overwhelmed by cravings and use.

The principle problem with naltrexone historically is that people will stop taking the medication when they get cravings to use so they can get high. Adherence rates are very low unless the patient must take the medication to obtain or retain something essential to them. Examples include a place to live, a job, or a marriage. Even these circumstances are not a guarantee, as cravings to use can be so strong that people will sacrifice housing, jobs, relationships, and freedom to use.

The effectiveness of naltrexone has improved some with the invention of a long-acting injectable (LAI) form of the medication. After being stabilized on oral naltrexone, patients can transition to a shot every three to four weeks. This can protect patients who have psychologically started the BUTA (building up to addict) phase of illness recurrence. Naltrexone protects patients while they obtain treatment and support to sustain their commitment to sobriety, to manage cravings, and manage the triggers that cause cravings. Patients receiving LAI naltrexone still return to addicting at a rate of up to 60%. Some patients use enough opioids at three weeks after their injection to break through the blocking effect of the remaining naltrexone. These people do better with injections administered every three weeks rather than every four weeks. As with oral naltrexone, supervision, structure, support, good treatment, and therapeutic consequences for both abstinence and addicting can improve the efficacy of this treatment. As with all addiction psychopharmacology, people have lower rates of addicting when providers pair medications with good treatment and supports.

People taking oral naltrexone typically take 50 mg a day. The LAI naltrexone dose is usually 380 mg every four weeks. Providers need to monitor liver function tests to ensure that naltrexone is not harming the liver.

Unlike methadone and buprenorphine, naltrexone does not take away the symptoms of PAWS. Some patients taking naltrexone experience strong cravings, depression, anxiety, irritability, unstable mood, fatigue, and insomnia. These symptoms result in higher recurrence rates due to medication non-adherence than for patients on methadone or buprenorphine. Patients on naltrexone often experience overwhelming urges to use to feel better, especially during the first few months of recovery. Naltrexone is extremely effective, however. Those with a strong commitment to recovery who take the medication despite their cravings and distress do well.

NICOTINE

You should combine addiction psychopharmacology for nicotine with other treatment modalities. Options include hypnosis, acupuncture, meditation, and cognitive behavioral therapy (CBT). You have a better chance of recovery when you have a strong commitment to abstinence, good recovery skills for managing triggers and cravings, and recovery supports.

Nicotine Replacement. Nicotine Replacement Therapy (NRT) does not work for smokeless tobacco products. For cigarette smokers, nicotine products act like methadone for opioids. They reduce nicotine withdrawal symptoms and cravings, thus improving mood and attention. They also reduce the reinforcing effects of smoking. Overall, NRT can increase the chances of quitting by up to 70%.[70]

Nicotine replacement products on the market include:

1. Nicotine patches
2. Nicotine gum
3. Nicotine lozenges
4. Nicotine inhalers
5. Nicotine nasal spray
6. Nicotine tablets that absorb under the tongue (not yet available in the US)

Nicotine patches reduce withdrawal symptoms, but do not eliminate breakthrough cravings, especially when triggered by smoking cues or stress. The patch is most effective when combined with craving management interventions and/or one of the other five nicotine replacement products listed above. These other products reduce intense cravings by delivering a surge of nicotine to the brain, like a cigarette.

A typical protocol for someone who smokes half a pack a day or more would be:

- Wear a 21 mg patch for 6 weeks.
- Wear a 14 mg patch for 2 weeks.
- Wear a 7 mg patch for 2 weeks.

This allows for a gradual tapering off nicotine. You may need more time to wean off nicotine. Some never succeed with this approach. For these people, wearing the patch indefinitely can prevent a recurrence of nicotine use. You can use nicotine gum, lozenges, inhalers, sprays, or tablets for breakthrough cravings. Use these products as a last resort when non-medication ways of managing cravings have failed. Otherwise, you may switch your addiction from cigarettes to these rapid nicotine delivery systems. Few people who use the patch stop smoking completely at first. Expect this. The patch makes it easier to stop smoking, recommit, and abstain. One study of five different smoking cessation medication protocols, which included bupropion (below), showed only the patch plus the nicotine lozenge increased abstinence rates after six months.[71]

Bupropion. Bupropion is an antidepressant. It increases levels of a neurotransmitter called dopamine. Dopamine is involved in motivation and reward systems in the brain. Studies indicate that bupropion reduces withdrawal symptoms, including depression, and cravings. Smokers can roughly double their chances of quitting by taking bupropion.[72] The recommended dose is 150 mg twice a day. Bupropion may also help by making cigarettes taste bad. Bupropion carries a small risk of seizures, especially in those with alcohol use disorder or eating disorders. People with these conditions should avoid taking bupropion.

Varenicline. Varenicline binds to nicotine receptors, partially stimulating them while also preventing nicotine from binding. While not as strong as nicotine, varenicline can still block withdrawal symptoms and the rewarding effects of smoking by blocking the effects of nicotine. In these ways, varenicline is like buprenorphine for opioid use disorder.

To tolerate varenicline, people must start with a low dose of 0.5 mg a day with food to avoid nausea. After a week, the dose increases to 0.5 mg twice a day. The dose then goes to 1 mg in the morning and 0.5 mg in the evening during the third week. Finally, the dose goes to 1 mg twice a day.

Varenicline can cause nausea and vivid dreams. Taking varenicline with food reduces the risk of nausea. Researchers have proven that initial indications that varenicline might cause depression, anxiety, or irritability are not true. Prescribers may need to lower the dose or increase the time between dose adjustments for people who are more sensitive to the medication.

The kidney excretes varenicline, so people with renal impairment need to take a lower dose. Varenicline doubles the chances of quitting. As with all other medications, combining varenicline with a comprehensive treatment program maximizes a person's chances of recovery.

COCAINE, METHAMPHETAMINE, AND OTHER STIMULANTS

No FDA-approved pharmacological treatments for cocaine use disorder or amphetamine-type use disorder exist at the time of this writing. Some respond well to substance abuse therapy, especially intensive individual therapy combined with substance abuse group therapy.[73] Some, however, simply cannot withstand the cravings they experience. Researchers have identified medications that can be helpful to these people.[74] These medications either calm the brain or provide a normalizing enhancement of brain activity. They modulate the activity of a variety of neurotransmitter receptors. Drugs that stimulate gamma-aminobutyric acid (GABA) receptors and beta-adrenergic receptors calm the brain. Drugs that activate and normalize brain functioning, thereby improving motivation and action, include glutamate, dopamine, and norepinephrine receptor promoters.

GABA produces a calming effect. The GABA-promoting medications **baclofen, tiagabine,** and **topiramate** may help reduce the risk of relapsing from cocaine by reducing stress-induced cravings.

Another drug that also calms physiological arousal and thus may reduce stress-induced cravings is **propranolol**, a beta-adrenergic blocker. Propranolol blocks outflow from the sympathetic nervous system—the system involved in your "fight or flight" response to stress and danger.

Glutamate serves as the main excitatory neurotransmitter of the brain. The drug **modafinil** indirectly promotes glutamate activity by stimulating histamine receptors and by inhibiting dopamine and norepinephrine transporters. By promoting glutamate activity, modafinil can reduce the fatigue and lack of energy people experience after stopping cocaine or other stimulants such as methamphetamine.[75,76]

Other drugs that increase norepinephrine in the brain include **doxazosin** and **nepicastat**. When given rapidly, doxazosin significantly reduces cocaine use.[77] Nepicastat is currently under investigation.

Novel medications that target the dopamine D3 receptor, may hold promise.[78] **Nalmefine**, a medication not yet available in the United States, reduced cocaine use in one case study.[79]

Citicoline is involved in the biosynthesis of the structural phospholipids of cell membranes. Citicoline also promotes dopamine activity. A recent study of citicoline (cytidine-5'-diphosphate) showed a significant reduction of cocaine use during the first 12 weeks of the study, showing a lessening of the addiction. Unfortunately, citicoline seemed to lose its effectiveness after 12 weeks. Citicoline may still play a useful role in helping people abstain from cocaine during the most vulnerable three months of recovery. It may provide space to make lifestyle changes and put recovery supports, structures, and practices into place.

People with ADHD and cocaine use disorder may benefit from treatment of their ADHD with stimulants that promote dopamine activity, with a simultaneous reduction in cocaine cravings. One study of high-dose extended release **mixed amphetamine salts** increased abstinence from cocaine from 7% without mixed amphetamine salts to 30% with mixed amphetamine salts.[80]

Even people without ADHD may benefit from other drugs that also promote dopamine activity in the brain. Some patients with a certain genetic makeup that gives them reduced activity of an enzyme called dopamine beta-hydroxylase have reduced dopamine activity. These people reduce their cocaine use significantly when given **levodopa**, another dopamine-promoting agent.[81]

Disulfiram, which increases levels of norepinephrine and dopamine, may hold the greatest promise in reducing cocaine cravings and recurrence rates. Several studies have shown disulfiram to reduce cocaine cravings and use, depending upon a person's particular genetics.[82,83,84,85]

Work has also occurred to develop a vaccine that prevents cocaine from entering the brain. Little work exists on medication treatments for other stimulants such as methamphetamine. **Topiramate** may reduce methamphetamine use in a subset of people with methamphetamine use disorder.[86,87] It may be that treatments for cocaine use disorder may also provide benefit for people suffering from amphetamine use disorder.

CANNABIS

Little research exists on medications for cannabis use disorder. One study showed a possible role for **naltrexone** in reducing the risk of a recurrence of addiction.[88] **Nabilone**, a synthetic cannabinoid used to treat nausea and vomiting in patients with cancer, and **dronabinol** (synthetic delta-9-tetrahydrocannabinol—THC) may reduce cravings.[89] Nabilone combined with naltrexone may reduce readdicting rates, cannabis self-administration, and the subjective effects of cannabis.[90,91]

Another study showed that **gabapentin**, a GABA-promoting agent, at a dose of 1200 mg a day, reduced cannabis use and withdrawal symptoms. It also increased mental functioning.[92] **Topiramate** appears to reduce the amount of cannabis used but not the percent of days used.[93] **N-acetylcysteine** in adolescents may also reduce cannabis use.[94]

Antidepressants may help with depression, thereby helping patients to work a recovery program and abstain from cannabis use. One study found that fluoxetine reduced both depression and cannabis use.[95] Caution should be exercised, because some antidepressants may worsen cannabis withdrawal symptoms, as was the case in studies of venlafaxine.[96,97]

People used to think cannabis produced only a psychological and not a biological dependence. We now know some people experience a significant biological withdrawal syndrome when they stop using cannabis. Up to 44% of people with cannabis use disorder report withdrawal symptoms, with up to 70% using cannabis to control their withdrawal symptoms.[98,99,100,101] Those who have used cannabis more often and for longer periods are more likely to experience cannabis withdrawal symptoms.[102] People can experience cravings, irritability, restlessness, depression, anxiety, insomnia, increased sleep, vivid and disturbing dreams, weakness, slowed movements, decreased appetite, and even nausea and vomiting. Most symptoms recede after three to four days, except for insomnia. Insomnia can get worse over time, suggesting a possible role for sleep agents in promoting recovery from cannabis use disorder. People with more severe cannabis use disorder experience more severe withdrawal symptoms, functional impairment because of withdrawal symptoms, and a greater rate of readdicting.[103]

Several studies have explored the medication treatment of cannabis withdrawal.[104,105] Researchers found **nabilone** to be effective for controlling cannabis withdrawal-induced nausea and vomiting. **Nabiximols**, a preparation of delta-9-tetrahydrocannabinol and cannabidiol that patients spray in their mouths on their inner cheeks, helps reduce cannabis withdrawal symptoms. It has no impact on long-term recovery rates, as is possible with naltrexone. **Dronabinol** and **bupropion** can also reduce withdrawal symptoms.[106,107] Withdrawal-induced insomnia can be treated with **quetiapine, zolpidem,** or **mirtazapine.**[108,109,110]

Chapter 12
Core Vulnerabilities and Virtues[111]

Defect	Virtue
Fear	Faith
Hate	Love
Egoism	Humility
Anxiety	Serenity
Complacency	Action
Denial	Acceptance
Jealousy	Trust
Fantasy	Reality
Selfishness	Service
Resentment	Forgiveness
Judgmentalism	Tolerance
Despair	Hope
Self-hate	Self-respect
Loneliness	Fellowship

The following tables contain more comprehensive lists of character virtues and vulnerabilities:

Character Virtues[112]

Acceptance: To consider circumstances, especially those that cannot be changed, as satisfactory.

Accountability: The quality or state of being accountable; especially, an obligation or willingness to accept responsibility or to account for one's actions.
Ambition: Having a strong desire for success or achievement.
Assertiveness: Disposed to or characterized by bold or confident assertion.
Beauty: The quality or aggregate of qualities in a person or thing that gives pleasure to the senses or pleasurably exalts the mind or spirit. Aesthetic harmony.
Benevolence: The disposition to do good.
Caring: To give care. A concern for someone or something.
Charity: Generosity and helpfulness, especially toward the needy or suffering. Aid given to those in need.
Chastity: Purity in conduct and intention.
Caution: Avoidance of rashness, attention to safety.
Cleanliness: Careful to keep clean; fastidious, habitually kept clean.
Commitment: The firm carrying out of purpose.
Compassion: Sympathetic awareness of others' distress, together with a desire to alleviate it.
Confidence: A feeling of one's powers or of reliance on one's circumstances. Faith in oneself.
Consideration: Thoughtful and sympathetic regard for the needs of others. Careful thought.
Contentment: The quality of feeling satisfied with one's possessions, status, or situation.
Cooperation: To associate with another or others for mutual benefit to achieve a shared goal.
Courage: A quality of spirit that enables you to face danger or pain without showing fear.
Courtesy: Polite, respectful, or considerate behavior; mindful of other people.
Creativity: The ability to create. A quality involving the generation of new ideas or concepts, or new associations of the creative mind between existing ideas or concepts.
Curiosity: A desire to find out and know things.
Defiance: Bold resistance (to what is evil or unjust).
Dependability: Reliable, worthy of reliance or trust.

Detachment: Freedom from attachments.
Determination: Firmness of purpose.
Devotion: A great love or loyalty, enthusiastic zeal.
Diligence: Conscientiousness in paying proper attention to a task; giving the degree of care required in a given situation. Persevering determination to perform a task.
Discernment: The ability to distinguish; judgment; discrimination; to distinguish between things; to perceive differences that exist.
Discretion: Being discrete in one's speech, keeping secrets.
Discipline: The trait of being well-behaved and under control.
Eloquence: Powerful and effective language. Fluent, persuasive, and articulate speech.
Empathy: Identification with and understanding of another's situation, feelings, and motives.
Enthusiasm: A feeling of excitement.
Excellence: The quality of excelling; possessing good qualities in high degree.
Exuberance: Overflowing with eager enjoyment or approval.
Faith: Complete confidence in a person, plan, or set of beliefs, etc.
Faithfulness: Steadfast in affection or allegiance; loyal.
Flexibility: Adaptable, able to be changed to suit circumstances.
Focus: Concentrated awareness and effort.
Forbearance: Restraint under provocation; patience; good-natured tolerance of delay or incompetence.
Forgiveness: To cease feeling angry or bitter toward a person or about an offense.
Fortitude: Strength of mind that enables one to endure adversity with courage.
Friendliness: A tendency to be pleasant and accommodating.
Frugality: Prudence in avoiding waste. Being economical with resources.
Generosity: Giving or ready to give freely, free from meanness or prejudice.
Gentleness: Moderate; mild, quiet; not rough or severe.
Grace: Elegance and beauty of movement or expression.
Gratitude: Being thankful.
Helpfulness: The quality of providing useful assistance.
Honesty: Truthful; sincere; not lying or cheating.
Honor: Not disposed to cheat or defraud; not deceptive or fraudulent.

Worthy of being honored.
Hope: The general feeling that some desire will be fulfilled.
Humbleness: Modest; not arrogant or boastful.
Humility: A disposition to be humble; a lack of false pride.
Humor: The ability to perceive, enjoy, or express what is amusing, comical, incongruous, or absurd.
Idealism: High mindedness; elevated ideals and conduct; the quality of believing that ideals should be pursued.
Integrity: Moral soundness; consistency of values and actions; unbroken completeness with nothing lacking.
Impartiality: Fair. An inclination to consider both views and opinions equally without bias.
Industry: Diligent, hardworking.
Innocence: Guileless, not guilty.
Joyfulness: The emotion of great happiness.
Justice: Fair, impartial, giving a deserved response.
Kindness: Friendly, helpful, well-meaning.
Knowledge: Part of the hierarchy made up of data, information, and knowledge. Data are raw facts. Information is data with context and perspective. Knowledge is information with guidance for action based upon insight and experience.
Liberality: An inclination to favor progress and individual freedom; the trait of being generous in behavior and temperament.
Love: A deep, tender, ineffable feeling of affection and solicitude toward a person, such as that arising from kinship, recognition of attractive qualities, or a sense of underlying oneness.
Loyalty: Steadfast in allegiance to one's homeland, government, or sovereign. Faithful to a person, ideal, custom, cause, or duty.
Magnanimity: The virtue of being great of mind and heart. It encompasses, usually, a refusal to be petty, a willingness to face danger, and actions for noble purposes.
Majesty: Great and impressive dignity.
Meekness: The feeling of patient, submissive humbleness; a disposition to be patient and longsuffering.
Mercy: Clemency; leniency and compassion shown toward offenders by a person or agency charged with administering justice.

Moderation: The avoidance of extremes in one's actions or opinions.
Modesty: Freedom from vanity or conceit. Not inclined to boast.
Obedience: Willingness to obey, to be controlled when necessary, to carry out orders.
Openness: Ready and willing to talk candidly, not secretive.
Orderliness: Neatness and tidiness. A personality trait which involves the organization of things into a state of order and symmetry. The quality of appreciating method and system.
Patience: The ability to endure delay, trouble, pain, or hardship.
Peace: Freedom from mental agitation; serenity.
Perseverance: Being persistent, refusing to stop despite failures, delays, and difficulties.
Persistence: Never-ceasing, relentless.
Piety: Humble devotion to a high ideal.
Prudence: Wise or careful in conduct. Shrewd or thrifty in planning ahead.
Punctuality: The quality or habit of adhering to an appointed time.
Purity: Freedom from defilement. Undiluted or unmixed with extraneous material. Unsullied by sin or moral wrong.
Purposefulness: Having a definite goal.
Reliability: Can be trusted to do something.
Resoluteness: The quality of being firm in purpose.
Resourcefulness: The ability to act effectively or imaginatively, especially in regard to difficult situations and unusual problems.
Respect: Admiration for others. Treating people with due dignity.
Responsibility: Having control over and accountability for appropriate events.
Restraint: Holding back.
Reverence: Profound awe and respect.
Righteousness: Adhering to moral principles. Holiness.
Selflessness: The quality of unselfish concern for the welfare of others.
Self-sacrifice: The giving up of one's own benefit, especially giving up one's life, for the good of others.
Service: Work done by one person or group that benefits another.
Sensitivity: Heightened awareness of oneself and others within the context of social and personal relationships.
Silence: Inner peace. Being silent.
Simplicity: Straightforward; not complex or complicated. Unpretentious.

Sincerity: Free from pretense or deceit in manner or actions.
Sobriety: Serious, solemn, and calm. Free from intoxication.
Spontaneity: Natural, not planned.
Steadfastness: Firm, resolute; determinedly unwavering.
Strength: Capable of exerting great force.
Tact: Consideration in dealing with others and avoiding giving offense.
Temperance: Moderation and self-restraint, as in behavior or expression. Restraint in the use of or abstinence from alcoholic liquors/intoxicants.
Thankfulness: Warm, friendly feelings of gratitude.
Thrift: The characteristic of using a minimum of something. Saving.
Tolerance: Tending to permit, allow, understand, or accept something; tending to withstand or survive.
Toughness: Strong and durable; not easily damaged.
Tranquility: Serenely quiet and peaceful; undisturbed.
Trust: Having confidence in others; lacking suspicion.
Trustworthiness: Able to be trusted or depended on; reliable.
Truthfulness: Accurately depicting what is real.
Understanding: Comprehension, assimilation of knowledge. The holistic awareness of facts.
Unity: Freedom from division. Oneness.
Vitality: Exuberant physical strength or mental vigor, energy.
Wisdom: The trait of utilizing knowledge and experience with common sense and insight.
Wonder: The feeling aroused by something strange and surprising.
Zeal: Ardor. A feeling of strong eagerness. Tireless devotion.

Character Vulnerabilities[113]
Abusive: Mistreating, hurting, or harming others.
Aloof: Being indifferent to or disinterested in others. Being apart from others.
Angry: Prone to strong feelings of displeasure over a perceived wrong or failure of others to meet one's expectations.
Antagonistic: Oppositional, hostile, unfriendly.
Anxious: Not as a clinical diagnosis but as a general way of viewing things with an eye toward what is wrong, what might be wrong, what has been wrong, or what is going to be wrong. Excessive worry, especially about things one cannot change.

Apathetic: Indifferent, unresponsive, having or showing little or no emotion.
Apologetic (overly): Apologizing for events beyond your control or for which you had no responsibility.
Appearances: (preoccupied or obsessed with.)
Argumentative: Tendency to disagree with or oppose the statements of others.
Arrogance: Offensive display of superiority or self-importance; overbearing pride.
Attention-seeking: A tendency to make oneself the center of attention with others, as opposed to giving attention to others.
Avarice: Insatiable greed for riches or material possessions.
Avoiding confrontation: Failure to assert one's needs or to address the harmful behavior of others.
Beating yourself up: Inappropriate self-condemnation and lack of self-acceptance of one's mistakes and imperfections.
Beauty: (obsession or preoccupation with.)
Bigotry: Stubborn and complete intolerance of any creed, belief, or opinion that differs from one's own.
Blaming: To hold others responsible or to condemn others for actions and events, particularly as a way of avoiding accountability for one's own role in bringing about these actions and events.
Boastful: To be predisposed to speaking with exaggeration and excessive pride, especially about oneself.
Boundaries (not setting): Either inappropriately sharing information about oneself or inappropriately asking others for personal information about themselves.
Busybody: Prying into or meddling in the affairs of others.
Cheating: To deceive, defraud, elude, or deprive someone of something that is rightfully theirs.
Closed-mindedness: Contempt prior to investigation. Disregarding things and ideas just because they are new and unknown. Being unwilling to try things or follow suggestions. Failing to remain teachable. Having a mind firmly unreceptive to new ideas or arguments.
Codependent: Maintaining a relationship that is harmful to oneself out of fear of losing the relationship.
Cold-heartedness: An inability to feel authentic warmth, care, or sympathy.
Communication (avoiding, poor): Not expressing oneself clearly, authentically, and respectfully. Engaging in hurtful speech.

Companions (seeking corrupt companions): Associating with people with negative or destructive behaviors (either to self, such as with addiction, or to others, such as with sociopathy).
Competitive (excessively): Excessive tendency to strive to outdo another for acknowledgment, a prize, supremacy, profit, etc.
Complaining: Negatively focusing on what is wrong. Lacking acceptance of what one does not like or prefer. Avoidance of problem solving or seeing how a situation can be improved or corrected.
Complacent: Pleased, especially with oneself or one's merits, advantages, situation, etc., without awareness of a potential danger or defect; unrealistically self-satisfied.
Conceit: Having an excessively favorable opinion of one's own virtue, ability, importance, wit, gifts, or talents.
Condemning: Excessively harsh negative judgments of others with a lack of compassion and understanding. Lack of acceptance of one's self or others' imperfections and humanity.
Confrontation: (avoiding out of fear or a lack of self-worth.)
Controlling attitude toward people, places, and things: Trying to control others by manipulation, bribery, punishment, withholding things, or tricking them into acting as you wish, even when you believe it is in their best interest to do so. Failing to be equal partners with others and to consider their knowledge and opinions.
Cowardice: Lacking in courage to face danger, difficulty, opposition, pain, etc.
Critical: Inclined to find fault or to judge with severity, often too readily.
Crude: Lacking in intellectual subtlety, perceptivity. Lacking culture, refinement, or tact.
Dependency, over dependency, codependency: Relying on others to provide for you what you ought to provide for yourself. Feeling you must be in a relationship or must hold on to others who want to move on. Letting others control you to an extreme due to your fear of being alone, abandoned, or independent.
Destructive: Causing harm to self or others.
Devious: Not being straightforward with others. Being shifty or crooked in one's dealings with others.
Different: (thinking you are.)
Disease: (feeling responsible for/taking credit for, making excuses for, not accepting.)

Dishonesty: Sins of omission and commission. Telling lies, hiding things, telling half-truths, or pretending something is so that isn't. Withholding important information. Adding untrue details to stories and situations.

Disorganized: Lacking organization or planning in one's daily affairs.

Egotistical: Given to talking about oneself; vain; boastful; opinionated, indifferent to the well-being of others; selfish.

Envious: Wanting what others have; feeling you don't have enough or deserve more. Wishing you had what others do instead of them. This applies to material possessions like houses, cars, money, and such. It also applies to nonmaterial things like relationships, a nice family, children, parents, friends and partners, and fulfilling work relationships. You can envy others—their looks and physical appearance, their talents and physical abilities or attributes such as thinness, tallness, sports ability, or musical talent.

Exaggeration: Embellishing or overstating the truth to enhance one's image with another, to impress others, or to make others or events out to be either worse or better than they really are.

Excess: Overindulgence in pleasurable activities. Acquiring more than what one needs.

Exploitative: To take advantage of others for one's own selfish gain.

Faith (lack of): Lacking confidence or trust in others or things. Lacking belief, such as in a code of ethics or in moral principles.

Fanatical: Extreme, uncritical enthusiasm or zeal. Often in religion or politics.

Fantasizing: Conceiving fanciful or extravagant notions, ideas, suppositions, or the like. Becomes a vulnerability when fantasizing becomes a substitute for Reality and purposeful action.

Favoritism (playing favorites): Not treating others equally. Not being impartial.

Fearful: Prone to excessive fear, dread, or apprehension.

Filthy-mindedness: Tendency to think about crude or degrading subjects.

Financial dependency: Failure to support oneself financially.

Financially insecure: Failure to save and budget.

Following through (failing to): Lack of accountability to do what one says one will do.

Forgiveness (lack of): An inability to let go of resentments for the perceived misdeeds of others.

Frustration: Feeling dissatisfied, often accompanied by anxiety or depression, resulting from unfulfilled needs or unresolved problems.

Gluttony: Excessive eating and drinking.
Greed: Wanting and taking too much food, sex, time, money, comfort, leisure, material possessions, attention, and security. Acquiring things (material things, relationships, attention) at the expense of others.
Gossiping: Speaking or writing about others in a negative manner, especially to get them in trouble or to feel superior to them and bond with someone else against the target of the gossip. When you find yourself talking about someone, pause and ask yourself why you're mentioning their name.
Guilt: Feeling excessive guilt about sexual fantasies or other socially unacceptable thoughts; excessive feelings of guilt out of proportion to the act; feeling guilty for things beyond your control.
Harshness: Being ungentle, unpleasant, stern, or cruel.
Hatred (of self, people, places, things, situations): Showing intense dislike, extreme aversion, or hostility.
Health (lack of responsibility for or neglect of): Engaging in actions that are harmful to one's health, such as not getting exercise, eating excessively, eating foods that are harmful to the body, and addicting.
Help (refusing/not asking for): An inability to recognize and accept one's need for assistance. An inability to ask for help or to allow others to offer help.
Hopelessness: A persistent feeling that what one wants cannot be had. That events will turn out for the worse. That nothing good can result from a situation.
Humility (lack of): Having an exaggerated opinion or estimate of one's own importance, rank, or status. Having a denial or disregard for one's own imperfections, weaknesses, or vulnerabilities.
Inaction: Failure to act according to the demands of a situation.
Inconsiderate: Lacking regard for the rights or feelings of others. Acting without consideration of others. Being thoughtless of the feelings or needs of others.
Indecisive: Inability to make a decision when faced with a choice.
Indifferent: Lacking interest or concern for people or events.
Ignorant: Lacking common basic life knowledge. Being uninformed or unaware.
Immodest: Being indecent, shameless, pretentious, or forward with others.
Impatience: Being frustrated by waiting, wanting often to be some time in

the future, wanting something to change or improve rather than accepting it as it is. Not accepting the pace at which things happen.
Impulsive: Acting or saying something without thinking through the consequences. Inability to inhibit urges or the expression of emotions.
Inadequate: Feeling deficient, inept, unsuitable, or ineffective in response to emotional, social, intellectual, or physical demands in the absence of any obvious mental or physical deficiency.
Insecure: Feeling fears or doubts about one's abilities, talents, thoughts, or feelings. Not feeling self-confident or self-assured.
Insensitive: Unresponsive to or unaware of the needs and feelings of others. Lacking human sensibility, feelings for others, or consideration of others. Being callous.
Insincere: Not being honest in the expression of actual thoughts or feelings.
Intolerance: Not accepting people or things for whom or what they are.
Irresponsible: Not being accountable for things that are within one's power, control, or management. Failing to meet promises or obligations. Behaving with disregard for what is appropriate or expected.
Isolative: Avoiding social contact with others.
Inventory-taking: Focusing on the actions, issues, traits, and flaws of others to avoid looking closely at oneself and take accountability for one's own actions, issues, traits, and flaws.
Judgmental: Noticing and listing out loud or to yourself the faults of others. Passing judgment on others without a full understanding. Condemning others for their mistakes and imperfections, often while disregarding one's own mistakes and imperfections. Having a lack of compassion for human imperfection.
Jealous: Upset or threatened by someone's attachment to or affection for another person, leading to feelings of hurt, anger, resentment, fear, or suspiciousness. Intolerance of rivalry for the affections of another person.
Knowing it all: A compulsive need to have an answer to everything. An inability to not know, to doubt, or to be open to the opinions, explanations, or observations of others.
Lazy: Not wanting to work, exert oneself, or engage in activities.
Leering: Looking at others with lustful interest or with sly and malicious intentions.
Lifestyles (not accepting others'): A belief that one's personal lifestyle is the

best and only appropriate lifestyle. An intolerance of the differing lifestyles and cultures of other people.

Love and friendship (refusal to accept): An inability to engage in mutual, caring relationships in which people give and receive love and friendship.

Lustful: Being driven by an intense sexual desire or appetite, with uncontrolled illicit sexual desires. An overwhelming craving for something (sex, power, money, possessions, etc.).

Manipulative: Attempting to influence the behavior or emotions of others for one's own purpose, often with a disregard for others' well-being.

Materialistic: Excessively concerned with physical comforts or the acquisition of wealth and material possessions, rather than with spiritual, intellectual, or cultural values.

Measuring self against others: Inability to accept oneself for who one is, leading to the comparison of oneself to others. When comparing oneself to others you see as better than you, this leads to feelings of inferiority, envy, and resentment. When comparing yourself to others less fortunate or talented than you, this leads to feelings of superiority, arrogance, or false pride.

Meddlesome: Involving oneself in a matter without right or invitation. Interfering in the affairs of others when this is not welcome.

Messy: Tendency to be dirty, untidy, or disorderly.

Miserly: To be stingy or greedy. To focus on gaining and hoarding material wealth or goods.

Negative body image: To have a lack of acceptance and appreciation for one's body. To be overly preoccupied with one's perceived bodily imperfections.

Negative: Seeing the dark side of a situation. Focusing on problems and defects rather than on opportunities, solutions, strengths, or assets.

Neglectful: Disregarding, indifferent, or careless. Failing to carry out duties and obligations to others. Failing to pay attention to others or to one's own needs.

Opinionated: Obstinate or conceited with regard to the merit of one's own opinions. Conceitedly dogmatic. Inability to consider the opinions, viewpoints, or observations of others.

Overcompensating (for projected wrongs, for weaknesses): Pursuing perfection or overachievement to cover up an underlying feeling of being defective, inadequate, or deficient in some way.

Perfectionism: Expecting or demanding too much from oneself or others. Treating things that aren't perfect as not good enough. Not recognizing a good attempt or progress.
Pessimism: Not as a clinical condition but to generally see the dark, negative side of things.
Physical appearance (obsession or preoccupation with): Overinvesting in one's physical appearance as a sign of one's value, appeal, attractiveness, or self-worth at the expense of a consideration of one's actions or character.
Playing God: Arrogantly attempting to control people, places, or things with a sense of grandiosity and entitlement; feeling that one's opinions, needs, and preferences are superior to others'.
Possessive: Jealously opposed to the personal independence and autonomy of another person. Being unwilling to share people or things with others.
Preachy: Tediously or pretentiously lecturing others.
Prejudiced: Pre-judging people based on a group they belong to. Negative feelings about someone based on their religion, race, nationality, age, disability, sexual orientation, accent, politics, economic status, or physical characteristics like height, weight, hair style, clothing style, and physical fitness.
Prideful (false, intellectual, spiritual): Excessively high or inordinate opinion of one's own dignity, importance, merit, or superiority, whether as cherished in the mind or as displayed in bearing, conduct, etc.
Procrastinating: Putting off or delaying doing things that need to be done.
Rationalizing, minimizing, and justifying: Avoiding responsibility or accountability for one's actions by making excuses.
Self-justification: Saying and/or believing one had good motives for bad behavior. Saying that one did bad things for good reasons or that what one did really wasn't that bad.
Stealing: Taking things that aren't yours and that you aren't entitled to.
Racist: Believing that one's own racial group is superior or that a particular racial group is inferior to the others.
Reckless: Unconcerned about the consequences of one's actions. Acting carelessly and without caution.
Remorseful: Excessive tendency to be absorbed in painful regret for wrongdoing. Inability to forgive oneself, learn from past mistakes and misdeeds, and resolve to do better in the future.

Resentment: The feeling of displeasure or indignation at some act, remark, person, etc., regarded as causing injury or insult.
Rigidity and fear of change: Stubbornly sticking to one belief, perception, habit, or way of doing things in the face of changing circumstances that call for changes to improve upon a situation.
Rudeness: Being deliberately impolite or discourteous.
Sarcastic: Tendency to make derisive, sneering, taunting, or cutting remarks.
Secretive: Tendency to withhold the truth from others, either out of fear, or to gain an advantage over others.
Self-absorbed: Focusing on one's own needs, feelings, and thoughts at the expense of attending to the needs, feelings, and thoughts of others.
Self-aggrandizing: A preoccupation with increasing one's own power and wealth, usually aggressively.
Self-centered: Concerned solely or chiefly with one's own interests, welfare, etc.; engrossed in oneself; selfish; egotistical.
Self-condemning: To excessively disapprove or negatively judge oneself. Driven by a lack of self-acceptance or a need to be perfect.
Self-deprecating: Belittling or undervaluing oneself; being excessively modest.
Self-hatred: Having an intense dislike or hostility toward oneself.
Self-important: Having or showing an exaggerated opinion of one's own importance; pompously conceited or haughty.
Self-indulgent: Indulging one's own desires, passions, whims, etc., especially without restraint.
Self-justifying: Justifying oneself, especially by offering excessive reasons, explanations, excuses, etc., for an act, thought, or the like.
Self-loathing: A strong dislike or disgust in oneself; intense aversion to oneself.
Self-pity: Pity for oneself, especially a self-indulgent attitude concerning one's own difficulties, hardships, etc.
Self-reliant: Relying on oneself or on one's own powers, resources, etc. This becomes a vulnerability when one refuses to ask for or accept help when facing a problem one cannot overcome alone.
Self-seeking: The seeking of one's own interest or selfish ends.
Selfishness: Spending excessive time thinking about oneself. Considering oneself first in situations. Not having enough regard for others or thinking about how circumstances hurt or help others. Thinking about what one can

get out of situations and people. What's in it for me? Spending too much time considering one's appearance, acquiring things for oneself, pampering oneself, indulging oneself.

Setting expectations: (too low or too high—of self or others.)

Sex: A vulnerability when compulsive, selfish, deceptive, or harmful to self/ others.

Skeptical: Prone to excessive doubt or disbelief.

Sloth: Not doing as much as is reasonable to do. Putting things off repeatedly. Not carrying one's own load as much as one is able. Letting others provide things that one ought to get for oneself.

Stepping on others to get to the top: Grasping for power at the expense of others.

Stewardship of assets (poor): Failing to conserve important resources.

Suspicious: A tendency to believe others are guilty, false, undesirable, defective, or bad, with little or no proof.

Thoughtless: Lacking in consideration for others; inconsiderate; tactless.

Thrill-seeking: Compulsive and excessive pursuit of excitement at the expense of other important life-goals.

Uncharitableness: Deficient in charity; unkind; harsh; unforgiving; censorious; merciless.

Uncleanliness: Tendency to be unclean, dirty, impure, evil, or vile.

Uncompassionate: Failure to experience a feeling of deep sympathy and sorrow for another who is stricken by misfortune, accompanied by a lack of desire to alleviate the suffering.

Undependable: Incapable of being depended upon; unworthy of trust; unreliable.

Undisciplined: Failing to keep to a task or obligation with order and control.

Unfaithful: Not fulfilling duties, obligations, or promises. Being disloyal to another person.

Ungrateful: Lacking gratitude for one's gifts.

Uniqueness (terminal): Believing that one has unique powers, qualities, or talents that make them different from and superior to others.

Unjust: Not treating others fairly or justly.

Unreliable: Failing to do what one says, to keep commitments, or to follow through.

Untrustworthy: Undeserving of trust; undependable; unreliable.
Vain: Excessively proud of or concerned about one's own appearance, qualities, achievements, etc.; conceited.
Vengeful: Desiring to inflict injury, harm, humiliation, or the like on a person who has harmed them; violent revenge.
Vulgar, immoral thinking: Thinking that lacks good taste, or is indecent, obscene, lewd, crude, coarse, or unrefined.
Wasteful: Given to useless and unnecessary consumption or expenditure.
Wishing ill of others: Possessing a strong desire for others to suffer.
Worry: Tendency to torment oneself or suffer from disturbing thoughts.

Success Habits

Confucius once said, "Men's natures are alike, it is their habits that carry them far apart." Success comes by virtue of the positive life habits you develop and maintain combined with passionate vision and strategy. Find the secret to success in your daily routine.

Much of recovery is about breaking bad habits and replacing them with good habits. There is a saying that "bad habits are easy to develop and hard to live with, while good habits are hard to develop but easy to live with." Developing good habits requires persistent effort.

A successful life is a focused, dedicated, intentional, and disciplined life. Without these qualities, you waste your life energy without harnessing it.

What follows are the key success habits needed to achieve your life vision.

1. **Persist.** Success comes not from an hour's effort, or even a year's effort; it comes from a lifetime's effort. As long as your goals remain realistic, you should not let fatigue or failure cause you to give up.
2. **Focus.** Direct your attention to the next positive action before you. Keep your mind's focus on your life vision and what that vision calls for in this moment.
3. **Cultivate passion.** Life brings innumerable distractions. If you lose sight of your vision, you will lose your passion. Take time daily to reflect on what is most important to you. What gives your life purpose and meaning? This is the source of your passion.
4. **Stay positive.** Work to keep an abundance mentality. Focus on your gifts, opportunities, and successes, no matter how small. Stay positive

by surrounding yourself with positive people. Shun both negativity and negative people.

5. **Break it down.** Break down tasks into individual actions. This makes the impossible possible.
6. **Act.** Start your journey by taking the first small step. Since you've broken down the big tasks into the many small tasks, you need only take action, accomplishing small tasks patiently, one by one. Act. Take the first step. This gives you momentum. Once you take the first step, the second step becomes easier.
7. **Pace yourself.** Rome wasn't built in a day. A marathon isn't run at a sprint. In the race between the turtle and the hare, it was the turtle who won. Going too fast leads to burnout, failure, or even readdiction.
8. **Take a break.** Your efficiency and productivity go up when you take breaks throughout the day. This is part of good self-care and is also an important part of pacing yourself. One practice is to work four 50-minute sessions, the first three followed by a 10-minute break, and the last work period followed by a 30-minute break. You may vary this schedule depending on your stamina. During breaks, get up and move around. Get a snack. Go to the bathroom. Stretch. Climb a few flights of stairs. Meditate. You may want to lean back and close your eyes for a few minutes.
9. **Practice patience.** It took Thomas Edison thousands of failed attempts before he finally found a filament to make a light bulb. Nothing of any value comes overnight. Life unfolds in its own time. Patiently come into step with Life.
10. **Enjoy.** Enjoy the journey to your life vision as you work on achieving your goals. Savor life along the way. If your passion is authentic and your life vision is true, you will do what you love.
11. **Prepare.** A carpenter would be a fool to come to the job without his tools. You will not learn what's needed to pass an important test if you do not study. Take time to prepare yourself for the tasks before you. Lack of preparation leads to failure.
12. **Learn.** Greatness comes not only from learning knowledge, but from learning from your mistakes. Successful people learn what they need to know and combine that with learning from experience. Prepare as much as possible. No amount of preparation, however, will teach you all you need to know. A key to success is to learn from experience. Learn what's

needed as you go along. New challenges require new knowledge. Become a student of life. Support your success by continuously learning what's needed to succeed.

13. **Work.** Success is 1% inspiration and 99% perspiration. Whatever you do, you should work hard, giving it 100% of your effort with complete commitment. Strive to do everything to the best of your ability. Accomplish each humble task as if it were great and noble.
14. **Play.** Great achievers often work fewer hours than others. They boost their energy and creativity by engaging in vigorous play that engages their brains in other ways.[114] They work intensely for fewer hours, and then do something fun that takes their mind off their work. Taking your mind off your work not only replenishes you, it creates the opportunity for "aha!" moments.
15. **Delay gratification.** By far the best gratification is delayed gratification. Children who can forego eating a candy bar for five minutes to get a second candy bar end up achieving more in life. They are more successful because they can put a higher goal before immediate gratification.
16. **Start early.** Those who get up early end up accomplishing more than those who get off to a late start.
17. **Touch it once.** Follow the "one-touch rule" as tasks arise. Try to handle everything only once. Either do it, schedule it, delegate it, delete it, or file it. If you can do a task in a few minutes or less, do it.
18. **Record it.** Write down ideas and insights that arise throughout the day. Carry a notepad and a pen with you. Write down your ideas. When you get to a break point, clarify, reprioritize, reorganize, readjust your schedule, change your plans, or take new action.
19. **Say "No."** Stay focused and distraction-free by filtering out what is not important to your life vision—what is not on your life plan. Purge all but the most essential tasks. Unclutter, delegate, and simplify. When telling someone "No," say, "I don't want to do that because . . ." vs. "I can't." This is more authentic.
20. **Schedule solitude and stillness.** Creativity comes from a quiet and reflective mind. Too much busyness dulls your awareness. Busyness blocks insight. Be still and silent for several minutes at least twice a day. More is better.
21. **Schedule tasks.** If you need to do something, either do it or schedule

it. Not scheduling tasks increases the risk of not doing what is on your to-do list. When you schedule a task, you know you will do it.

22. **Create accountability.** Accountability to others helps you meet your commitments. Let others know of your goals and plans. When getting into recovery, for example, people experience a boost in their motivation to cease addicting by announcing their plans to quit to their friends and family. This creates accountability. Don't keep your dreams a secret. Once you've written your life plan, share it with your world. This solidifies your commitment.
23. **Keep the inbox empty.** Whether it's a physical inbox or an email inbox, empty the box every day if possible. Follow the one-touch rule, either doing, scheduling, deleting, delegating, or filing. This enables you to keep up with the inflow. It prevents you from getting overwhelmed and behind. Better to spend a small amount of time daily on your inbox. Avoid having to plow through a backlog of items, some of which you should have handled when they arrived in your inbox.
24. **Prioritize the day.** To be successful, schedule your priorities instead of prioritizing your schedule. Don't let tasks creep into your schedule that are not important and consistent with your priorities. In scheduling the day, first schedule your recovery activities. This is your highest priority. This might include journal work, reading, meetings, therapy, or connecting with recovery supports. After scheduling your recovery, schedule your self-care, as you will not thrive and prosper if you are not first taking care of yourself. This means scheduling time for your spiritual practice, exercise, meals, leisure, and rest. It may seem counterintuitive to schedule self-care before work, but you are more productive if you first take care of yourself. After scheduling recovery and self-care, schedule your work. First take care of items that are both urgent and important. Then attend to what is non-urgent and important. Schedule the most important, most difficult, and most unpleasant tasks first, when you are fresh. The benefits of doing this are several. First, you get what's more important and difficult out of the way, leaving you with feelings of relief and accomplishment. Now you have the rest of the day to reward yourself by working on items that are more rewarding or less challenging and unpleasant. If you have a very large task that will take several days, block out time every day to chip away at it. Then you spend at least a little time each day on each of

your most important, big goals. This technique works well for step work, which can take months to years to complete. If you're doing step work, schedule a small amount of time, for example 30 minutes a day, for step work. Write in your step journal. Schedule an hour a week to go over your step work with your sponsor.

25. **Fix the time or the goal.** When scheduling your priorities, you must do some tasks today. Some tasks take so much time you cannot accomplish them in one sitting. If you must do something today, you fix the task with your goal. Then work at the task until you achieve the goal. For example, if you have a report due tomorrow morning, make it your goal to complete the report today, no matter how long it takes. Otherwise, fix the time you will spend on the task today so you can also attend to other priorities. You might schedule two hours a day to work on a presentation so it will be ready on time.
26. **Stay true.** It is easy to get sidetracked from realizing your life vision. Competing demands and opportunities arise daily. To succeed, stay true to your life vision, using that vision as the guide to setting and then scheduling your priorities. Harness your passion to stay motivated to do what is before you. If you let life's distractions deflect you from your life vision, your passion and motivation will weaken. Staying true to your life vision both focuses you to maximize your efficiency and energizes you to maximize your productivity.
27. **Value failure.** Your many daily mistakes and failures are the stepping-stones to your success if only you commit to learning from experience. Proficiency comes from practice. Give yourself permission to do something poorly the first time, and several times after that. This is how you learn and grow. If you wait until you can do something perfectly, you will wait the rest of your life. While preparation is important, you must then jump in and do what needs to be done, knowing you can fix it later. This "just do it" attitude works well to develop skills and create refined work products. You need this attitude to achieve a full and stable recovery from addiction.
28. **Ask for help.** It is the weak person who cannot ask for help. Two or more heads are better than one. All great achievements, including achieving recovery, occur through a combination of your efforts and the help, support, and guidance of others. Asking for help is essential not only for

recovery, but for success in life in general.

29. **See the forest.** Large projects consist of a thousand and one details. You can lose sight of the forest if you get caught up in seeing just the trees. Don't get lost in the details. While success requires attention to detail, always maintain "double vision," seeing both the grand plan and the many details of that plan. This will protect you from the details leading you astray. Seeing the forest lets you prioritize the details and sort out what is important and what you can disregard and discard.
30. **Take care.** You are a highly complex, dynamic, living system. You need certain conditions for your well-being to achieve optimal performance. Take care of yourself by getting enough sleep, taking breaks, slowing down, having fun, exercising, and carving out time for quiet reflection. Take care of yourself to the degree necessary to optimize your well-being, without stepping over into self-indulgence.
31. **Grow.** As a student of Life, commit to your own personal growth and development. Reflect on the events of your life, looking for opportunities to learn from difficulties, mistakes, and failures. Take on new challenges. Learn new skills. Through your spiritual practice and daily recovery work, cultivate your character and awareness. Keep yourself sharp through the daily practice of the skills of your hobbies and profession.
32. **Firewall.** Tasks requiring sustained concentration and effort require protection from distractions. Eliminate distractions by protecting yourself from interruptions. Shut the door. Silence your phone and shut down your email. Go to an office or library instead of staying at home. Turn off the TV and radio. If passersby on the street distract you, close the window and the shades. Start work early to get things done before others get up. The same goes for late at night if you have the energy. Whatever your situation, create a quiet, protected environment to maximize productivity.
33. **Eliminate time-wasters.** Charles Darwin once said, "A man who dares to waste one hour of life has not discovered the value of life." While rest, relaxation, and fun are necessary, there comes a point when you can go beyond fulfilling these needs to wasting time. Along with your to-do list, keep a "to-don't" list. Make a list of negative habits and other unproductive activities you will forego out of your dedication to your life vision.
34. **Organize.** Successful execution of a plan requires organization. This is

why you schedule your priorities. When you schedule a task, you literally put it in a place in time when it will get done. Some people create tickler files of their important events, tasks, and deadlines. A good scheduler on a smart phone or computer can serve the same purpose. Create a good filing system so you can find things when you need them. Whether it be a physical document or a scheduled task, make a place for everything, with everything in its place. Stay organized by spending a little time each day scheduling, filing, and purging to keep yourself organized.

35. **Achieve daily goals daily.** Make meaningful, measurable progress by achieving what you set out to do each day. This is easier said than done, but is still possible with skillful scheduling and discipline. Through skillful scheduling, you not only schedule what is important, but you also set a realistic pace that respects your time and energy constraints. Then you don't set yourself up for unnecessary failure. With discipline, you maintain focus and persevere until you accomplish your goals. Avoid derailing distractors.
36. **Open yourself to feedback.** You cannot fix a problem of which you are unaware. No one has full awareness of everything they say and do and the consequences. You can also be blind to defects, conflicts, issues, and problems right in front of you. You need the eyes of others to see what you cannot see. Grow and learn by asking for feedback from others. Humbly acknowledge that you cannot see and know everything.
37. **Monotask.** Multitasking dilutes your performance and sets you up for mistakes. Sometimes multitasking is unavoidable, such as when you must watch the children while making dinner. When possible, give each task 100% of your attention. This reduces mistakes, improves efficiency, and eliminates the wasted time jumping from one task to another.
38. **Get a jump on the week.** Prepare for your work week the night before. Go over your schedule for the week. Note events, important tasks, appointments, and deadlines. Change your schedule as needed. If possible, dispose of any leftover tasks from the week before. Taking just a small amount of time to get a jump on the week can promote a smooth and successful week.
39. **Not right now.** Besides external distractions, you also have internal distractions. You may be in the middle of completing a project when you realize you didn't finish something else you need for tomorrow. You may

have a flash of insight into some other difficulty. Whatever the distraction may be, whether external or internal, stay on track by saying, "Not right now." Keep a notepad for writing ideas and concerns that arise while you are working. Then, when you get to a break, review what you have written and adjust your schedule as needed. Rearrange your schedule based upon new priorities, or make a change of plans given the new information or new ideas. Go through the "one-touch" method with your new list, either doing, deleting, delegating, scheduling, or filing each item that came to mind. Then get back to work with a clear mind.

40. **Manage deadlines.** One technique that sets superior students apart from their peers is their management of deadlines. Every day, when they get home from classes, they work on their new assignments that evening, instead of waiting until the night before they're due. For large projects, such as a term paper or research project, they start on the task as soon as possible. They work on it steadily and complete it as soon as possible. Apply these strategies to your work. Boost your productivity and success by starting tasks as soon as possible. Don't wait until the last minute. Stay ahead of the work, getting things done as quickly as possible so that things don't pile up. When planning, look ahead. Anticipate the work ahead of you. Get things done on time. Don't procrastinate. Avoid the chaos of the last minute when you are vulnerable to both mistakes and to not completing tasks.
41. **Be disciplined.** To succeed, stay focused, consistent, and persistent. Fueled by your life vision, do what you must regardless of your mood at the moment. Keep your commitments. Do what is right despite what you're feeling. This is the essence of recovery. Don't give in to temptations. Instead, delay gratification and fend off distractions. Keep yourself focused and on track. Be disciplined, but not rigid. Be flexible when new conditions and constraints arise.
42. **Follow through.** Do what you say and say what you do. Establish the consistency, transparency, and accountability required for others to trust you. If you say you will do something, then either do it or renegotiate if constraints arise. Wrap up the final details of projects. Don't leave things unfinished. Enable yourself to follow through by practicing these success habits. Once you have completed a task, follow up with others to make sure you've satisfied their needs.

43. **Cultivate interdependence.** Taking accountability for your life entails first moving from dependence on others to independence. Go beyond independence to interdependence, because no one is an island, isolated and apart from others. You need healthy interdependence to achieve your life vision. Life is a team sport. You need others to succeed. Because you live both for yourself and others, nurture positive relationships with those around you. Cultivate people's trust in your integrity and your good will. Keep your promises and commitments, or renegotiate when you cannot follow through due to factors beyond your control. Invest in caring for others by connecting, listening, seeking to understand, and empathizing. Work to know others' needs and concerns and then ask yourself what you can do to help. Then, look for win-win solutions. Let go of the need to be right. Practice humility. Keep your focus on what's best for everyone. Give more than you get. Look for the good in others. Welcome disagreements and differences of opinion. Practice respectful tolerance of different ways of living and thinking, and of different beliefs. Focus on the most positive outcome for everyone. Reach out to others instead of waiting for them to reach out to you. Develop positive connections with people in which everyone benefits.
44. **Abandon quick fixes.** No one achieves anything of substance or value overnight. Greatness requires great effort. There are no quick fixes. A life vision requires a lifetime to achieve. Recovery takes time. There is a saying that, if you walk ten miles into the woods, you have to walk ten miles out. Again, the virtues of patience, persistence, and hope come into play.

Managing Fear

Self-Assessment: A Fear Inventory Journal

The first step in healing from unhealthy fear is to identify what you are afraid of. Often, it's not what you think. Anger, hurt, jealousy, envy, and greed can mask fear. At their core, all of these negative emotions spring from fear about your safety and well-being. Examples include:

- You may have a fear of doing the work of recovery out of a fear of failure, rooted in a false belief that failure is final.

- A spouse may experience anger toward her partner because of his neglect of her. This anger may be rooted in a fear of losing the relationship, being alone, and a fear of never being properly loved by another person.
- Many feel anxious when speaking in public, when asking someone out, or when socializing with strangers. They fear others will judge, criticize, or reject them. Their distress arises from a belief that others' judgments of them are true—that they are unlovable, unlikable, defective, or inadequate. This fear comes from a lack of self-love.
- Trauma-based fear arises when someone has hurt you. Fear of engaging in relationships arises from a fear of being hurt again. This feeds isolation.
- Some suffer from phobias. Phobias are extreme fears of things such as heights, crowds, flying, snakes, needles, or spiders, to give a few examples. These fears may prevent someone from flying on an airplane, going to the mall, or going on a hike. In each case, the brain magnifies an appropriate fear of potential harm out of proportion, causing impairment.
- You feel anger when someone disrespects you. This anger comes from hurt. Hurt comes from a natural need for others to value you. When others threaten this need, fear of others not valuing you arises.

Create your own inventory of fears, writing down not only what you fear, but also the root cause: failure, rejection, harm, or loss. For each fear, describe:

1. Who or what you are afraid of
2. When you have this fear
3. What makes it worse or better
4. What causes you to be afraid
5. What you fear will happen

In this way, you dissect the anatomy of your fears. To resolve fear, get to the "why" of the fear.

Write down all your untrue or unrealistic beliefs. Ask someone who knows you well to help you. Examples include the belief that:

- You are bad if you make a mistake.
- Failure is final.
- Rejection means you are unlovable.
- Distress is unbearable.

When constructing a fear inventory, look at your other destructive emotions, such as anger and hurt. Fears of not being valued and safe give rise to compulsions to achieve, to acquire, and to have power over others. Fear of harm drives the compulsion to control people, places, and things. All destructive emotions arise from fear.

Processing Fears

Once you have named your fears, you can process them. By processing them, you come to understand them. With understanding, unhealthy fear either dissolves or transforms to healthy fear that you can manage, confront, and overcome.

The first step in processing fear is to look into its validity. You ask yourself, "Is it true?" Is it true that flying is dangerous, given that you have a greater chance of dying on the trip to the airport? Is it true that I am a failure if I fail, or a reject if I am rejected? Is it true that no one will ever love me? How do I know this is true? Is this fear rational or irrational? What is the realistic risk? See the actual validity of your fears. Note the realistic risks you actually face. This shrinks unhealthy fear down to size.

Unhealthy fear may come from unrealistic expectations. Examples include:

- "I cannot take a risk."
- "I must never fail."
- "I cannot make mistakes."
- "Everyone should respect me."

Unhealthy fear fades with the awareness of the unReality of these and other expectations.

Whenever contemplating any course of action, think through all possible outcomes, from the best case to the worst case.

People suffering from unhealthy fear often "catastrophize," imagining unrealistic dire outcomes. This fear lessens when you ask yourself, "What is the worst thing that could happen?" followed by, "What will that mean?" If you are afraid of needles, the worst thing that could happen is that it will hurt for an instant as the needle goes in. What will this mean? It will mean that you have a brief moment of mild to moderate distress. If you are afraid of giving your heart to someone, the worst-case scenario is that they will hurt or abandon you. What will this mean? It means that you either made the wrong choice or you must work on your relationship skills. By thinking through the worst-case scenario and its true meaning, you see that what you fear is manageable. This will give you courage to do what's best.

Finally, talk out your fears. If a future event worries you or if you are afraid of doing something, talk it through with someone. Examine with them the validity of your fears. Sort out unrealistic expectations. Think through the worst-case scenarios.

Who do you talk to? Therapists and recovery mentors are good choices. They can question your beliefs and expectations. Really, any good listener can ask the right questions, reflect back the Reality of things, and help you gain clarity. What you want to avoid is someone who blocks your processing by brushing off your fears or resorting to giving unhelpful advice.

Unhealthy fear is fear not yet fully understood. Through investigation, you discover and correct the sources of unhealthy fear in your unrealistic beliefs, expectations, and predictions. Processing fear brings clarity. With clarity, you gain the freedom to act according to what is in everyone's best interest.

Make Peace with Fear

Making peace with fear requires practice. Clarity is not something that comes overnight while you are sleeping.

Let's look at how to make peace with the four core fears.

To make peace with the fear of failure, embrace failure as inevitable, necessary, and valuable. See that failure is success in disguise, because you take one step closer to achieving your goals.

For the fear of rejection, accept that rejection is inevitable. You risk rejection by being true to yourself. Living a life of respectful authenticity and integrity involves doing and saying what is true, right, and good. Not everyone will value your actions and beliefs. Not everyone will value you.

Let go of the unrealistic expectation that everyone value you. When it comes to rejection, "QTIP" (quit taking it personally). While rejection may result from your actions, it says nothing about your value as a person.

Like failure and rejection, harm is also inevitable. Accept this as a part of life. No one goes through life harm-free (emotional or physical). Harm comes from many sources. While you can minimize harm by not taking unnecessary risks (e.g., walking down a dark alleyway at night), you cannot avoid risk entirely. Some risk-taking is necessary, such as when you risk driving to work to make a living.

Finally, everyone fears loss. No one wants to lose what they value. Fear of loss coupled with doubt makes change difficult. We all experience ambivalence about change. Everyone wants things to be different without changing. We want something new without giving up the old.

Loss imposes change, whether it be of a job, the ability to run a mile under five minutes, or a loved one. Loss is a pervasive and inevitable part of life. Loss comes from impermanence. Everything changes, and everything will ultimately be lost. Make peace with the fear of loss by accepting this fact and appreciating the tremendous value of loss. Loss is the vehicle of change. Through loss, old doors close, but new ones open. Loss brings the gifts of change, growth, and hope.

Accept unavoidable losses beyond your control. Especially welcome the loss of aspects of your life that brought you more harm than good, such as your addiction and destructive relationships.

Quell Fear

Even after you gain clarity on your unhealthy fears and make peace with them, fear will still arise, as it takes practice and repetition to understand and accept your fears. There is often a gap between what you know to be true and what you feel. Although understanding fear is of great benefit, you can do other things to quell your fears.

To quell fear and anxiety, be sure you are safe. Establishing safety and security is the first order of business for reducing fear. You may need to remove yourself from an unsafe situation. You cannot resolve fear and anxiety if you are in danger.

After establishing your safety as much as possible, the first practice for quelling anxiety is that of acceptance and surrender. If you get cancer, you will be anxious about whether you will die and how much you will suffer. Although you can do many things to increase your chances of survival, you do not have complete control. Not having control is a prime cause of anxiety. Acceptance and surrender are the antidotes. When you accept the Reality that you have little or no control, anxiety eases. Do your best. What will happen will happen.

Second, reframe fear as positive, such as the healthy fear that keeps you safe. Make friends with fear. Value and respect fear, even as you work to manage it. Fear is OK if you face it and work through it. Growth and change often come with fear. Fear comes with challenges. Quell the fear of challenge by focusing on the upside more than the downside. Practice positive action, recognizing that a positive anything is better than a fear-driven negative nothing. Get comfortable with being uncomfortable. This is when growth happens. The fear of venturing into the unknown says you're on track. Welcome it.

Another technique for dealing with fear is mindfulness. When you're mindful, you look and listen. You note what's happening inside and out without judgment. You practice loving awareness of this moment. When mindful, Awareness comes out of its usual immersion in thoughts and feelings. In this state, you are not your fear. You just experience fear. Ask yourself what it is that you fear. Then, face the fear, rather than avoid it. Surrender to it. Let it pass through and beyond you. As Thich Nhat Hanh says, "Every time your fear is invited up, every time you recognize it and smile at it, your fear will lose some of its strength." Mindfulness involves living in the Present, or the "Now." Quell anxiety about the future by focusing on the immediate moment, not the rest of your life. If you dwell on negative "what if" projections, note them. Let them go. Come back to this moment. Ask, "What does this moment call for?"

Worrying about the future differs from planning for the future. Planning is a constructive act. Worrying is a wasteful, destructive act that robs you of your vitality. Through mindfulness, you can practice noting your habit of worrying. Through returning Awareness to the Present, worry slowly dissolves. This practice takes time and repetition. With time and effort, mindfulness gradually becomes a lifelong habit. As you become more mindful, fear and worry weaken their hold on you.

Another technique for quelling fear is to practice self-reassurance and self-affirmation. Make a list of your past successes and the past failures you overcame. Reduce your fear of failure by reframing failure as a necessary stepping-stone to success. You have endured and survived setbacks, disappointments, and even tragedies. Seeing this, reassure yourself that everything will be all right. You are all right, no matter what.

Part of self-reassurance and self-affirmation is the practice of positivity discussed earlier in the Touchstone on taking accountability. When you are positive, you let your optimism and hope shape your actions, and not your fears. Rather than focusing on all the reasons something won't work, focus on all the reasons why it will. If you stay positive, you will strengthen your courage and resolve to do what needs to be done.

Self-calming techniques can help quell anxiety. These include progressive muscle relaxation, deep breathing, meditation, and yoga. Therapists and instructors can teach you these techniques, or you can learn and practice them by learning online or with videos.

Aerobic exercise is another effective way to reduce anxiety. Exercising 25-50 minutes every day releases chemicals in your brain that promote calm, energy, and positivity.

Talking out fears and anxiety with a support helps you to process your anxiety and fear. Talking can often dissolve fear by inquiring into its roots. Others can help you develop a more positive reframing of your situation to reduce fear. Finally, since a concern shared is a concern halved, you feel better by not being so alone with your fears. By sharing, others can support you in your efforts to cope.

Some people suffer from high levels of baseline anxiety that causes significant suffering and impairment. A therapist and a psychiatrist can help when anxiety is severe and persistent. Therapists can teach cognitive behavioral techniques, including relaxation techniques, to help you learn to quell fear. Psychiatrists can help you reduce fear through the use of antidepressants, beta blockers, alpha-2 adrenergic drugs, and anticonvulsants. While benzodiazepines are useful for severe, overwhelming anxiety in acute situations, the harm from long-term use generally outweighs any benefits. Most people should not use benzodiazepines long term. People with addiction are at risk with benzodiazepines, so most prescribers discourage their use other than for detoxification.

Finally, reduce your anxiety by connecting with Nature. A walk through the woods, for example, can help to settle your troubled mind, as you let the stillness of Nature enhance your own internal stillness. Placing plants in your work and living environments can also reduce tension, as plants have a soothing effect. Pets can also bring comfort and relief through their affection and companionship.

Make Friends with Risk and Failure

Risk and failure are part of life. Don't let them hold you back. Feel free to fail. All great athletes know that losing is an unavoidable part of winning. Winners have an abundance mentality. They view failure as a gift—an opportunity to learn and grow. They do not fear failure. Failure is just invaluable feedback on changes needed to improve. This attitude is especially important in processing slips and recurrences of addicting.

While you want to minimize danger, you cannot completely avoid it. Avoiding danger is no better in the long run than exposing yourself to what you fear. Achieving goals involves risk. Those who don't take risks risk even more.

Practice boldness in your conviction to do the right thing, regardless of your fear. If you don't take a chance, you won't have a chance. Go out on a limb to get the fruit.

Those who go the farthest are those who take calculated, reasonable risks. They take the most challenging route. They don't wait until the time is "just right." That time never comes.

The most challenging task is likely the most rewarding. If you let fear prevent you from acting, then you give up greatness. You create an ending in which you say, "I might have," and, "I should have." By letting go of your fear of risk and failure, you position yourself to do great things. By welcoming challenge and change in your life, you open yourself up to reap the fruits of your positive actions, including the fruits of recovery. Daring to do the next right thing brings freshness, novelty, excitement, and reward.

Reduce your fear of risk and failure by planning, preparing, and working hard. If you are afraid you will fail a test, reduce that fear by studying. If you're nervous about a job interview, reduce your anxiety by researching the job, the company, and the interviewer. Make sure you have a clean, pressed outfit to wear to the interview. If you're afraid you'll get lost, go the day before to learn the way. Planning and preparation go a long way toward reducing risk.

Plan, but don't project the outcome, as the outcome is only partially within your control. Even with impeccable preparation, you may still not get the job you want. In life, do your best and hope for the best, but don't expect the best. While we make our own luck and blessings, nothing in life is guaranteed. Each day, you should judge yourself not by what you achieved, but by the effort you made.

Deepen Faith

When you're in fear, you're not in faith. Lack of faith multiplies fear. Review the section on faith in the Touchstone on perseverance.

Commit to a Passionate Vision

While action without vision is a nightmare, vision without action is just a daydream. You need a passionate vision of the life and world you want. Without enthusiasm, you lack the energy to pursue your dreams. Overcome fear and enable yourself to act by having a passionate vision of the life you want. This is where meaning and purpose can help you face and overcome unhealthy fears. With passion, you can do anything within your ability. Sustained passion over a lifetime makes for a successful life.

Passion comes from identifying and pursuing your dreams. You redefine yourself according to the vision you have of your new self, living a better life. Visualize success. Stay committed to your dreams. Keep your focus on the rewards that will come from your efforts, if you only persist. Replace negative thoughts with positive reasons to make a better life for yourself.

Your passion drives you on to overcome life's obstacles. Succeed by devoting your entire self to your life—to what you do and to whom you love.

Emboldened by your vision, you want that vision more than you fear it. Vision with passion creates courage, commitment, and determination. With courage, you can face and overcome fear. With commitment and determination, you can do the difficult and unpleasant. This is what transforms people into winners.

Faith and a will to act bring success. With a passionate vision, you gain both will and faith, making it possible to overcome even the greatest of fears.

Take Action (Despite Fear)

There is a saying that some make it happen, some watch it happen, and some ask, "What happened?" Working through fear requires action to make it happen. While action does not guarantee success, inaction guarantees failure. Anxiety can cause indecision, procrastination, and inaction, poisoning both your happiness and your recovery. Unhappy people don't like the way things are and they don't like change. Their fear stops them from making the changes they need to make to improve their lives. They do the same things over and over, getting the same results.

Changing your life requires action. Your life won't change unless you change. Get a little outside your comfort zone. Face your fear. Once you face your fear, investigate it, embolden yourself with faith and vision, and do what you can to quell fear, although you will still have fear. This fear, however, is manageable. You can act despite your fear. Leverage your courage and convictions to act.

Take action now, not when the time is "right." The right time is now. The longer you let fear hold you back, the greater the grip fear has on you. You may not be great when you start, but you will never become great if you do not start. If you find yourself in a difficult position, you should remind yourself that success comes from making a strong foundation out of the bricks thrown at you. Begin now, making the best of your circumstances.

Make plans and deliberate before acting. Consider all options, best- and worst-case scenarios, and the risks and rewards involved. When you are done deliberating, act.

Face your fears every day. As Ralph Waldo Emerson once said, "He who is not every day conquering some fear has not learned the secret of life." Action eases anxiety, thus the saying, "A fear faced is a fear erased." Every time you take a courageous step in the right direction, you experience the most wonderful feeling of accomplishment.

Face your fears and work through them by taking small steps. Cognitive behavioral therapists use what is called a "fear ladder," in which they help clients break down fears into smaller, manageable steps that get progressively more difficult. Each step becomes either longer in exposure to fear, or a little scarier than the step before. Anxiety fades with time and exposure. If you are afraid, for example, of snakes, you might first get comfortable with a book about snakes. You would read it and gaze at the pictures until the fear goes away. You might then watch a movie on snakes, again, watching it over and over until your fear dissipates. You might then go into a pet store and stand some distance from a snake in a glass enclosure, gradually getting closer as you become more comfortable. Eventually, you might sit with someone who is holding a snake, and eventually touch the snake yourself. This process is called "graded exposure." Fear lessens with exposure to each successive step.

Sustain faith and hope by keeping your focus on what's needed now, not on what went wrong in the past. Acknowledge, but don't obsess over past mistakes and failures. While learning from the past is essential, dwelling on the past only increases fear.

Overcome fear by doing what you fear. You have a choice, to either face it or run from it. Not all fears have to be conquered. You don't have to learn to skydive if you don't want to. Still, conquer what must be conquered to advance your life. You gain confidence in yourself and build up your courage every time you face your fear and take the right action. With practice, you will do things you never thought possible.

Overcome fear by faking it until you make it. Practice confidence, smiling when you want to run away. Act as if you are not afraid. Work your way into feeling right by acting right.

Working through fear requires courage, faith, vision, passion, clarity, practice, patience, and persistence. By welcoming failure and setbacks as friends, you gradually lose your fears as you work through them and learn from experience.

Chapter 13
Life Principles

- **Accept:** Make friends with the present moment, no matter how great your distress. Gently let go of negativity.
- **Be accountable:** Take accountability for your life and for your actions. Do not blame others. Do not take the victim role.
- **Adapt:** Everything changes constantly, requiring you to change. Life that adapts to changing circumstances flourishes. When you hit an obstacle, improvise a way around or a way through. Make lemonade out of lemons.

- **Ask for help:** No one does recovery or life alone.
- **Autonomy:** Respect the rights of others to choose their own actions, to believe what they will, and to live their lives as they see fit.
- **Balance:** Care for yourself by balancing work, love, and play.
- **Care:** Invest yourself in caring for others.
- **Choose wisely:** Make decisions carefully and thoughtfully. Ask for the council of others. Take the time necessary for the best course of action to appear.
- **Commit:** If you start something, see it through to the end. If you commit to a life habit or practice, stay with it.
- **Conserve:** Do not waste your own or others' resources.
- **Practice consideration:** Carefully observe and take into account others' feelings. Consider how your actions will affect others.
- **Courage:** Do what is right despite fear.
- **Dedication:** When you do something, give it your all.
- **Discipline:** Similar to commitment. Stick with what you set about to do. Don't let lesser distractions take you away from doing the work at hand.
- **Do good:** Help yourself and others. Use good means to accomplish good ends.
- **Effort:** Work hard. All worthwhile achievements come from great effort.
- **Encourage:** Show others support and affection. Appreciate others' virtues and contributions. Look for opportunities to give specific praise. When appropriate, give hugs.
- **Enjoy:** Live in and savor each moment.
- **Equality:** Respect that everyone should have equal rights and opportunities. Promote equality. Although we have different gifts and blessings, no one is more or less deserving of humane and fair treatment. We all deserve our fair share of the blessings of society.
- **Explore:** See new things. Have new experiences. Learn.

- **Fairness:** Treat others equally without discrimination. Play by the rules. Take turns. Don't exploit others. Don't play favorites. Be just.
- **Faith:** Cultivate your faith in yourself, in others, and in the world. See that goodness dominates over destruction and evil. Believe in goodness. Believe in Life.
- **Focus:** Do things 100%, one at a time.
- **Forgive:** Yourself and others for being human.
- **Friendship:** Invest in friends in both good times and bad. Maintain connections. Be in it for the long haul. Do not betray others. Be loyal. Accept friends' limitations and shortcomings.
- **Fail:** Make friends with failure, seeing it as the pathway to success. Take intelligent risks. Try new things, knowing you get nothing right the first time. Recognize that, no matter how hard you try, you make mistakes every day and will continue to do so for the rest of your life. Be willing to learn and grow from failing.
- **Give:** Practice generosity. Give more than you get, knowing you get the most from giving.
- **Golden rule/platinum rule:** Treat others as you wish to be treated. Better yet, act with love and treat others according to what most enhances their well-being.
- **Gratitude:** Take time every day to take account of your blessings and to show gratitude to others who have benefitted you.
- **Grow:** Stay open to what life has to teach. Make it a discipline to practice these principles and other virtues for a lifetime.
- **Harm-free life:** Do not harm yourself or others. Combine good intentions with intelligent perception of what is needed. Act with care. Do not gossip. Do not judge others.
- **Honesty:** Do not lie, defraud, deceive, or mislead.
- **Humor:** Look for the humor in all things. Take every opportunity possible to laugh.
- **Kindness:** Treat others with kindness, remembering that all are sacred and that everyone, in their own way, is just trying to get by

as best they can. Cultivate compassion through understanding.

- **Integrity:** Keep your promises and agreements. Walk your talk. Do the next right thing.
- **Interdependence:** The greatest challenge of human relationships is to be simultaneously autonomous and interdependent. Open your heart to others. As you help others, let them help you. Cooperate, collaborate, and compromise.
- **Patience:** Let go of wanting things now. Be willing to wait. See that things happen in their own time. Be willing to delay gratification.
- **Perseverance:** Get up when you fall down. Do not give up.
- **Privacy:** Respect personal privacy and confidentiality.
- **Positivity:** Practice focusing on the good aspects of bad situations. Look for blessings and silver linings. Cultivate positive, affirming thoughts. Let go of negative thoughts and judgments.
- **Rational intuition:** Cultivate creativity and intuition through the practice of stillness and presence. Open your mind to reflection. Create the opportunity for insight. Combine insight with knowledge and reason to apprehend truth as best you can.
- **Reason:** Make decisions according to an analysis of the facts and their logical consequences.
- **Recovery:** Make recovery the first of life's priorities, knowing all other priorities depend on this.
- **Respect:** Treat others with courtesy out of an unconditional commitment to be respectful in all circumstances, because you are a respectful person.
- **Respond:** Respond intelligently rather than react emotionally. Do not act on destructive urges. Think things through.
- **Restraint:** Practice moderation. Do not overindulge. Keep to the middle way between extremes.
- **Service:** No matter what you do, make it a practice of service. Volunteer.
- **Simplify.** Stay focused on your life vision. Don't clutter it with unnecessary distractions.

- **Spiritual practice:** Make spiritual practice a daily commitment and nonnegotiable priority.
- **Stewardship:** Life does not belong to you. You belong to Life. It is your role to be a steward of Life so that you may pass it on.
- **Synergize:** Combine the differing strengths and assets of a group to do what no individual could do on their own. Practice teamwork. Dedicate the "me" to the "we."
- **Tolerance:** Appreciate that there is no one right way, right answer, right opinion, or right belief. Life flourishes because of diversity. Respect and value those who differ from you. Agree to disagree.
- **Understand:** Look closely. Listen closely. Ask questions. Seek to understand another person's concerns in a conflict out of your authentic concern for them rather than engage in a fight to be right. First give others the gift of understanding before asking for understanding in return.
- **Win-win:** Try to change win-lose into win-win. Keep everyone's interests in mind. Be creative in finding the best solution for all involved. Maximize the ratio of benefit to harm for everyone.
- **Keep the faith—in yourself and others:** Maintain a relentless optimism. Remember that it is always darkest before dawn.
- **Maintain spiritual vision:** Tap into stillness through exercise, yoga, meditation, prayer, contemplation, or other spiritual practices. Read spiritual literature. Get involved with a spiritual/religious community.
- **Process it:** Write out your thoughts in a journal to get clarity, or talk to the wise people—your "Reality network"—to get perspective.
- **Renew and reground:** Take a "time out" to refresh and for renewal. Stop thinking about something for a while. Let the correct perspective come. Downtime, relaxation, exercise, and play can all help to restore your sanity.
- **Laugh:** If you look, you can always find humor in difficult situations.

- **Easy does it:** Be gentle with yourself, with others, and with your circumstances. Don't force things. Practice patience. Do the next right thing and let life unfold in its own time.
- **This too shall pass:** Just as you should savor the good times, knowing they will pass, so you should remind yourself that even the darkest of times are not forever. Everything changes.
- **One moment at a time:** True to your mindfulness practice, make a consistent, gentle effort to live in the moment. Extend this to one day at a time. Plan for the future, but don't project. Don't harm yourself with unnecessary worry. Take care of today to take care of tomorrow.
- **Plan for and accept the worst:** While you can hope for the best, perspective involves seeing things, in proportion, exactly as they are. Ask yourself, "What is the worst possible outcome?" Then plan for it. Accept the worst ahead of time. This will help you prepare while giving you peace in this moment.
- **Take the long view:** Ask yourself if what is happening now will matter in the end.
- **Take others' perspectives:** Get perspective by investigating other people's perspectives. Listen. Strive to understand with care and concern.
- **Practice positivity:** Recognize that negativity and complaining only make matters worse. Life is difficult enough without adding negativity.
- **Befriend difficulties:** Welcome stress, problems, and losses as opportunities for learning and growth and as the ultimate pathway to success.
- **Do what works:** Look back into your past to see what you did in similar circumstances to cope. Build on your prior successes, including your prior recovery successes.
- **See your place:** See your place in this vast Universe. Your life is both infinitely sacred and a miniscule part of the Whole. From this perspective, see that your problems are tiny.

- **Keep the larger Reality of things in mind:** For major life problems such as death, disability, and disease, recognize that these are universal. You are not alone. Everything must come to an end. Be mindful of your own imminent death. These truths are part of the perfection. Understand and accept change and impermanence.
- **Don't fight Reality:** Stop struggling to make Reality conform to your wishes. Change what you can and accept the rest. See and respect the way things are.
- **Celebrate:** Celebrate life and love, especially when things are rough. There is always much to celebrate, even in the midst of sadness and grief.
- **Less is more:** Simple is good. More is not always better.
- **Embrace imperfection:** Do your best. Accept the rest. Accept imperfection and mistakes as part of the perfection.
- **Move on:** If you are going through hell, keep going. Do what needs to be done. Don't dwell on the negative. Focus on your positive life vision. If you are suffering from terminal illness, say your goodbyes and prepare for a good death. If a loved one dies, grieve and invest yourself in your other relationships before it's too late.

Spiritual Practices—Silence, Solitude, Stillness, Intentions, and Affirmations

Meditation: A common meditative technique is to concentrate on just one aspect of this moment. This can be the sensation of your breath going in and out of your nostrils. People call concentrating on just one aspect of the Now, such as your breath, "concentrative meditation." As your busy mind repeatedly immerses Awareness back into thought, you gently and persistently return Awareness back to the breath, or some other aspect of the Now. This might be sights, sounds, smells, tastes, or physical sensations. Some meditators practice rotating their attention from seeing, to hearing, to smelling, to tasting, and to feeling.

In more advanced states, you develop the ability to experience your thoughts without becoming lost in them. When you open the focus of Awareness to all your experiences, you move from concentrative meditation to "mindfulness meditation." You are "mindful" of all aspects of your experience, including your thoughts.

Prayer: In prayer, you can either pray with words, or engage in silent, contemplative prayer. The intent of prayer is to connect with a transcendent life force, which some call God. There are three types of prayer: "Help," "Thanks," and "Wow."

When asking for help, don't ask for a particular outcome. Ask for strength, faith, hope, guidance, peace, insight, wisdom, and acceptance.

When you say, "Thanks," you express gratitude for the gift of your life and for your many blessings.

When you say, "Wow," you experience the wonder, the sacredness, and the awe of existence.

With word prayers, focus on the meaning of the words. Go beyond the words to experience the truth to which they point. In contemplative prayer, you ask a question or silently repeat a word or phrase. A question might be, "What does Life need from me?" Then listen carefully for the silent answer. As Father Thomas Keating says, "God speaks to us in silence. Everything else is a bad translation." In contemplation, you ask. When you go into the stillness of contemplative prayer, you listen for the answers. In repeating a mantra, such as "one" or "surrender," you focus on the meaning of the word and then listen for the wordless response.

A Morning Spiritual Practice: I recommend a daily morning practice of 15 minutes to an hour of Silence, Solitude, and Stillness with daily intentions and affirmations (AMSSS practice). This practice cultivates insight, wisdom, clarity, and a joyful reverence for the gift of existence.

Healing from trauma, addiction and other psychiatric illnesses is in part about healing the experience of Bare Reality. This is the experience before thought. It is the experience of existence, Pure Awareness, or Bare Consciousness, when the mind is still and silent. Many experience a sense of a connection to a loving life force.

If we are spiritually vital, have a healthy brain, and are happy, bare existence is joyful. The Now is Good. There is a sense of wonder and awe at the miraculous experience of consciousness. The experience is safe, grounding, and reassuring. We can take refuge in bare consciousness. We feel grateful for the gift of conscious existence. Some intuit a feeling of an intelligent love force that envelops us and flows through us. We experience Grace. There is a subtle experience of gratitude and joy.

Those with trauma, addiction, and other psychiatric difficulties often endure a painful experience of the Now. The Now is not good. Pure consciousness is filled with distress. An overactive amygdala sends out fear alarm signals, even when no imminent threat exists. It is the healing of this existential distress—this fear-based experience before thought—that is the focus of the healing phase of recovery.

How can a spiritual practice help heal the pain of bare existence? How do we make the Now good and cultivate a reverence for Reality? There are many ways, including the ways outlined in the Touchstone on Healing. Healing is also promoted by an AMSSS practice.

People with neglect and trauma histories have a damaged experience of the joy of bare experience. They are in distress, feeling alternately hyper aroused, hyper vigilant, or numb. They do not feel safe. Many experience intrusive memories and nightmares of their trauma. Their thinking patterns are fear-based. For these people, the lure of addictive substances and behaviors can be irresistible because of their ability to alter consciousness and ease distress.

The problem is, Addiction just doesn't work to heal psychological pain. It only makes it worse, adding yet another struggle to an already difficult life. This is why I encourage my patients to renounce addicting in all ways. Addicting prevents healing and growth.

Start each day with an AMSSS practice—Silence, Solitude, and Stillness. You can do whatever feels right for you during this time, as long as it is in silence, is solitary, and is performed with a still mind. Options include meditation, yoga, tai chi, qi gong, meditative journaling (free writing), contemplative spiritual reading (Lectio divina), or meditative walking. It might just be sitting alone with a cup of coffee in the morning, practicing complete presence with the drinking of the coffee.

The point is to still the Mind, bring Awareness to the Present, and cultivate a positive experience of the Now. In stillness, we can take some refuge and respite from the painful thoughts and emotions that our brains may be generating. With practice, we recognize we are not our thoughts and feelings, but the still Awareness that experiences them. With time, we learn to take refuge in this stillness, allowing the contents of mind to be as they are with acceptance. In this key action, we reduce suffering, even as we continue to be in distress. We take a kind of meditative freedom that is liberating.

In stillness, there is healing. There is the capacity to feel safely grounded. Stillness allows for the Mind to rest, even if for just a few seconds at a time at first. There is the capacity to intuit being enveloped in a Loving Intelligent Universe." Stillness cultivates the experience of Love in the heart.

Thought colors our emotional experience, so managing thought also cultivates the Joy of Existence. I recommend beginning and ending each spiritual SSS period with a recitation of written affirmations and intensions. These can be any that feel most healing of the pain of existence and that bring you the most joy.

Some examples that I recommend include:

1. "I am of immeasurable worth."
2. "At the center of my pain I am whole."
3. "I vow to care for myself today as if I were my own child."
4. "Today I will not addict. I will practice other ways to feel better. I will ask for help."
5. "I vow this day to live with integrity."
6. "I will treat each person I meet today with reverence and respect."""
7. "May I be a channel for Love from my Higher Self to flow through me."

There are thousands more. Just look deep within yourself and see what affirming and loving things need to be said.

The trick to this practice is just that: practice. Remember that recovery is learning to live intentionally and not by our default mode of being, seeing and doing; that only led us into addiction. Recovery means swimming against the stream of our default ways of living with a gentle, consistent intentional practice. Rewiring the brain takes practice and consistency. This requires a commitment borne out of a faith that this practice will lead to healing, growth, and transformation.

Whether your spiritual practice involves meditation, prayer, a combination of both, or some other practice of silence and stillness that connects you to the wordless Now, be sure to practice daily. Spiritual growth requires a regular spiritual practice. Make it a priority and schedule it into your daily routine. As with your recovery practices, do not let life get in the way of your spiritual practice.

Set a goal of practicing an AMSSS practice ninety times in ninety days—90 in 90. You will likely see that in just ninety days you will feel calmer, clearer, and more open hearted. With sustained practice—along with living skillfully—you will change. You will develop spiritual intelligence. You will have a reverence for the Now and will be at peace much, if not all, of the time—even while in distress.

End each day with another period of meditation or prayer. Review the day. Ask yourself if you fulfilled your morning intentions this day. Some people write their daily reflections in a journal. One friend of mine ends his days asking, "Did I addict today?" and "Was I a 'dick' today?" Allow yourself to feel contentment and satisfaction for a day well lived. If you were less than skillful, reflect on what you could have done differently. Make a commitment to doing better tomorrow. When the morning comes, make your affirmations and intentions for the day with a renewed intention to do better this day.

I hope you will introduce this practice into your life, if you are not already doing so. If you are in pain, renounce using anything addictive to manage your pain. Seek professional, abstinence-based treatment. Use your spiritual practice to develop the capacity to be in pain and yet not suffer.

Look around you and have faith. Join a community that will support you in your practice. See that with a daily spiritual practice, along with the other practices in this book, you can slowly heal and experience the Joy of Existence…the Joy of Recovery.

Blessings to you.

NOTES

1. David B. Allison, PhD; Kevin R. Fontaine, PhD; JoAnn E. Manson, MD, Dr PH; et al. Annual Deaths Attributable to Obesity in the United States. *JAMA.* 1999;282(16):1530-1538. doi:10.1001/jama.282.16.1530.
2. https://www.cdc.gov/tobacco/data_statistics/fact_sheets/health_effects/tobacco_related_mortality/ Accessed/4/17.
3. Degenhardt, L, Charlson, F, Mathers, B, Hall, WD, Flaxman, AD, Johns, N, Vos, T. The global epidemiology and burden of opioid dependence: results from the global burden of disease 2010 study. Addiction. 2014 Aug; 109(8): 1320–33.
4. Kalant, H, Kalant, OJ. Death in amphetamine users: causes and rates. Can Med Assoc. Feb 8, 1975; 112(3): 299–304. www.cdc.gov/tobacco/data_statics/fact_sheets/health_effects/tobacco_related_mortality/index.htm#cigs.
5. cdc.gov/alcohol/fact-sheets/alcohol-use.htm. Accessed 9/13/16.
6. http://womenforsobriety.org/beta2/new-life-program/13-affirmations/
7. Chodron, Pema. *Getting Unstuck: Breaking Your Habitual Patterns and Encountering Naked Reality.* Sounds True. 2005.
8. Dodes, L. Breaking Addiction: *A 7-Step Handbook for Ending Any Addiction.* 2011. Harper. New York.
9. Felitti, VJ, Anda, RF. The Relationship of Adverse Childhood Experiences to Adult Medical Disease, Psychiatric Disorders, and Sexual Behavior: Implications for Healthcare. In: *The Hidden Epidemic: The Impact of Early Life Trauma on Health and Disease.* R. Lanius & E. Vermetten editors. Cambridge University Press, 2009.
10. Johnson, A. *Eating in the Light of the Moon: How Women Can Transform Their Relationship with Food Through Myths, Metaphors, and Storytelling.* 2000. Gurze Books. Carlsbad, CA.
11. Kelly, JF. et al. Spirituality in Recovery: A Lagged Mediational Analysis of Alcoholics Anonymous' Principal Theoretical Mechanism of Behavior Change. Alcoholism: Clinical and Experimental Research. Volume 35, Issue 3, pages 454–463, March 2011.
12. Galanter, Marc MD; Dermatis, Helen PhD; Post, Stephen PhD;

Sampson, Cristal BA. Spirituality-Based Recovery. From Drug Addiction in the Twelve-Step Fellowship of Narcotics Anonymous. *Journal of Addiction Medicine*: May/June 2013 - Volume 7 - Issue 3 - p 189–195. doi: 10.1097/ADM.0b013e31828a0265.

13. Peteet, JR. A Closer Look at the Role of a Spiritual Approach in Addictions Treatment. *Journal of Substance Abuse Treatment*. Volume 10, Issue 3, May–June 1993, Pages 263–267.
14. Carroll, S. Spirituality and Purpose in Life in Alcoholism Recovery. *Journal of Studies on Alcohol*, 54(3), 297–301 (1993).
15. Pardini, DA. et al. Religious Faith and Spirituality in Substance Abuse Recovery: Determining the Mental Health Benefits. *Journal of Substance Abuse Treatment*. 19(4), 2000. Pp 347-354.
16. Lesley L. Green, Mindy Thompson Fullilove, Robert E. Fullilove. Stories of Spiritual Awakening: The Nature of Spirituality in Recovery. *Journal of Substance Abuse Treatment*. Volume 15, Issue 4, July–August 1998, Pages 325–331.
17. Davidson, RJ1, Kabat-Zinn, J, Schumacher, J, Rosenkranz, M, Muller, D, Santorelli, SF, Urbanowski, F, Harrington, A, Bonus, K, Sheridan, JF. Alterations in brain and immune function produced by mindfulness meditation. *Psychosom Med.* 2003 Jul-Aug;65(4):564-70.
18. Netta Weinstein a,*, Kirk W. Brown b, Richard M. Ryan, A multi-method examination of the effects of mindfulness on stress attribution, coping, and emotional well-being. *Journal of Research in Personality* 43 (2009) 374–385.
19. Segal, Z, et al. "Antidepressant Monotherapy vs Sequential Pharmacotherapy and Mindfulness-Based Cognitive Therapy, or Placebo, for relapse Prophylaxis in Recurrent Depression." Archives of General Psychiatry. December 2010, Vol. 77 (12), 1256-1264.
20. Elizabeth Cohen. Mindfulness Behind Bars. May 26, 2010. http://greatergood.berkeley.edu/article/item/mindfulness_behind_bars/. Accessed 6/3/17.
21. James W. Carson, Kimberly M. Carson, Karen M. Gil, Donald H. Baucom. Mindfulness-based relationship enhancement. Behavior Therapy. Volume 35, Issue 3, Summer 2004, Pages 471–494.
22. Hölzela, BK, et al. Mindfulness practice leads to increases in regional brain gray matter density. Psychiatry Research: Neuroimaging. Volume

191, Issue 1, 30 January 2011, Pages 36–43.
23. Kida, Thomas. *Don't Believe Everything You Think*. Promethium Books. 2006.
24. https://www.ncbi.nlm.nih.gov/books/NBK64258/.
25. Brown, S. and Lewis, V. *The Alcoholic Family in Recovery: A Developmental Model.* New York: Guilford Press, 1999.
26. Reilly, D.M. Drug-abusing families: Intrafamilial dynamics and brief triphasic treatment. In: Kaufman, E., and Kaufmann, P., eds. *Family Therapy of Drug and Alcohol Abuse*. 2d ed. Boston: Allyn and Bacon, 1992. pp. 105–119.
27. http://fairfieldbhs.org/sites/fairfieldbhs.org/files/Family%20Roles%20in%20Addiction%20(1).pdf.
28. Treatment Improvement Protocol (TIP) Series, No. 39. Center for Substance Abuse Treatment. Rockville (MD): Substance Abuse and Mental Health Services Administration (US); 2004.
29. Brooks, C., and Rice, K.F. *Families in Recovery: Coming Full Circle*. Baltimore: Paul H. Brookes Publishing, 1997.
30. https://www.ncbi.nlm.nih.gov/books/NBK64441/.
31. Child Welfare. 1994 Sep-Oct;73(5):405-30. Preventing child abuse and neglect: programmatic interventions. Daro D, McCurdy K.
32. https://archives.drugabuse.gov/NIDA_Notes/NNVol13N2/exploring.html.
33. Treatment Improvement Protocol (TIP) Series, No. 39. Center for Substance Abuse Treatment. Rockville (MD): Substance Abuse and Mental Health Services Administration (US); 2004.
34. https://www.aacap.org/AACAP/Families_and_Youth/Facts_for_Families/FFF-Guide/Children-Of-Alcoholics-017.aspx.
35. Giglio J.J., Kaufman E. The relationship between child and adult psychopathology in children of alcoholics. International Journal of the Addictions. 1990;25(3):263–290.
36. Johnson J.L., Leff M. Children of substance abusers: Overview of research findings. Pediatrics. 1999;103(5 Pt 2):1085–1099.
37. Sher K.J. Psychological characteristics of children of alcoholics. Alcohol Health and Research World. 1997;21(3):247–254.
38. Hoffmann J.P. The effects of family structure and family relations on adolescent marijuana use. *International Journal of the Addictions.*

1995;30(10):1207–1241.

39. Werner E.E. Resilient offspring of alcoholics: A longitudinal study from birth to age 18. *Journal of Studies on Alcohol.* 1986;47:34–40.
40. Wolin, S.J., and Wolin, S. *The Resilient Self: How Survivors of Troubled Families Rise Above Adversity.* New York: Villard Books, 1993.
41. https://www.addiction.com/3003/will-alcohol-abuse-lead-divorce/.
42. http://www.medicaldaily.com/heavy-drinking-will-lead-divorce-unless-both-partners-are-equally-alcoholic-263648.
43. http://www.dualdiagnosis.org/codependency-substance-abuse/.
44. https://www.bjs.gov/content/pub/ascii/vbi.txt.
45. Hoffmann J.P. The effects of family structure and family relations on adolescent marijuana use. *International Journal of the Addictions.* 1995;30(10):1207–1241.
46. Alexander D.E., Gwyther R.E. Alcoholism in adolescents and their families: Family-focused assessment and management. Pediatric Clinics of North America. 1995;42(1):217–234.
47. Treatment Improvement Protocol (TIP) Series, No. 39. Center for Substance Abuse Treatment. Rockville (MD): Substance Abuse and Mental Health Services Administration (US); 2004.
48. Alexander D.E., Gwyther R.E. Alcoholism in adolescents and their families: Family-focused assessment and management. Pediatric Clinics of North America. 1995;42(1):217–234.
49. Center for Substance Abuse Treatment. Treatment of Adolescents With Substance Use Disorders. Treatment Improvement Protocol (TIP) Series 32. DHHS Publication No. (SMA) 99-3283. Rockville, MD: Substance Abuse and Mental Health Services Administration, 1999e.
50. Anderson, J.Z. Stepfamilies and substance abuse: Unique treatment considerations. In: Kaufman, E., and Kaufmann, P., eds. Family Therapy of Drug and Alcohol Abuse. 2d ed. Boston: Allyn and Bacon, 1992. pp. 172–189.
51. Treatment Improvement Protocol (TIP) Series, No. 39. Center for Substance Abuse Treatment. Rockville (MD): Substance Abuse and Mental Health Services Administration (US); 2004.
52. National Institute on Drug Abuse. Prescription Drugs: Abuse and Addiction. National Institute on Drug Abuse Research Report Series. Rockville, MD: National Institute on Drug Abuse, 2001. http://www.

nida.nih.gov/PDF/RRPrescription.pdf [Accessed February 11, 2004].

53. Center for Substance Abuse Treatment. A Guide to Substance Abuse Services for Primary Care Clinicians. Treatment Improvement Protocol (TIP) Series 24. DHHS Publication No. (SMA) 97-3139. Rockville, MD: Substance Abuse and Mental Health Services Administration, 1997a.
54. Center for Substance Abuse Treatment. Substance Abuse Among Older Adults. Treatment Improvement Protocol (TIP) Series 26. DHHS Publication No. (SMA) 98-3179. Rockville, MD: Substance Abuse and Mental Health Services Administration, 1998d.
55. Brook, D.W., and Brook, J.S. Family processes associated with alcohol and drug use and abuse. In: Kaufman, E., and Kaufmann, P., eds. Family Therapy of Drug and Alcohol Abuse. 2d ed. Boston: Allyn and Bacon, 1992. pp. 15–33.
56. Smoking Thwarts Positive Outcomes in Opioid Addiction. American Society of Addiction Medicine (ASAM) 43rd Annual Medical-Scientific Conference. Article session 6, presented April 20, 2012.
57. Arch Gen Psychiatry. 1991;48(12):1069-1074. doi:10.1001/archpsyc.1991.01810360033005.
58. Changes in Mental Health After Smoking Cessation: Systematic Review and Meta-analysis. www.bmj.com/content/348/bmj.g1151.
59. Jørgensen, CH, Pedersen, B, Tønnesen, H. The Efficacy of Disulfiram for the Treatment of Alcohol Use Disorder. Alcohol Clin Exp Res. 2011 May 25.
60. Garbutt, JC, Kranzler, HR, O'Malley, SS, et al. "Efficacy and Tolerability of Long-Acting Injectable Naltrexone for Alcohol Dependence: A Randomized Controlled Trial." JAMA. 293(13): 1617-1625, 2005.
61. [1]Rösner, S, Hackl-Herryourth, A, Leucht, S, et al. Acamprosate for alcohol dependence. Cochrane Database of Systematic Reviews 2010, Issue 9. Art. No.: CD004332.
62. Johnson, BA, Rosenthal, N, Capece, JA, et al. Improvement of physical health and quality of life of alcohol-dependent individuals with topiramate treatment: PEOPLE multisite randomized controlled trial. Arch Intern Med. 168(11):1188-99, 2008.
63. Johnson, BA, Roache, JD, Javors, MA, et al. Ondansetron for

reduction of drinking among biologically predisposed alcoholic patients: A randomized controlled trial. JAMA. 284(8):963-71, 2000.

64. Addolorato, G, Leggio, L. Safety and efficacy of baclofen in the treatment of alcohol-dependent patients. Curr Pharm Des. 16(19):2113-7, 2010.
65. *The Journal of Addiction Medicine* (ncbi.nlm.nih.gov/pubmed/23728065).
66. Mason, BJ, Quello, S, Goodell, V, et al. Gabapentin treatment for alcohol dependence: A randomized clinical trial. *JAMA Intern Med.* Published online November 4, 2013.
67. Pregabalin, Tiapride, and Lorazepam in Alcohol Withdrawal Syndrome: A Multi-Centre, Randomized, Single-blind Comparison Trial, Martinotti G, et al. 2010.
68. Adv Ther (2012). DOI 10.1007/s12325-012-0061-5. Pregabalin for Alcohol Dependence: A Critical Review of the Literature Riccardo Guglielmo, Giovanni Martinotti, Massimo Clerici, Luigi Janiri.
69. Buprenorphine Is a Weak Partial Agonist That Inhibits Opioid Receptor Desensitization. Michael S. Virk, Seksiri Arttamangkul, William T. Birdsong, and John T. Williams. The Journal of Neuroscience, 3 June 2009, 29(22): 7341-7348; doi: 10.1523/JNEUROSCI.3723-08.2009.
70. Stead, LF, Perera, R, Bullen, C, Mant, D, Lancaster, T. Nicotine replacement therapy for smoking cessation. Cochrane Database Syst Rev. 2008 Jan 23. CD000146.
71. Piper, ME, Smith, SS, Schlam, TR, Fiore, MC, Jorenby, DE, Fraser, D, et al. A randomized placebo-controlled clinical trial of 5 smoking cessation pharmacotherapies. Arch Gen Psychiatry. 2009 Nov. 66(11):1253-62.
72. Hughes, JR, Stead, LF, Lancaster, T. Anxiolytics and antidepressants for smoking cessation. Cochrane Database Syst Rev. 2000. CD000031.
73. Crits-Christoph, Psychosocial Treatments for Cocaine Dependence. P. Arch Gen Psychiatry. 1999;56(6):493-502. doi:10-1001/pubs. Arch Gen Psychiatry-ISSN-0003-990x-56-6-yoa8244.
74. Kampman, KM. New Medications for the Treatment of Cocaine Dependence. Psychiatry (Edgmont). 2005 Dec; 2(12): 44–48.

75. Kampman, KM, et al. A double blind, placebo controlled trial of modafinil for the treatment of cocaine dependence without co-morbid alcohol dependence. Drug Alcohol Depend. 2015 Aug 14. pii: S0376-8716(15)01596-3. doi: 10.1016/j.drugalcdep.2015.08.005. [Epub ahead of print].
76. Shorter, D, Domingo, CB, Kosten, TR. Emerging drugs for the treatment of cocaine use disorder: a review of neurobiological targets and pharmacotherapy. Expert Opin Emerg Drugs. 2015;20: 15-29.
77. Shorter, D, Lindsay, JA, Kosten, TR. The Alpha-1 Adrenergic Antagonist Doxazosin for Treatment of Cocaine Dependence: a pilot study. Drug Alcohol Depend. 2013;131:66-70.
78. Keck, TM, et al. Identifying Medication Targets for Psychostimulant Addiction: Unraveling the Dopamine D3 Receptor Hypothesis. J Med Chem. 2015 Jul 23;58(14):5361-80. doi: 10.1021/jm501512b. Epub 2015 Mar 31.
79. Grosshans, M (1), Mutschler, J, Kiefer, F. Treatment of cocaine craving with as-needed nalmefene, a partial ⊠ opioid receptor agonist: first clinical experience. Int Clin Psychopharmacol. 2015 Jul;30(4):237-8. doi: 10.1097/YIC.0000000000000069.
80. Levin, F.R., et al. Extended-Release Mixed Amphetamine Salts vs. Placebo for Comorbid Adult Attention-Deficit/Hyperactivity Disorder and Cocaine Use Disorder: A Randomized Clinical Trial. JAMA Psychiatry. 2015 Jun;72(6):593-602. doi: 10.1001/jamapsychiatry.2015.41.
81. Liu S, Green CE, Lane SD, et al. The influence of dopamine beta-hydroxylase gene polymorphism rs1611115 on levodopa/carbidopa treatment for cocaine dependence: a preliminary study. Pharmacogenet Genomics. 2014;24:370-373.
82. Shorter, D, Domingo, CB, Kosten, TR. Emerging drugs for the treatment of cocaine use disorder: a review of neurobiological targets and pharmacotherapy. Expert Opin Emerg Drugs. 2015;20: 15-29.
83. Kosten, TR, Wu, G, Hjuang, W, et al. Pharmacogenetic randomized trial for cocaine abuse: disulfiram and dopamine beta-hydroxylase. Biol Psychiatry. 2013;73:219-224.
84. Carroll, KM, Nich, C, Ball, SA, et al. Treatment of cocaine and alcohol dependence with psychotherapy and disulfiram. Addiction.

1998;93:713-727.
85. George, TP, Chawarski, MC, Pakes, J, et al. Disulfiram versus placebo for cocaine dependence in buprenorphine-maintained subjects: a preliminary trial. Biol Psychiatry. 2000;47:1080-1086.
86. Ma, JZ, et al. Fine-grain analysis of the treatment effect of topiramate on methamphetamine addiction with latent variable analysis. Drug Alcohol Depend. 2013 Jun 1;130(1-3):45-51. doi: 10.1016/j.drugalcdep.2012.10.009. Epub 2012 Nov 9.
87. Elkashef, A, et al. Topiramate for the treatment of methamphetamine addiction: a multi-center placebo-controlled trial. Addiction. 2012 Jul;107(7):1297-306. doi: 10.1111/j.1360-0443.2011.03771.x. Epub 2012 Feb 28.
88. Shoenfeld, N, et al. Six-month follow-up study of drug treatment for cannabis addiction: comparison study of four drugs. Harefuah. 2011 Dec;150(12):888-92, 937.
89. Bedi, G, Cooper, Z, Haney, M, et al. Subjective, Cognitive and Cardiovascular Dose-Effect Profile of Nabilone and Dronabinol in Marijuana Smokers. Addict Biol. 2013;18(5): 872-881.
90. Haney, M, Cooper, Z, Bedi, G, et al. Nabilone Decreases Marijuana Withdrawal and A Laboratory Measure of Marijuana Relapse. Neuropsychopharmacology. 2013;38(8): 1557-1565.
91. Haney, M, Ramesh, D, Glass, A, et al. Naltrexone Maintenance Decreases Cannabis Self-Administration and Subjective Effects in Daily Cannabis Smokers. Neuropsychopharmacology, 2015;40(11):2489-2498.
92. Mason, BJ, et al. A proof-of-concept randomized controlled study of gabapentin: effects on cannabis use, withdrawal and executive function deficits in cannabis-dependent adults Neuropsychopharmacology. 2012 Jun;37(7):1689-98. doi: 10.1038/npp.2012.14. Epub 2012 Feb 29.
93. Miranda, R, Treloar, H, Blanchard, A, et al. Topiramate and Motivational Enhancement Therapy for Cannabis Use Among Youth: A Randomized Placebo-Controlled Pilot Study. Addict Biol. January 11, 2016. [Epub ahead of print.]
94. Gray, K, Carpenter, M, Baker, N, et al. A Double-Blind Randomized Controlled Trial of N-Acetylcysteine in Cannabis-Dependent

Adolescents. Am J Psychiatry. 2012;169(8): 805-812.

95. Cornelius, J, Bukstein, O, Douaihy, A, et al. Double-Blind Fluoxetine Trial in Comorbid MDD-CUD Youth and Young Adults. Drug Alcohol Depend. 2010;112(1-2), 39-45.
96. Kelly, M, Pavlicova, M, Glass, A, Mariani, J, et al. Do Withdrawal-Like Symptoms Mediate Increased Marijuana Smoking in Individuals Treated with Venlafaxine-XR? Drug Alcohol Depend. 2014;144: 42-46.
97. Levin, F, Mariani, J, Brooks, D, et al. A Randomized Double-Blind, Placebo-Controlled Trial of Venlafaxine-Extended Release for Co-Occurring Cannabis Dependence and Depressive Disorders. Addiction. 2013:108(6);1084-1094.
98. Greene, MC, Kelly, JF. The prevalence of cannabis withdrawal and its influence on adolescents' treatment response and outcomes: a 12-month prospective investigation. J Addict Med. 2014 Sep-Oct;8(5):359-67. doi: 10.1097/ADM.0000000000000064.
99. Lee, D, et al. Cannabis withdrawal in chronic, frequent cannabis smokers during sustained abstinence within a closed residential environment. Am J Addict. 2014 May-Jun;23(3):234-42. doi: 10.1111/j.1521-0391.2014.12088.x.
100. Hesse, M, Thylstrup, B. Time-course of the DSM-5 cannabis withdrawal symptoms in poly-substance abusers. BMC Psychiatry. 2013 Oct 12;13:258. doi: 10.1186/1471-244X-13-258.
101. Hasin, DS, et al. Cannabis withdrawal in the United States: results from NESARC. J Clin Psychiatry. 2008 Sep;69(9):1354-63. Epub 2008 Sep 9.
102. Gorelick, DA, et al. Diagnostic criteria for cannabis withdrawal syndrome. Drug Alcohol Depend. 2012 Jun 1;123(1-3):141-7. doi: 10.1016/j.drugalcdep.2011.11.007. Epub 2011 Dec 7.
103. Allsop, DJ, et al. Quantifying the clinical significance of cannabis withdrawal. PLoS One. 2012;7(9):e44864. doi: 10.1371/journal.pone.0044864. Epub 2012 Sep 26.
104. Allsop, DJ, et al. Cannabinoid replacement therapy (CRT): Nabiximols (Sativex) as a novel treatment for cannabis withdrawal. Clin Pharmacol Ther. 2015 Jun;97(6):571-4. doi: 10.1002/cpt.109. Epub 2015 Apr 17.

105. Lam, PW, Frost, DW. Nabilone therapy for cannabis withdrawal presenting as protracted nausea and vomiting. BMJ Case Rep. 2014 Sep 22;2014. pii: bcr2014205287. doi: 10.1136/bcr-2014-205287.
106. Levin, F, Mariani, J, Brooks, D, et al. Dronabinol for the Treatment of Cannabis Dependence: A Randomized, Double-Blind, Placebo-Controlled Trial. Drug Alcohol Depend. 2011;116(1-3):142-150.
107. Penetar, D, Looby, A, Ryan, E, et al. Bupropion Reduces Some of the Symptoms of Marihuana Withdrawal in Chronic Marihuana Users: A Pilot Study. Subst Abuse. 2012;6:63-71.
108. Cooper, Z, Foltin, R, Hart, C, et al. A Human Laboratory Study Investigating the Effects of Quetiapine on Marijuana Withdrawal and Relapse in Daily Marijuana Smokers. Addict Biol. 2013;18(6): 993-1002.
109. Herrmann, E, Cooper, Z, Bedi, G, et al. Effects of Zolpidem Alone and in Combination with Nabilone on Cannabis Withdrawal and A Laboratory Model of Relapse in Cannabis Users. Psychopharmacology (Berl). 2016; 233(13):2469-2478.
110. Haney, M, Hart, C, Vosburg, S, et al. Effects of Baclofen and Mirtazapine on a Laboratory Model of Marijuana Withdrawal and Relapse. Psychopharmacology (Berl). 2010;211(2):233-244.
111. Bill, P, Todd, W. *Drop the Rock: Removing Character Defects* – Steps Six and Seven. 2005. Hazelden, Minnesota.
112. Abstracted in part from http://www.virtuescience.com/virtuelist.html. Accessed 10/18/16.
113. Abstracted from: https://realisticrecovery.wordpress.com/2009/05/03/194-character-defects/. https://realisticrecovery.wordpress.com/2009/04/24/list-of-character-defects-and-assets/ http://www.stepsfoundation.com/Step6CharacterDefects.htm. http://www.barefootsworld.net/aaonsteps4567.html. Accessed 10/27/16
114. Soojung-Kim Pan, Alex. *Rest: Why You Get More Done When You Work Less*. Basic Books, 2016.

FREE EBOOK!

Can't wait to release the suffering and start creating more joy in your life?

Go to drmichaelmcgee.com and download your **free copy** of *20 Ways to Realize Joy in Your Life* now!

CPSIA information can be obtained
at www.ICGtesting.com
Printed in the USA
BVHW040250230719
554057BV00023BA/1526/P

9 781946 928160